JOHN S.

COMMITMENT

CW00816146

Themes from the life and work of
a socialist historian

JOHN SAVILLE
COMMITMENT AND HISTORY

*Themes from the life and work of
a socialist historian*

Edited by David Howell, Dianne Kirby
and Kevin Morgan

Lawrence & Wishart in association with
the Socialist History Society

LONDON 2011

Socialist History Society Occasional Publication No. 27
ISBN 9781907103 216

British Library Cataloguing in Publication Data.
A catalogue record for this book is available from the British Library

Typeset by e-type, Liverpool
Printed in Great Britain by MPG-Biddles, Kings Lynn

Contents

Illustrations are between pp128 and 129

Foreword

'...we always grossly exaggerate the speed at which volumes of this kind can be produced...'. John Saville's remark on editing the pioneering collection *Democracy and the Labour Movement* will strike a chord with anybody who has attempted similar undertakings. There is therefore no greater testimony to the wide respect in which John was held, and the wide circles of people who experienced his influence, assistance or friendship, that the present collection could be devised, commissioned and completed in just a year. If the collection, as we hope, provides at least a flavour of John's varied interests and commitments, our thanks as editors are due in the first place to our contributors, for their enthusiasm for the project and for their willingness to accommodate its very tight deadlines.

Thanks are also due to the Socialist History Society for adopting the collection as its occasional publication for 2010. As the essays here remind us, John was one of the most distinguished participants in the society's predecessor, the CPGB Historians' Group of the immediate post-war years. Following his break with Stalinism in 1956, John's energies were channelled into a range of other bodies, from the Oral History Society to the Society for the Study of Labour History and the Council for Academic Freedom and Democracy. With the establishment of the SHS on a more inclusive basis in 1992, the enduring achievements of the Historians' Group were recognised, along with the need to respond to current historiographical challenges and avoid the temptations of mere revivalism or antiquarianism. An inspiring but occasionally daunting compensation for editing the society's journal *Socialist History* was to receive the comments on its contents of Historians' Group veterans (like Victor Kiernan, an editorial adviser whose erudition John described as unequalled, and Brian Pearce, who was closely associated with John at the time of his break

7

with the CPGB). John himself was keen, supportive and occasionally (and not unjustifiably) acerbic, and, as the bibliography in his autobiography records, among his final writings were the 'Books to be remembered' items he contributed to the journal for as long as health and personal circumstances allowed.

Very much in the spirit of the Historians' Group, the SHS is a collective endeavour dependent on the individual commitments of its members. Thanks are especially due in this instance to members of the society's occasional publications team: Francis King (who compiled the index), David Morgan (who assisted with copy-editing) and Willie Thompson. Thanks are also due to Sally Davison and Lawrence & Wishart, for agreeing to this experiment in collaboration; to John's family, for their encouragement and their assistance with the illustrations; and, among the many libraries and archives drawn upon, to the newly established Hull History Centre, which provides magnificent accommodation for John's personal papers and for the labour history collections he built up at Hull.

Above all we are grateful to the memory of John Saville himself. In the spirit of his own work, the treatment here is critical, not reverential; issues of contention are not brushed aside; there is no pretending that a socialist history will look the same today as in the earlier years of his career or even in the later ones. Nevertheless, there are not many academics' lives whose themes, commitments and engagements could give rise to such varied reflections. 'Every one of the contributors to this book, and scores of other investigators of the past, can testify to the patient help and unfailing stimulus which she has given them.' When Christopher Hill penned this dedication to Dona Torr in 1954, a less expansive colleague amended 'scores' to 'many others'. In John's own case, over his much longer career as a historian, the phrasing can be left exactly (gender apart) as it stands.

Kevin Morgan for the editors, September 2010

PART ONE

Commitments

The good old cause

Kevin Morgan

Around the time of John Saville's death in June 2009, academics in Britain were becoming sorely exercised by the measurement of so-called research 'impact'. Sceptics warned of research becoming still further constrained, commodified and instrumentalised, and of intellectual enquiry becoming subordinated to inimical values and tendentious assessment criteria. Socialist historians might have added that notions of a wider user community, and of 'benefits to the wider economy and society', were liable to be constructed according to the carnivorous business logic so characteristic of the New Labour years. Among his many commitments, John Saville took academic freedom seriously; among his keenest intuitions, corroborated by experience in India and during the Cold War, was a forensic clarity regarding the modus operandi of the British state. One may be sure that he would have had some telling thoughts to contribute to the present discussion, and we are the poorer for not having had them.

Even so, if any academic career exemplified a genuine quality of 'impact', both within and beyond the academy, it was Saville's. A substantial historian of the British labour movement, where his contribution was truly exceptional was in the promotion and enrichment of a wider field of scholarship which at the outset of his career was barely marked out at all. In the establishment of labour history as an academic discipline it is hard to overstate the importance of ventures like the *Dictionary of Labour Biography* (*DLB*), the *Essays in Labour History*, the labour archives at Hull and the reprints of numerous labour and radical texts, in all of which Saville had a major hand. There could be no complaining here from the standpoint of conventional notions of impact. At the same time, Saville was a life-long socialist, whose understanding of economic and social well-being

11

was a world away from what Collini calls the 'economistic officialese' of those fixated on the market and its outcomes.[1] For nearly thirty years he not only co-edited the annual *Socialist Register* but, as Colin Leys describes here, provided it with a regular flow of essays, attesting either the continuing topicality of labour history themes or else the importance of historical perspective in understanding the times we live in.[2] The hundred or so items in the bibliography attached to his autobiography, *Memoirs from the Left*, was anything but exhaustive. Nevertheless, it represents a formidable body of activity over some half a century.

Between the bibliography and the narrative which preceded it there was nevertheless a paradox; for while all these major projects and publications date from after 1956, as do ninety per cent of the items in the bibliography, the text of the *Memoirs* itself is heavily weighted towards the much shorter period Saville spent, at a much lower level of prominence, as a member of the British Communist Party (CPGB). There might of course be incidental reasons for this. The persisting wider interest in communist party history is one. That even the most purposive academic endeavours make for less than enthralling reading is another. More fundamentally, Saville's was a life which in crucial ways remained defined by formative communist values and commitments for decades after he had left the party itself behind him. Along with Edward Thompson, he was a crucial figure in the formation of the New Left, and in the categorical repudiation of Stalinism which provided its original rationale. As Madeleine Davis describes here, however, when Saville and Thompson first produced *The Reasoner* in 1956 they did not at first envisage that this meant removing themselves from the CPGB; when forced out by the leadership's recidivism over Hungary, they departed, according to Saville, 'with great reluctance'.[3] For Saville in particular, neither theory nor practice of communism could be reduced to Stalinism, and the communist experience remained both emotionally and intellectually a critical point of reference. As late as 1991, with the collapse of Europe's communist systems, he felt compelled to bring to bear a sort of personal witness, combining elements of reaffirmation with critique and repudiation.[4] In a very real sense, of which he was himself perfectly conscious, Saville's career as a labour and socialist historian was one he saw as carrying through values and precepts learnt, and never subsequently unlearnt, as a communist.

COMRADE STAM AND JOHNNY SAVILLE

He certainly did not owe these values to his family background. Another peculiarity of Saville's autobiography, which is otherwise conventionally structured, is that its somewhat perfunctory account of his birth and childhood is interpolated some twenty pages into the narrative, where it offers little in the way of insight into his later political attachments. Born Orestes Stamatopoulos in April 1916, Saville was the only son of a well-born Greek attached to a Lincoln engineering firm and a not-so-well born Lincolnshire domestic worker. His father having been killed in the war, his mother found a second husband in a Romford master tailor for whom she had taken up work as a housekeeper. Saville was six when they met, ten when they married; previously he had lived with a surrogate 'Gainsborough Mammy', for whom he expressed a real sense of loss, and with a maiden aunt, who, recalled a little less fulsomely, provided 'what must have been a sense of security and affection'. This might have been an unsettled childhood, but Saville gave little indication that it was an unhappy one. He was a keen and very able sportsman, who by the time he left school had represented his county at football, swimming and athletics. Following his mother's example, he was also an active member of the Anglican church, and the diverse rituals and forms of association it allowed for.

Already in the early 1930s, the issues were fermenting which were to lure so many of the younger generation towards communism. They do not, however, appear to have disturbed the peaceful tenor of the Saville household. Strenuously though Saville would later insist on the reality of the slump, in Romford, still a 'small country town', it must have seemed at one step removed; and even the nearby Becontree estate and Ford motor works are nowhere mentioned in Saville's memoirs. In his wider survey of the period, he did refer to the 'extraordinary spate' of literary bestsellers which expressed a powerful mood of war revulsion in 1928-31.[5] Saville himself, however, appears to have encountered this literature only in his last months at school, in the shape of Beverley Nichols's *Cry Havoc!*, published in 1933, and a volume of Wilfred Owen's war poems borrowed from the local public library. That was rather characteristic of children from such conservative backgrounds. Saville's mother was an avid Dickens reader, his stepfather took the reactionary *Daily Mail*. It took a teacher, again in his last years at school, to introduce him to Malraux's *La Condition Humaine*, and even then he could not fully make sense of it.[6]

Life, or at least its reconstruction in his autobiography, thus began for Saville when he arrived at the London School of Economics in the autumn of 1934. Enrolling for the broad BSc (Econ) degree with a specialism in economic geography, his studies were in due course to secure him a First. On his arrival in Houghton Street, however, such provident considerations were quickly put to the back of his mind. Student communism at this time was entering upon its most active period of recruitment, and London was one of its centres. Swept along by the current, within a fortnight Saville had joined the LSE Socialist Society and within a couple of months the CPGB itself. By his second year, Comrade Stam, as he was known, was the LSE's student communist organiser and a somewhat daunting figure to later intakes of students.[7] Lectures, with the exception of Harold Laski's, were invariably skipped; writing skills were not as yet honed on student essays. Far more compelling was the 'political excitement' of student communism, pulling him into the library and out again in search of that unity of theory and practice which never seems more attainable than to the student activist.[8] Only continuing prowess on the football pitch provided significant diversion from what was more or less a full-time activity.

Saville was never much taken with Raphael Samuel's emphasis on themes of conversion and a surrogate religiosity in his evocations of British communism's 'lost world'.[9] With his extensive experience as a labour historian, he was certainly sure of his ground in urging how implausible it was to think of militants at the heart of the British labour movement joining the communists out of craving for a sense of belonging.[10] That Saville's own adhesion to the party was as 'matter-of-fact' a decision as he came to believe is perhaps more contestable, and Saville himself conceded that his instant attachment to the student movement was something he was unable to explain.[11] Communism was never for him akin to a religious order; but in its sense of comradeship and common purpose it might well have had the sort of associational compensations which he had continued to find in England's actual established church for some years after he had lost all sense of the religious beliefs on which it was supposed to rest. In casual discussions of communism as a surrogate religion such distinctions are too easily overlooked.[12] 'It would not have been difficult to feel oneself lonely at LSE', Saville recorded, again with a certain obliquity; and as he made each day the forty-mile round trip from what remained his family home in Romford, one can well believe that he had personal authority for the statement. To join the communists at the LSE, in any case, was 'to belong immediately to a network of comrades and friends whose intellectual sophistication was both encouraging and intimidating'.[13]

Deeply impressed by the communists he encountered, Saville was to continue to express a strong sense of identification in much of his work as a labour historian. As the *DLB* so splendidly demonstrates, he was second to none in his appreciation of the importance of activists' life-histories, and he can be found discussing the (in Britain) neglected subject of labour prosopography as early as 1973.[14] If the CPGB historians were more generally marked by a sensitivity to the issue of political agency, experiences like Saville's own in the party itself were doubtless a significant contributory factor. As Saville pointed out, and as Samuel would certainly have concurred, communists were by no means alone in the commitments they made to social and political movements, which were indeed hardly conceivable without such commitments. From the volumes of the *DLB* Saville singled out the example of the Durham miner Tommy Ramsay, a staunch nonconformist, and from his later experience in Hull the non-communist secretary of the trades council, Jack Nicholson.[15] In later years he was to be curtly dismissive of a literature downplaying the role of such activist minorities, on the grounds of its naivety as to how radical social and political movements were necessarily constructed.[16]

Graduating in the summer of 1937, Saville's initial hopes of a research scholarship were to be disappointed. The three years that followed were something of a hiatus. Voluntary political work and an ill-fated venture into supply teaching were followed by posts for the Dictaphone Company and the British Home Stores. Respectively recalled as 'quite uninteresting' and 'hard but endurable', these at least provided the necessary financial independence to share a flat with Constance Saunders, whom Saville had met at the LSE and who was to remain his lifelong partner, despite her leaving the CPGB some seventeen years earlier than him, over the Nazi-Soviet pact.[17] Had war not intervened, quite conceivably his life course might have taken a very different direction, and detained us much more briefly.

Saville's six years in the army provided a second major formative experience and were presented as such in the second chapter of his autobiography. Called up in April 1940, his first four years were spent in anti-aircraft batteries in Britain, and the latter two in India. Together they represented a significant extension of his personal frame of reference. In defiance of current communist policy, Saville refused to apply for a commission on the grounds that his place in the event of trouble – and communists in 1940 were certainly expecting that – was with the 'rude and licentious soldiery'.[18] It was among these that he consequently found himself, from his earliest stationing at an AA training barracks near Wokingham. With his family roots in Gainsborough, to which he had periodically returned, Saville was not as innocent of working-class life as some of his contemporaries. Nevertheless, student communism by the late 1930s could appear a relatively self-contained world. Earlier in the decade, communism had meant for some a conscious orientation towards the proletariat, expressed in adaptations of dress, demeanour and accent as well as forms of political engagement. With the onset of the popular front, on the other hand, students and intellectuals were valued for what they could achieve in their own more restricted sphere of work. In the last winter before the war, Saville had assisted the National Unemployed Workers' Movement (NUWM) in the spectacular demonstrations it organised in London's West End of London, and he himself had taken part in a 'small lie-down' in Piccadilly Circus.[19]

It was in the army, nevertheless, that one has the sense of his crossing some invisible divide. Towards the end of his student days he had assumed his stepfather's name of Saville, possibly influenced by the CPGB's current embrace of Englishness. He also took the forename John, which, one imagines – though without a source to corroborate – must have reflected the inspiration which student communists of his generation drew from the example of the brilliantly gifted John Cornford, who at the age of twenty-one had been killed at Cordova in December 1936. No longer Comrade Stam, except to those who knew him in his student days, Saville found himself transmuted into Johnny Saville, and out of discretion or camaraderie having to modify his previous accent. 'We thought', one of his new confederates told him, 'you were a snotty bastard'. One of the sharpest impressions of his army years was of how deep the class divisions ran in British society, particularly as reinforced and accentuated by rank and segregation.

In India it was even worse, but there was another lesson too. If the universities of the 1930s were restricted in their social intake, in terms of students' national origins they did allow for encounters which did not occur in the average English town or industrial suburb. Saville had associated most closely with American students, and developed a taste for American novelists like Hemingway and Dos Passos. Other friendships were established with political refugees like the Austrian Teddy Praeger and the Spaniard Manuel Azcarate. Exposure to the politics of international solidarity, to which Spain of course was central, was to be reinforced following Saville's graduation, when he worked for a time for the China solidarity campaigns of the Union of Democratic Control. Saville's two years in India, however, made an unforgettable impression that was to mark him all his life. On the one hand, there was the exposure to brutal levels of poverty and exploitation, and the deep-dyed racism of the British in India. On the other, there was the example of the Indian communists, with whom he made immediate contact and whom he was able to assist in the production of pamphlets and the party weekly *People's War*. What most impressed him were the 'self-sacrifice and dedication of the full-time Party workers', and listening to their stories of underground work and prison was an experience at once exhilarating and sobering – but 'much more the latter than the former'.[20] Saville's associations with Indian students in Britain had been constrained by fear of the consequences they might run. In India itself, however, contacts with communists like Mohan Kumaramangalam, a future minister under Indira Gandhi, developed into close friendships. In his discussion in this volume of relations between Indian and British communists, Sobhanlal Datta Gupta notes the perception in India that a commitment to colonial liberation was in Britain a burning issue only for a minority. Through the contingency of his Indian posting, Saville was nevertheless part of that minority, and his wider political outlook was to be strongly marked by this insight into the realities of western colonial rule. He returned to England in the spring of 1946, he later wrote, having seen imperialism at its revolting worst and with his communist convictions strengthened.[21] Whatever his reactions to the Cold War, he was never going to idealise the West.

For a period after his return he was employed in operational research at the Ministry of Works. More fatefully, in the autumn of 1947 he took up the lecturing post in Hull in which he was to spend his entire academic career. Settling into the area, he was to accept the obligations of local party work, delivering the *Daily Worker* and chairing his local branch of the British-Soviet Friendship Society. The beginning of his university career, however, also coincided with the activation of the most effective of the party's professional groups, the CPGB Historians' Group. This was to provide a third and indelible formative experience, one requiring further discussion in its own right.

THE LINGERING WORLD OF BRITISH COMMUNISM

What the Historians' Group exemplified for Saville was a method of work whose influence can clearly be traced in his later activities. If that was one major legacy of his communist years, the other was a *Weltanschauung*, or world-view, which may have been modified, and in some aspects even transformed, in 1956, but in other crucial features was to be consistently upheld until his death.

There was, of course, no single communist *Weltanschauung*. The different phases of communist policy and different moments of engagement made for varying cohort experiences of the party, which were further complicated by personal disturbances like war service or even university. Across his twenty-two years of CP membership, Saville not only experienced these successive phases of the communist *mentalité*, from popular front to cold war, but through his appetite for history and theory encountered the still-surviving texts of an earlier period. To sum up even the individual communist world-view is therefore no simple matter. If one has, nevertheless, to compress the matter, one might hazard that Saville was emotionally a communist of 1930s mould, but politically as deeply marked by the Cold War.

Comparison with Edward Thompson, his sometime closest collab-orator, is in this respect instructive. Born in 1924, Thompson's adhesion to communism post-dated Saville's by eight years, and in the course of their association Saville was repeatedly reminded of his own identity as one of 'the generation of the Red Decade'.[22] The commu-nist narrative of the 1930s was one of Manichean clarity, and in essays like his 'May Day 1937' (1979) Saville gave as emphatic a rendition of this narrative as his condemnation of its revisionist alternatives was severe. Except in the matter of their support for Stalinism in the USSR, the communists in this period continued, in Saville's estimate, to have the best of every argument: though prisoners of their party's past and of the directives it received from Moscow, theirs were the energy, the inspiration and the outstanding personalities behind what Saville always held to be the decade's major campaigns and social movements.[23] Within the *DLB*, while a negative bias was never consciously intruded, a positive tribute was admissible through entries on key figures and influences in Saville's own life history. Jack Cohen (volume nine) was from 1936 the CP's national student organiser; Don Renton (also volume nine) was the London organiser of the NUWM at the time of Saville's involvement; Clive Branson (volume two) was the sometime International Brigader whose *British Soldier in India* made such a powerful impression on Saville during the war years; even Mohan Kumaramangalam (volume five) crept in on the strength of his student activities.[24] All were of the 'generation of the 1930s', and in Cohen's and Branson's cases their biographies required co-operation with surviving partners who were also of that generation and had remained in the CPGB. It was similarly with the assistance of Margot Heinemann, John Cornford's former girlfriend, that Saville launched his memorable and effective broadside against the misrepresentation of the communists' efforts in Spain in *The Penguin Book of Spanish Civil War Verse*.[25] Even Harry Pollitt, an obvious target for critics during the CPGB's Stalinist rearguard action of 1956, was at Saville's urging to be spared *The Reasoner*'s personal attacks in deference to these earlier struggles: 'To me', as he wrote to Thompson, 'Harry is linked with Spain, anti-appeasement and the Hunger Marches'.[26] Even at the height of his political disillusionment with King Street, for Saville these remained the indispensable elements of a shared collective memory.

Though to this extent a communist of 1930s vintage, joining as the Seventh World Congress was already on the horizon, Saville was in other respects rather untypical of the popular-front recruit. In particular this was true of his unrelenting suspicion of the Labour Party. Without dissatisfaction with Labour's official policies and leadership one would hardly have been a communist at all, and indignation over issues like non-intervention in Spain was also widely felt within Labour's own ranks. For many of Saville's contemporaries, these internal tensions encouraged a distinct ambivalence towards the Labour Party, graphically illustrated by their willingness to enter the party in their hundreds, particularly in London and the

Home Counties. Saville himself, on the other hand, could never have done this, and he never entertained the idea even after leaving the CPGB.[27]

In some respects this is surprising, for it was Laski, at that time an epitome of the thinking Labour left, whom Saville described as the most important influence in his own intellectual life, and as an inspiration to him as a student.[28] At the same time, self-directed reading allowed a space for heterodoxy which is often underestimated. Like others of his generation, Saville was particularly impressed by the astringency of R Palme Dutt – it was only later that he saw him as a disastrous influence – and the continued attention that he gave to issues of empire and colonialism.[29] Among the books that influenced him, moreover, he singled out John Strachey's *Coming Struggle for Power*, originally published in 1932, and Theodore Rothstein's *From Chartism to Labourism*, published in 1929. Both carried a flavour of more sectarian times; neither encouraged confidence in the British Labour Party. On the contrary, wrote Strachey, 'those very organizations of working-class revolt, which the workers have gradually and painfully created over nearly half a century … are today by far the most formidable obstacle in the way of an early victory'.[30] What Saville saw as the feebleness of the 1930s Labour Party impressed upon him a scepticism towards social democracy which never abated, and which as late as the 1980s saw him introduce Rothstein's neglected study to a new generation of readers.[31]

If Saville had misgivings about his party's concessions to social democracy during the later war years, he was to find his own underlying antagonism vindicated by the onset of the Cold War. Disillusionment with Bevin's foreign policy was instantaneous. Support for the maintenance of empire and colonial wars was one major factor. The suppression of the communist resistance in Greece, discussed below by John Sakkas, was another, as important in Saville's estimation as Spain had been in the 1930s.[32] Spain itself, with the persistence of the Franco regime, was a third: 'To allow this butcher of so many thousands of his own people to remain in power … was for me a confirmation of the conservative iniquities of British labourism'.[33] While in the New Deal era Saville had looked with optimism towards the USA, Labour's supine atlanticism now seemed to him the key to these further iniquities, and he was later to describe Britain's subjection to US foreign policy as the outstanding feature of its post-war history.[34] There was to be no change of heart in this respect. Renewed through the New Left and in his criticisms of the Wilson governments, the analysis was to receive emphatic confirmation in Saville's final years, and he was to conclude his autobiography with a ringing denunciation of Blair's war in Iraq. How unfortunate it is that we shall never have Saville's assessment of Blair's own lamentable and self-serving autobiography. At Hull, however, he encouraged pathbreaking research into cold war history, including the doctoral research of Dianne Kirby and John Sakkas, who contribute to the present collection. We also have some of the fruits of Saville's own research into Labour's post-war foreign policy following his retirement in 1982. As well as articles on Attlee and Bevin in the *Socialist Register*, in 1993 Saville published his major study *The Politics of Continuity*, which John Callaghan evaluates here. The two further volumes he envisaged, however, were never to be published.

Unlike many of his contemporaries, Saville was almost as unimpressed by the Attlee government's domestic achievements. The significance of the governments' welfare reforms was a crucial issue for socialists in the 1950s and Saville at one stage proposed a Historians' Group publication on the welfare state. Even Maurice Dobb, the CPGB's most eminent economist, expressed a certain diffidence in the matter: 'This may be because I find it, politically, a harder nut, and am uncertain quite what line we take on the matter – that the welfare tendencies of recent decades are all a cunning liberal manoeuvre to corrupt the workers, or that they are to be welcomed as the products of working class pressure etc and a sign of what determined effort can do even under Cap^m, or some synthesis of the two?'.[35] Saville, like everybody else, recognised that there were indeed contradictory elements in the phenomenon.[36] To an unusual degree he nevertheless leant towards the 'cunning manoeuvre' interpretation, and, as Madeleine Davis describes here, on subsequently expounding this view in the *New Reasoner* prompted rebuttals from among his closest collaborators.[37]

The issue was also to register in Saville's later writings, for it was on these premises that he was to develop the analysis of labourism which was to prove one of his most characteristic and influential contributions to British labour history. 'It is not only that the social composition of the Labour leadership is increasingly middle class, or that the top and middle level trade union leadership displays the unmistakable characteristics of a bureaucracy; but it is also that among the rank and file of the movement the dynamism for radical social change has steadily weakened', he wrote in 1957. 'Those who see the growth in numbers and physical strength of the movement as a considerable achievement too often miss the equally important point that these improved instruments of working class organisation and power have today become much blunted in purpose.'[38] Evaluated here by David Howell, the analysis of labourism was to assist the smooth working relations Saville had with Ralph Miliband, with whom for twenty-three years he was to co-edit the *Socialist Register* and whose *Parliamentary Socialism* (1961) embodied a similarly sceptical view of the British Labour Party.

If elements of a communist world-view remained discernible in what Saville published, still more important was the experience of collective work which influenced how he published, and how, more generally, he approached his wider responsibilities as a socialist academic. In some ways, that can be traced back to his earliest activities as a communist. 'In personal terms what I learned from my communist years at LSE was intellectual discipline and a strong commitment to party work', he wrote of his student experiences.[39] Though the party mantra 'Every communist a First' sounds like a virtual parody of socialist competition, Saville was careful to describe how forms of mutual support and discussion, from the borrowing of notes and shared reading tasks to the release from political responsibilities in one's final year, gave even the pursuit of academic excellence something of the character of a shared endeavour.[40] To lasting effect, extending far beyond its immediate members, this was also to be the experience of the CPGB Historians' Group.

THE HISTORIANS' GROUP AS WORKING MODEL

The story of the group has been told many times.[41] Its nineteenth-century section, of which Saville along with Eric Hobsbawm was one of the most active members, provided the setting in which Saville conducted the researches into the Chartist movement which provided his first major contribution to British labour historiography. Reflected in the coverage of the *DLB*, and picked up again in another important monograph, *1848*, Saville's analysis of Chartism is worthy of attention in its own right, and is discussed as such below by Malcolm Chase.

In the bibliography in his memoirs, nevertheless, it is interesting that these individual writings are listed only after Saville's diverse editorial undertakings. That, too, may be seen as in the spirit of the Historians' Group, and of the strong conception of collective work that Saville himself developed within it. The proposed collection on the welfare state, for example, was one of three such volumes which he put forward in the form of a '4 Year plan' intended to provide a renewed sense of purpose and direction for the group's nineteenth-century section:

> Briefly I am ... arguing that our published work is by no means commensurate with our intellectual forces, and that the Dona Torr volume [see below] has shown real possibilities of co-operative activity. If we can persuade our people to write one 'co-operative' essay per year, we could, within a couple of years, start publishing one of these volumes.

In this first four-year plan, it is not difficult to see one of the sources of such future enterprises as the *DLB*, the *Essays in Labour History* and the annual exercise in co-operative essay writing, the *Socialist Register*. Only on such a basis, Saville continued, could a vigorous tradition of Marxist historical scholarship ever be established in Britain.[42]

The 'Dona Torr volume' was *Democracy and the Labour Movement*, a pioneering collection of labour history essays published under Saville's editorship in 1954. With Kiernan, Hobsbawm and Hill among the contributors, the project exemplified this spirit of collective endeavour and discussion: exactly as do the discussions on the early modern period which David Parker has recently edited.[43] As Hobsbawm emphasises in his essay on its activities, the group was not 'a "school" built round an influential teacher or book' but – again those words – a 'genuinely co-operative' enterprise of equals and as such probably without precedent in British historiography.[44]

For Saville, far more than for Hobsbawm, the dedication of this first major group production was nevertheless rather more than just an incidental formality. Like Christopher Hill, who prepared the volume's preface, he had an unabashed regard for Torr as a sort of role model whose contribution far exceeded anything she had actually put into print. As originally conceived by Hill, the volume's foreword thus ascribed the continuing delay to Torr's long-awaited biography

of Tom Mann, not just to her meticulous attention to detail, but to
the less individualised conception of scholarly endeavour to which she
was so committed:

> and … to the selfless and sacrificial way in which she has put her
> learning and her wisdom at the disposal of others. The 'History in
> the Making' Series [of historical documents] … is the most obvious
> result of her genius for collective work … But her help and guidance
> have been extended in countless other directions, which cannot be
> traced, with results which cannot be measured. Hers has been a
> pervading influence for a whole generation of Marxist historians, of
> whose extent the modest Dona herself can have no conception.
> Every one of the contributors to this book, and scores of other inves-
> tigators of the past, can testify to the patient help and unfailing
> stimulus which she has given them.

Here at least there was explicitly the sense of a 'whole school of
Marxist historians [having] grown up around her', with its principles
defined as those of a lived history of the common people.[45] To this
extent, Hobsbawm's rather different recollection may be seen as a
conscious disclaimer.[46]

With its combination of genius, wisdom and modesty, the foreword's note of late Stalinist excess was prudently modified in the
published version.[47] Nevertheless, Saville's regard for Torr went
beyond such rhetorical flourishes. Though Hill had drafted the
foreword, the original idea for the book had been Saville's, and it
was he who undertook the work of organising it, as 'secretary' to its
editorial committee, and without at first assuming responsibility
for editorial decisions. 'I have offered to do this', he explained,
'because nobody including me wants additional work of this kind,
but I am most anxious to get things moving'.[48] It took over three
years to produce the book, with Saville from Hull co-ordinating an
editorial committee based in Oxford, Cambridge and Birmingham.
In the same period he also found time to organise a seventieth
birthday dinner for Torr in addition to his work with the nineteenth-century section. In justice to his editorial efforts, it was
Saville's name, very properly, which eventually appeared on the
title page with Torr's.[49]

Revising these words in the week of JH Newman's implausible

beatification, there is no need to extend such treatment to either Torr or Saville himself. With a young family and no independent income, Saville understood that conflicting pressures of both time and expense were involved, and that collective goals could not be achieved at the expense of professional self-immolation. After the protracted experience of *Democracy and the Labour Movement* he observed that 'we should not expect our people to concentrate wholly on co-operative work of this kind', and that equally in his own case, with 'two quite separate projects … running years behind schedule', he felt obliged to keep the following year clear to complete them.[50] One of them was indeed to see publication in 1957 as the scholarly monograph *Rural Depopulation in England and Wales*. Whatever the advantages of leaving the CPGB, however, they did not include release from the sense of collective responsibility he had learnt there. In the midst of their efforts with *The Reasoner* in 1956, Saville confided to Thompson how much he wanted to get back to writing history.[51] In practice, however, *The Reasoner* was followed by the *New Reasoner*, and the *New Reasoner* by the *Socialist Register*. Even as he did get back to history, it was with that marked disposition to forms of collective activity that he had internalised as a communist. As a lecturer at Humberside, Tony Adams, one of the contributors to the present volume, notes the commitment Saville made to the wider promotion of labour history, co-ordinating research discussions and contributing to day schools for predominantly working-class mature students. One result, Saville recalled, apparently without regret and certainly without bitterness, was that major studies like his *1848* appeared some twenty years later than they might otherwise have done.

You could take the historian out of the party, but you couldn't take the party out of the historian. In ways they may not have suspected, and might even have strenuously denied, this was true of many of the historians who left the CPGB in 1956-7. Of none, however, was it truer than of Saville, and to none was this less a matter for embarrassment, apologia or dissimulation. Even half a century on Saville described the Historians' Group as 'the most productive, useful and helpful period of my intellectual career', one that enlarged his intellectual horizons and sharpened his historical wits. Of the monumental enterprise of the *DLB*, which at the time of writing has reached its thirteenth volume, he traced the primary inspiration neither to the trailblazing *Maitron* in France nor to the files he inherited from GDH Cole, but to the Historians' Group of the CPGB.[52]

In 1991, as Colin Leys reminds us, Saville declared that the time had come to repudiate the name of communism. At the same time, however, he reaffirmed the need for 'a comradeship that will sustain and support the self-discipline and self-sacrifice without which the principles, and the aims, of the Good Old Cause will never be achieved'.[53] The passage recalls Ralph Miliband's tribute on the occasion of Saville's *festschrift* in 1979, and its recognition of the commitment Saville had made 'once and for all, some forty-five years ago', when he set foot in the LSE.[54] There were not many entries in the *DLB*, Miliband continued, which recorded lives of greater integration and integrity. Eric Hobsbawm recalled these words in his *Guardian* obituary, and very properly. Three decades on there are dozens more *DLB* entries, and very soon, one imagines, Saville will have his own. Few socialist academics, as Miliband rightly intimated, have done more to merit their place in such company.

Notes

1. See Collini's discussion of 'impact', *Times Literary Supplement*, 13 November 2009.
2. It was characteristic, as Colin Leys notes, that a contribution in 1982 ostensibly on recent labour historiography in reality provided an analysis of the state of the socialist project in the UK. But to a lesser degree this was true of other contributions too; Saville could no more write an essay on Hugh Gaitskell (1980) without bringing it to bear on Labour's current predicament than he could discuss the record of the Wilson governments (1967) without a historical frame of reference, in this instance including his key historical concept of labourism.
3. Saville, 'The Communist experience: a personal appraisal' in Ralph Miliband and Leo Panitch, eds, *Communist Regimes: the Aftermath, Socialist Register 1991*, Merlin, 1991, p22.
4. Saville, 'Communist experience', pp1-25.
5. Saville, 'May Day 1937' in Asa Briggs and John Saville, eds, *Essays in Labour History 1918-39*, Croom Helm, 1977, p250.
6. All details from Saville, *Memoirs*, pp21-6.
7. This at least was the experience of Betty Matthews as interviewed by the author
8. Ralph Miliband, 'John Saville: a presentation' in David E Martin and

David Rubinstein, *Ideology and the Labour Movement*, Croom Helm, 1979, p18.

9. See Samuel, *The Lost World of British Communism*, Verso, 2006.
10. *Memoirs*, pp9-11.
11. Saville, *Memoirs*, p9; Miliband, 'John Saville', p16.
12. See the observations in Kevin Morgan, Gidon Cohen and Andrew Flinn, *Communists in British Society 1920-91*, Rivers Oram, 2007, ch2.
13. Saville, *Memoirs*, p8.
14. In the *Social Science Research Council Newsletter*. The item was included in the bibliography of his writings compiled for *Memoirs from the Left*.
15. Saville, 'Communist experience', pp9-10.
16. Saville, 'The crisis in labour history: a further comment', *Labour History Review*, 1996, pp322-3.
17. Constance died two years before him, in 2007. For this period see Saville, *Memoirs*, pp27-32.
18. Unless otherwise stated, material here is drawn from Saville, *Memoirs*, ch2.
19. Saville, *Memoirs*, p31.
20. Saville, 'Communist experience', p17.
21. Saville, 'Communist experience', p19.
22. Saville, 'Edward Thompson, the Communist Party and 1956' in *Socialist Register*, 1994, p25.
23. Saville, 'May Day 1937', pp247-8 and passim.
24. Saville, *Memoirs*, p56; Saville, 'Books to be remembered', *Socialist History*, 19, 2000, pp82-4.
25. See the discussion by Colin Leys in this volume. It must have confirmed Saville's low opinion of the editor, Valentine Cunningham, when his *British Writers of the Thirties* (1988) failed to uphold his earlier assertions, but without once referring to Saville's critique – while finding place in his extensive bibliography for his own somewhat less effective response to the critique.
26. Saville, 'The Twentieth Congress and the British Communist Party' in Ralph Miliband and John Saville, eds, *Socialist Register 1976*, Merlin, 1976, p18.
27. Saville, 'Communist experience', p12.
28. Saville, *Memoirs*, p98.
29. Saville, *Memoirs*, p11.
30. Strachey, *The Coming Struggle for Power*, Gollancz, 1932, chs 17-18; also Saville, 'Communist experience', p13.
31. See the discussion by Malcolm Chase below; also Saville, *Memoirs*, p8; Saville, 'Communist experience', pp11-12.
32. Saville, *Memoirs*, p62.
33. Saville, *Memoirs*, pp75-6.
34. 'John Saville and the *Dictionary of Labour Biography*: interview by Malcolm Chase', *Socialist History*, 19, 2000, p80.

35. Saville papers U DJS/10, Dobb to Saville, 19 November 1954.
36. See for example the assessment of his collaborator in the Historians' Group, Eric Hobsbawm, 'The taming of parliamentary democracy in Britain', *Modern Quarterly*, 6, 4, autumn 1951, pp336-9.
37. Saville, 'The welfare state', *New Reasoner*, 3, winter 1957, pp5-25; also Stephen Hatch and Dorothy Thompson, 'Discussion: the welfare state', *New Reasoner*, 4, spring 1958, pp124-30.
38. Saville, 'The welfare state', p25.
39. Saville, 'Communist experience', p14.
40. Saville, *Memoirs*, pp17-18.
41. See for example Eric Hobsbawm, 'The Historians' Group of the Communist Party' in Maurice Cornforth, ed., *Rebels and their Causes: essays in honour of AL Morton*, Lawrence & Wishart, 1978, pp21-47. The fullest account is Antony Howe, '"The past is ours." The political uses of English history by the British Communist Party, and the role of Dona Torr in the creation of its Historians' Group, 1930-56', Sydney: PhD, 2004.
42. Saville papers, U DJS/10, Saville to Sam Aaronovitch, 3 November 1954.
43. David Parker, ed., *Ideology, Absolutism and the English Revolution. Debates of the British communist historians 1940-1956*, Lawrence & Wishart, 2008. The other contributors to *Democracy and the Labour Movement*, were Henry Collins, Steven Mason, Ronald Meek and Daphne Simon.
44. Hobsbawm, 'Historians' Group', p43.
45. Saville papers U DJS/106, Hill to Saville with enclosure, 13 January 1954. E P Thompson expressed his own regard for these qualities in the foreword to his *William Morris: romantic to revolutionary*, Lawrence & Wishart, 1955, p8.
46. For Hobsbawm's more downbeat assessment of Torr's contribution see 'Eric Hobsbawm's Interesting Times: an interview with David Howell', *Socialist History*, 24, 2003, p8
47. See Saville, ed., *Democracy and the Labour Movement*, Lawrence & Wishart, 1954, foreword by George Thomson, Maurice Dobb, Christopher Hill and John Saville, pp7-9.
48. Saville papers U DJS/106, Saville to Maurice Cornforth, 24 October 1950.
49. A curious detail is that Torr objected 'violently' to the inclusion of a photograph of her in the collection (Saville papers, U DJS/106, Cornforth to Saville, 27 January 1954). Though Saville evidently allowed the inclusion of such a portrait in his own *festschrift* in 1979, he was also adamant that no photographs should be included in his own published memoirs. With the assistance of John's family, the omission is rectified in the present collection.
50. Saville papers, U DJS/10, Saville to Joan Simon, 27 November 1954 and Saville to Edwin Payne, 27 November 1954.

51. Saville, 'The Twentieth Congress and the British Communist Party'.
52. 'John Saville and the *Dictionary of Labour Biography*', pp75, 80.
53. Saville, 'Communist experience', p25.
54. Miliband, 'John Saville', p30.

The *New Reasoner* and the early New Left

Madeleine Davis

The story of the origin of the British New Left is reasonably well-known. Khrushchev's denunciation of Stalinism, followed by his own crushing of dissent in Hungary, touched off a crisis in world communism in which thousands of party members resigned. Angered by the refusal of the British Communist Party (CPGB) to allow open debate of the Khrushchev revelations, two of its members, John Saville and his fellow historian EP Thompson, from July 1956 produced and distributed three issues of an unofficial discussion journal, *The Reasoner*. In November, under threat of suspension for flouting party rules, its editors resigned their membership in protest at the British leadership's refusal to condemn Soviet actions in Hungary. Outside the party and assembling an enlarged editorial board of former communists, Thompson and Saville established a more substantial quarterly, the *New Reasoner*, which ran for ten issues until its merger with *Universities and Left Review* (ULR) on the cusp of the 1960s.[1] ULR was also born of reaction to 1956 events, although for the young intellectuals – Stuart Hall, Raphael Samuel, Charles Taylor and Gabriel Pearson – who founded it at Oxford in early 1957, British and French imperial aggression over Suez was at least as important an influence as the crisis in communism. Finding common ground – especially in their support for the Campaign for Nuclear Disarmament (CND) – and each facing organisational and financial difficulties, the two organs merged to form *New Left Review* (NLR). First appearing in 1960, this was intended as the mouthpiece and pivot of a novel New Left 'movement', with mobilising as well as intellectual ambitions.[2]

It is, then, a staple of scholarship on the New Left to locate its origins in the events of 1956. Yet we must avoid slipping into a kind of shorthand in which 'the moment of 1956', with all that we know it implies, is too hastily cited as a ready-made explanation for the emergence of a distinct New Left current, springing forth to proclaim 'socialist humanism' in place of Stalinist orthodoxy. In fact, the term 'New Left' was not used by either journal until the autumn of 1958, two years after *The Reasoner* was first published, and almost two years into the life of ULR. Initially, it was often used in inverted commas. A persistent tendency to view the history of the New Left as divided into two distinct phases or 'generations' (often referred to as the 'first' and 'second' New Lefts), separated by the transfer of editorship and ownership of NLR to Perry Anderson in 1962-3, is also unhelpful. It exacerbates a tendency to oversimplify into the distilled formula of 'the first New Left' a range of different positions and impulses. And it lends itself to the application of a retrospective teleology to accounts of the early New Left, in which it appears as a formation whose demise was inevitable, and/or as a prelude to later movements.[3] These tendencies in the historiography of the New Left have meant that NLR's predecessor journals are too often passed over as just that, and rarely given the attention each deserves in its own right. My purpose in this chapter, then, is to examine the nature of the project that John Saville, along with Thompson, embarked upon in *The Reasoner/New Reasoner*, and to explain how that journal came, with ULR, to take up a position at the centre of an emergent, complex agenda that became known as the 'New Left'. In doing so I hope to shed new light on what Saville certainly regarded as an important phase in his intellectual and political career.

BIRTH OF *THE REASONER*

Prior to their collaboration on *The Reasoner*, Saville and Thompson had, according to Saville, been 'friends for half a dozen years or so, but not close'.[4] Both were committed CPGB members of some years standing. In April 1956, Saville, by then lecturing in economic history at the University College of Hull, wrote to Thompson, and received a long response in Thompson's distinctive epistolary style. It began:

Dear John

Thank God for your letter. Never have I known such a wet flatfish slapped in the face as our 24th (National Congress). It is the biggest Confidence Trick in our Party's history. Not one bloody concession as yet to our feelings and integrity; no apology to the rank and file, no self-criticism … no indication of the points of Marxist theory which now demand revaluation … no promise of a loosening of inner-party democracy, and of the formation of even a discussion journal so that this can be fought out within our ranks …[5]

The two were part of a significant CPGB minority dismayed by the leadership's inadequate response to the Khrushchev revelations, and its determination to quash debate. Saville had a letter published in the party weekly *World News* in May, but a second was refused. Meanwhile, Rajani Palme Dutt described the 'mistakes' of Stalin as 'spots on the sun'.[6] Belatedly, in May, the Party's Executive Committee released a statement ('The lessons of the 20th Congress of the CPSU') expressing shock at events in the Soviet Union but glossing over revelations of mass murder and purges. It announced the formation of a special commission to examine the methods and workings of inner-party democracy. Moving slowly and under tight leadership control, a majority of the commission eventually endorsed a position that admitted 'errors' in the application of democratic centralism, but refused to reject it or admit the need for a thorough overhaul of party structures and practices. Faced with this intransigence, Saville and Thompson, unwilling to publish in the non-communist press, decided to produce their own publication in hopes of pressuring the leadership into allowing a full debate. They had no intention, at this point, of leaving the party.

The Reasoner, whose first issue appeared in July, its thirty-two pages painstakingly typed by Thompson and duplicated by Saville, was thus 'written by and addressed to members of the Communist Party': 'It is a discussion journal. Our first aim is to provide a forum for the far-reaching discussions at present going on within and close to the Communist Party – on questions of fundamental principle, aim and strategy'.[7] Under a quotation from Marx – 'to leave error unrefuted is to encourage intellectual immorality' – it comprised two editorial pieces, a critique of democratic centralism by Ken Alexander (a fellow dissenter with whom Saville corresponded regularly), correspondence, and documents of other communist parties, the last included to furnish British communists with information on the international scene unavailable through party channels. Some 650 copies were distributed through bookshops and contacts. Among the issues of which the editors called for the 'fullest discussion' were the 'very meaning of Marxism', the structure of the party, and even 'what is socialism?'. All this, though, could be addressed *within* the Marxist and communist tradition:

> We take our stand as Marxists. Nothing in the events of past months has shaken our conviction that the methods and outlook of historical materialism … provide the key to our theoretical advance … although it should be said that much that has gone under the name of Marxism-Leninism is itself in need of re-examination. History has provided a chance for this re-examination to take place, and for the scientific methods of Marxism to be integrated with the finest traditions of the human reason and spirit which we may best describe as humanism.[8]

Comrades Saville and Thompson were requested to cease publication, and on their refusal, summoned to King Street in August. Saville's recollection was of a leadership uninterested in any issue other than whether party rules were being broken.[9] The miscreants were given time to reconsider, though neither needed it: they drafted their responses, refusing to cease publication, on the train back north. The second, September issue was ready just before the leadership instructed they close down or face suspension. A pasted-in statement recorded this, and the editors' willingness to give way to an official discussion journal as a solution to what they acknowledged to be 'the problem of our unofficial publication'.

Initiating *The Reasoner* brought its editors hundreds of letters from other party members, most of which survive among Saville's personal papers. While the majority were supportive, some of the correspondence published in the second issue was critical. Ronald Meek (who later sat on the *New Reasoner* board) found the decision to publish independently irresponsible, and the editors' tactics 'incredibly bad', but disagreed with its suppression.[10] Others saw the purpose of the journal as an attack on the party leadership – a tactic one correspondent found 'peevish and negative'.[11] The editors were themselves unsure what to do next, eventually deciding to publish one more issue at the same time as announcing that they would cease publication in the interests of the Party. However they planned to appeal against their inevitable suspension, envisaging that this would help to keep the debate alive. It is clear from their correspondence that their instinct at this point, and their advice to others, was to keep the fight within the party. Yet the nucleus of a 'New Left' project could already be seen in their assessment of the priorities for British socialists, to 'recreate … a much clearer understanding of the character of socialist society – not only in its economic basis but also in its social relations and political institutions, and in its relation to contemporary British conditions'.[12]

Events in Hungary altered the context. As the last *Reasoner* was being duplicated, Soviet forces moved to crush the popular uprising in Budapest. An editorial statement dated 31 October announced their intention to close, to give way to a 'serious socialist journal' with a larger editorial board. In a final plea to keep matters within the party, it invited the leadership to 'take steps adequate to the political crisis and itself … initiate the formation of such a journal'.[13] But in a separate piece hastily included after the attack on Budapest, a harder line superseded. Soviet intervention marked 'a turning point' and meant that 'the crisis in world communism is now different in kind'. Thompson and Saville called on the CPGB leadership publicly to condemn the Soviet action and demand the withdrawal of troops. Failing this, they urged 'all those who, like ourselves, will dissociate themselves completely from the leadership of the British Communist Party, not to lose faith in socialism, and to find ways of keeping together'.[14] The issue also contained an impassioned piece by Thompson, 'Through the smoke of Budapest', in which he began to elaborate the moral standpoint he later called 'socialist humanism', declaring 'Stalinism is socialist theory and practice which has lost the ingredient of humanity'.[15] Rejection of Stalinism did not, however, imply rejection of communism, whose essentially humanist principles and values Thompson saw as perverted by dogmatism. These communist values were to be recovered and reaffirmed, yet to do so it was necessary to break out of party confines. Their suspension rendered irrelevant, Saville and Thompson resigned their party membership.

A 'MOST REMARKABLE JOURNAL'

It was Alasdair MacIntyre who described the *New Reasoner* (NR) as a 'most remarkable journal', some time after his own break with Marxism and many years after he debated socialist humanism with Thompson in its pages.[16] Yet, as Bryan Palmer notes, the NR is a publication 'much alluded to but seldom read', its project often subsumed by commentators in the larger enterprise of the New Left.[17] More central to the identity of the NR than its gradually emergent New Left character, however, was its role as an arena for negotiating a complex transition from communism, in which older ideas and habits coexisted, often productively, yet sometimes awkwardly, with the development of new theoretical and practical commitments. This dynamic was evident in the key preoccupations of the journal (discussed below), while their experiences of communism no doubt also contributed to the intense sense of commitment and practical purpose that Saville and Thompson brought to the journal. As an exchange of letters in early 1957 showed, their ambitions – both intellectual and political – for the new publication were high. Thompson saw it as a journal which 'states and develops positions – affirmative positions – unstated elsewhere, and which we believe to be profoundly important; an intellectual movement which must be kept alive, and which must maintain certain international contacts, and which without us would be seriously dispersed or without any vehicle'.[18] With their collaboration now well-established, NR's political stance did not require negotiation; there was, though, some discussion of tone. Thompson found Saville's initial proposals for the content of the first issue 'too concerned with a respectable intellectual audience', saying 'the chief thing I want in this journal is *attack*'; and that: 'I want specialists who write in such a way that serious non-specialists can not only understand what they mean, but (if the subject requires it) can be stimulated, roused or moved by what they say. This is NOT the learned or academic tradition; it IS the tradition of a certain sort of politico-cultural journalism (Swift and Hazlitt) in Britain.'[19]

In keeping with this vision, the new publication sought to bridge gaps between the Marxist/communist and other socialist tendencies in Britain, and to play a mobilising and educative role for a renewed socialist left. Its first editorial appealed to:

that great body of socialists who desire not only to act but to understand the context and aim of their actions. The energies of the labour movement have been weakened by the snapping of links between socialist intellectuals and those who bear the brunt of the practical work of the movement.

The NEW REASONER hopes to make some contribution towards re-establishing these links and regenerating these energies … we take our stand with those workers and intellectuals in the Soviet Union and E. Europe who are fighting for that return to Communist principle and that extension of liberties which has been dubbed 'de-Stalinisation'; in Britain with those socialists on the left wing of the Labour Party, or unattached to any party, who are fighting under very different conditions, for a similar rebirth of principle within the movement.

The first issue was weighty, at around 140 pages, but with a varied texture. Looking back, Saville thought it 'as good as anything the left were capable of at the time'.[20] It comprised substantial essays by Hyman Levy on Soviet socialism, Peter Worsley on Mau Mau in Kenya, Eric Hobsbawm on 'Marx's Victorian Critics', and Thompson's keynote discussion article on 'Socialist humanism', interspersed with literary content including a short story from Hungarian dissident Tibor Dery, and Polish and American poets Adam Waszyk and Tom McGrath. A 'Chronicle, Polemic, Discussion' section carried shorter pieces by Malcolm MacEwen, Peter Fryer and others – including Saville's own 'A note on dogmatism'; and 'Documents' included a translation of Sartre's 'Is this the time?', calling for transformation of the PCF. A similar mix continued through subsequent issues, which cultivated a direct, informal – even chatty – editorial tone with a regular 'Letter to readers' in which appeals for donations and later, updates on the merger discussions, were typical items.

Saville and Thompson were joined on the board by other former communists: initially Ken Alexander, literary figures Randall Swingler and Doris Lessing, and economist Ronald Meek; and later Alfred Dressler, the scientist DG Arnott, the anthropologist Peter Worsley, economist Michael Barratt-Brown, the writer Mervyn Jones, and Ralph Miliband, then lecturing at LSE and the only board member not to have been in the Communist Party. However, the two initial editors continued to shoulder the main burden of producing the quarterly. As their correspondence attests, they found this burden at times extremely heavy, especially since both had other major work and publishing commitments, and Saville at the time a young family. With a subscription price of fifteen shillings a year, the NR was distributed first among contacts acquired through publication of *The Reasoner*, and then more widely, with Saville in charge of organising sales and distribution. The second issue recorded a circulation of 2000. In total ten issues were produced, comprising some 165 signed contributions.[21] In this considerable body of work, four key themes predominated: an attempt to elaborate a libertarian, 'socialist humanist' agenda to counterpose to Stalinism; a commitment to internationalism; attention to culture and problems of political organisation.[22]

Socialist humanism

Socialist humanism was first defined by Thompson as the 'positive content' of the revolt against Stalinist ideology and inhumanity that began in 1956:

> It is *humanist* because it places once again real men and women at the centre of socialist theory and aspiration, instead of the resounding abstractions – the Party, Marxism-Leninism-Stalinism, the Two Camps, the Vanguard of the Working-Class – so dear to Stalinism. It is *socialist* because it reaffirms the revolutionary perspectives of Communism, faith in the revolutionary potentialities not only of the Human Race or of the Dictatorship of the Proletariat but of real men and women.[23]

The key elements of the position elaborated by Thompson were a rejection of the twin 'philistinisms' of Stalinism and western social democracy; a critique of the dogmatic 'economic automatism' of Stalinist Marxism, and against this an assertion of human historical agency and individual moral capacity. Its most original theoretical feature was the attempt to fuse the humanist content of Marxism with the moral consciousness exemplified by English romanticism, especially William Morris, whose biography Thompson had recently completed, and whose 'insights' and 'discoveries about man's potential moral nature' were 'not icing on the Marxist gingerbread but were complementary to the discoveries of Marx'.[24]

In the subsequent rejection of early New Left positions by Anderson's cohort, Thompson's writings of this period were sharply critiqued as 'moralist', 'populist' and lacking theoretical rigour. The famous polemic between Anderson and Thompson was also to be seen later as emblematic of the spread of anti-humanist, Althusserian structuralist thought from the mid-1960s, and of the controversies that ensued between adherents of humanism and/or 'culturalism' and structuralism. The tendency to view socialist humanism in terms defined by this subsequent debate has contributed to some misunderstanding of its significance for the early New Left. As the milieu took shape, socialist humanism became, as was intended, a kind of rallying point to bring disaffected communists and independent socialists together, and the term was taken up in ULR. But Thompson's theoretical position was far from consensual either within the wider New Left or among his *Reasoner* colleagues. Even Saville, his closest collaborator, dissented to some degree, though he did not publish his criticisms within the NR. Others however, including Alasdair MacIntyre, Charles Taylor and Harry Hanson, did. That their discussion is so often neglected is unfortunate, for it was a theoretically rich and lively debate in which the question of the relationship of socialism and Marxism to ethics and morality (later to re-emerge in better-known 1980s exchanges that barely registered the New Left contribution) was central.

Charles Taylor, of ULR, questioned Thompson's presentation of a compatibility between humanism and Marxist communism, arguing that the latter was 'at best an incomplete humanism' whose values needed not reaffirmation but fundamental reconsideration.[25] From a different perspective, Harry Hanson's critique anticipated elements of Anderson's later diagnosis of Thompsonian moralism and populism in his observation that 'you ... serve up your Marxism in a kind of watered down Christian sauce without being aware that you are concocting a very curious dish'.[26] The most significant and penetrating critique came from Alasdair MacIntyre, then a Marxist philosopher on the fringes of the New Left. MacIntyre attempted to develop socialist humanism, and to provide an alternative to 'moral individualism' as a standpoint from which to criticise Stalinism, by offering a moral theory grounded in Marxism. Key to this was a more developed humanist reading of Marxism than that offered by Thompson, in which he emphasised Marx's conception of human nature/essence as historicised human possibility.[27] Thompson's reply to his critics robustly defended his position, declaring 'human needs are the only valid criterion by which to assess ... economic and social arrangements'; but he did not fully address their points.[28] The incompleteness of the debate reflected the fact that Marxism itself was not in general subjected to sustained theoretical scrutiny by the *Reasoner* grouping. Writers of the NR shared in the wider enthusiasm for Marx's early work, then becoming more widely available, and the ideas of thinkers new to the British left, such as Gramsci, were well-received. Thompson himself, though he engaged seriously with Marx's thought and offered important reconceptualisations of base/superstructure and class, was primarily interested in demonstrating the compatibility of (British) romantic humanism and Marxism, the better to restore a libertarian and humanist lineage to communism, than he was in elaborating a specifically Marxist ethics, and he did not engage with the ideas of humanist thinkers elsewhere. Of all his critics he gave most ground to Taylor: saying 'I can now see more clearly that if Stalinism is a mutation of Marx's ideas, the very fact that they are capable of undergoing such a mutation while still remaining in a direct relationship indicates an original weakness which goes beyond mere ambiguity', and he was eventually to conclude that Marxism could not adequately encompass moral concerns.[29] In his correspondence with Saville, Thompson also referred to differences between the two in terms of the extent of their commitment to Marxism, requesting that Saville, in a meeting to discuss progress on the NR, should not 'overstress NR as a journal fighting for "Marxism" as a known and given position, since this would only lead to unnecessary disagreements between you and me in the meeting'.[30]

Socialist humanism as developed by Thompson was political rather than philosophical in inspiration. It allowed a moral critique of Stalinism and a partial rehabilitation of Communism, while seeking to root the values of the latter more firmly in British soil. It did though contain theoretical problems. These were only partially explored during the lifespan of the NR, both because to do so would have undermined emergent alliances, and also because the language of humanism and moral regeneration of socialism was sufficiently broad to appeal to rather different constituencies. It thus functioned as a (temporarily) unifying agenda around which a 'New Left' could gather.

Internationalism

The emphasis placed by Thompson on indigenous influences in his articulation of socialist humanism, the fame of Anderson's critique of the early New Left as parochial and British-orientated, and his well-known reorientation of NLR as a conduit for Marxist ideas developed elsewhere, has too often caused the *New Reasoner*'s marked internationalism to be overlooked. In fact, Anderson's criticisms were more justly applied to the early model of NLR, which did indeed become much more domestic in focus than its predecessor journals as the imperative to build a British-based New Left movement took precedence. Prior to the merger, NR's editors, in keeping with communist tradition, saw coverage of the international socialist scene as a primary duty.

Not surprisingly, events in Eastern Europe were a key concern. Though obvious difficulties of political access made systematic chronicle impossible, the NR's coverage was considerable. The Hungarian revolt was discussed by Peter Fryer, and Imre Nagy's execution deplored by Malcolm MacEwen and commemorated a year later with a tribute from Tibor Meray. The Programme of the League of Yugoslav Communists was first excerpted then subjected to a sober analysis by Miliband, while Royden Harrison reported from the Yugoslav Congress of Workers' Councils. East German revisionism was the subject of a piece by Dora Scarlett, who also contributed an account of her experiences in Hungary. Ronald Meek reported back from a lecture tour in Poland and the Soviet Union during which he tried to assess the effects of 'anti-revisionism' on intellectual debate. Coverage of the USSR itself was inconclusive: Hyman Levy's piece on Soviet socialism was succeeded by a 'symposium on Sputnik', pieces on 'Contemporary Soviet psychology' and 'The Russian economy'; but no sustained analysis of Soviet politics was offered by a member of the editorial board. No doubt the editors were wary of being seen as 'anti-communist' but the absence perhaps also spoke of unresolved problems: working through the lessons of 1956 would prove a complex and lengthy project. As well as political coverage, the NR became an important outlet for the expression of literary voices of dissent, publishing fiction and poetry from Tibor Dery, Adam Waszyk, W. Woroszylski and Alexander Yashin.

Internationalism was also expressed via a foreign policy agenda dubbed 'positive neutralism' and promoted as a realistic and immediate alternative to what was seen as Labour's shamefully acquiescent stance on the Cold War and nuclear weapons. The key elements of this position included support for nuclear disarmament (and of course CND) and British withdrawal from NATO. As well as setting an example of moral leadership, it was thought that British opt-out from the Cold War in favour of a neutral stance would be 'a policy which capitalist Britain could pursue and yet survive. And thus it would be a policy which the Left in the Labour Movement could impose on the Labour leadership, the Tories, or both.'[31] It was further recommended that in place of entry into the 'West-End European capitalist club' of the Common Market, Britain should plan its international trade through a system of agreements with trading partners, and especially with non-aligned countries newly emerged from colonial rule whose governments were pursuing a national-populist agenda.[32] The ultimate aim was to create 'a political space in which, globally, superpower hegemony could be dismantled and colonized peoples could free themselves – the prerequisites for ending world poverty and abolishing the bomb'.[33]

A cornerstone of positive neutralism was support for movements of self-determination and national liberation in what was beginning to become known as the 'Third World'. Peter Worsley and John Rex were the main contributors, discussing African developments in the main, though Keralan Communism, Arab nationalism and Japanese Marxism were also covered by other writers. Rex and Worsley attended conferences in Ghana, Rex reported on the 1958 Accra conferences of former colonies and those struggling for independence, and Dorothy Thompson reported back from a 1958 congress of the new *Parti d'Union de la Gauche Socialiste* (UGS) convened by Claude Bourdet and attended by European and African socialists. Little wonder then, that EP Thompson reacted furiously when Anderson's team scolded their New Left predecessors for neglect of Third World struggles. In fact it was its sometimes uncritical 'Third Worldism', under the influence of writers such as Fanon and Sartre, that was among the aspects of the new NLR that Thompson found most odious, lambasting tendencies to glorify violence, denigrate the record of European radicalism, and transfer the thwarted revolutionary hopes of the West to new arenas.[34] As he made abundantly clear, NR's internationalism was founded on a belief in the common interests of exploited peoples worldwide. Saville was later to make a similar – if much briefer –

defence of the record of the *Socialist Register* against a charge that it had
failed to welcome third world revolutionary struggles with sufficient
enthusiasm.[35] Of the various New Left currents post-1963, it was the
Socialist Register, under Saville and Miliband, that remained truest to
the original spirit of the NR in this (and other) respects.

Cultural coverage

NR devoted a significant proportion of its output to cultural
coverage, especially original fiction and poetry. Saville was later irked
by Doris Lessing's disavowal of communist influence – in fact she was
a regular correspondent from the inception of the *Reasoner*, served on
the NR editorial board and contributed two short stories.[36] East
European literature was a particular interest, although NR also
published North American and Turkish poets as well as home-grown
talent. Literary romanticism was well-represented, with a Blake bicentenary supplement (written by Thompson under a pseudonym), a
piece on Wordsworth and invocations of Morris. The role of the
visual arts was discussed, and there were occasional comments on film
and drama. NR's cultural coverage, which, in line with Thompson's
socialist humanist agenda, was often concerned with literature and art
as expressions of socialist desire, or in educating the 'moral consciousness', was rather different in emphasis from ULR's. Indeed the latter's
more experimental and contemporary approach, embracing such
forms as popular music and youth culture, and tentatively embarking
on an ambitious project to theorise and practice a new kind of left
cultural politics, was regarded with suspicion as lightweight and
overly 'fashionable'. Raymond Williams' *Culture and Society* was
greeted as a 'fascinating and important' but at the same time criticised
as lacking 'a firm framework of historical fact'[37] – a point Thompson
later developed more fully in a two-part NLR review of *The Long
Revolution* that criticised Williams for insufficient attention to questions of power, struggle and materialism.[38]

Political organisation

Saville and Thompson's original purpose in founding *The Reasoner*
was emphatically not to make a new political movement, since they
retained their communist convictions. Yet their resignation from the

party placed them in an organisational limbo. From the NR's inception they engaged in constant discussion of its purpose and orientation, always seeing it as more than solely an intellectual project. As the journal broadened its appeal beyond former communists, two possible outlets for its 'organisational impulse' became apparent. [39]

The first was Labour leftism. Having left the CPGB, the NR's editors looked naturally toward the labour movement as a means of advancing socialism in Britain. The (re)establishment of Victory for Socialism (VFS), a Labour left grouping with which Ralph Miliband was involved and which aimed to 'fight apathy', 'stimulate fresh socialist thinking' and press for nuclear disarmament, was therefore of interest.[40] Miliband proposed a link between VFS and the NR. But though happy to explore areas of mutual interest, the two main NR editors refused any organisational tie-up. Thompson particularly was wary of being pulled into the orbit of the Labour left, saying 'it is the old old mistake of the labour left to think that socialism can be won simply by jumping into the movement and pushing leftwards'. The NR, he said, could and should influence the Labour left through the quality of its output, but must not be pulled into heading a new faction.[41] There was some difference of emphasis between Saville and Thompson, with the latter already considering some kind of non-party society or association as the best way forward. In January 1958 he asked Saville, on a visit to London, not to turn down approaches from ULR for joint initiatives such as reading groups, remarking: 'I think you would tend to turn down anything of an extra-party character which I might favour, while I would tend to turn down anything involved with the Labour left and V for S groupings which you might favour.'[42] Saville too, though, told Miliband he did not want to see the NR 'become the official organisation of the VFS'.[43]

NR did however intervene increasingly in Labour debates, especially as the Croslandite prospectus for the renewal of Labour threatened to sever its link with common ownership. Thus John Hughes published detailed proposals for steel nationalisation, ULR's pamphlet 'The Insiders' (a detailed critique of Labour's 'Industry and Society') was greeted with approval, and a joint ULR/NR pamphlet by Hughes and Ken Alexander outlined ambitious proposals for 'A socialist wages plan'. And Miliband began to develop the critique of Labour that would eventually lead to his dismissing it as any kind of vehicle for socialism. In 'Transition to the transition' he argued that reforming measures and state intervention undertaken by Labour, far from representing progress toward socialism, actually functioned to stabilise capitalism. This 'marginal collectivism', he wrote, 'state intervention, help and control, is now the price which capitalism has learnt it must pay as a condition of its survival as a more or less going economic concern'.[44] Saville made the same point in a discussion of the welfare state as contributing to capitalist efficiency by raising labour productivity: it was, he argued, 'essentially bourgeois' in nature.[45] This somewhat 'old left' dismissal of the significance of welfarism did not find favour with some colleagues: Ken Alexander, EP and Dorothy Thompson all offering pre-publication critiques that Thompson felt Saville took insufficient account of, even telling him: 'I am rather fed up about your whole reaction'.[46] In the event Dorothy Thompson published a sharp rejoinder arguing that aspects of the welfare state represented 'victories for working class values within capitalism'.[47] The debate over Saville's article hinted at, but did not thrash out, continuing differences within the *Reasoner* cohort on questions of organisation and strategy. Miliband especially, though forced to give up the idea of linking NR and VFS, remained convinced of the need for party organisation and saw a very clear distinction between capitalism and socialism.[48] Notwithstanding his sharp criticisms of Labour, he was convinced that the best immediate option for socialism was 'to get in and push' to radicalise the party.[49] He regarded the question of the 'transition to socialism' (on which topic Saville and Thompson had asked him to write) as abstract and remote. Thompson, on the other hand, increasingly suspicious of party organisation, was interested in the possibilities of a 'democratic revolutionary strategy' consisting of a conscious acceleration of 'reforming pressures in many fields, which are designed to reach a revolutionary culmination' and to push Britain to 'a kind of tipping-point from which full-blown socialism could develop'.[50] Thompson's view attracted him increasingly to the second possible outlet for the *Reasoner*'s organisational energies; the experimental and activist milieu developing around CND and ULR.

A PRECARIOUS FUSION

From its inception, the NR's project coexisted and interacted with a broader and more diffuse agenda. At the end of 1956 Raphael Samuel

wrote to Saville requesting a contribution by the NR editors to a new
publication to be called 'New University Left' (actually ULR) and
proposing 'some sort of division of labour' between the journals.
Practical co-operation began early in 1958, the year CND was
formed. Thompson immediately saw in CND a vehicle for 'positive
neutralism' and socialist humanism to reach a broader audience, while
the ULRers had a more organic connection with the disarmament
movement, whose grassroots activism and loose organisational format
mirrored that of the nascent ULR club network. As their correspondence shows, it was Thompson rather than Saville who was initially
keener on a merger with ULR, in part because of pressure of work. As
the NR ended its first year, he wrote to him: 'I think we have done a
good whack of work in '57, quite creditable, and we haven't quar-
relled, at least not disastrously, and we needn't in '58. But '58 is my
limit. We must get a change of editorship in '59, perhaps some loose
society behind the journal.'[51] By spring 1958 he was pressing the case
more forcefully, despite recording some less than favourable impressions of the ULR group following a meeting: 'the ULR boys are rather
cautious young men, with excellent ideas and attack where the
students and young intelligentsia are concerned, but with very little
experience and knowledge of the labour movement; and that while we
welcome their initiative among young people, we think that their
unstated but implicit claim to provide intellectual leadership in the
general socialist movement ought to be tempered by a rather more
cooperative and responsible attitude'. Perhaps he was annoyed by
their reluctance to consider amalgamation, for in the same circular he
noted '[they] clearly want to run their own show'.[52] He also proposed
his own and Saville's replacement as NR editors from the eighth
number, and warned Saville again in April: 'I *can't* go on as now
beyond no 8 … I am very sorry you won't take the ULR merger question more seriously because with all its colossal drawbacks it might
contain a solution.' Exasperated, Saville told Thompson 'NR is not
any longer a private venture of you and me and the decision about the
future of it is a most serious political matter. So … we must look
forward and plan for a third year, and a fourth year'.[53] But a couple
of months later he changed his view, saying that as he could not keep
NR going without Thompson: 'I am with you about the approaches
to ULR; and I think we should make definite advances to them.
There are lots of other reasons I now see for amalgamation – the

renewal of the Left is a slow business and we ought to be working together.'[54] The choice eventually came to be seen as merger or closure.

There were also strong positive reasons for amalgamation. During 1958-9, both journals intervened more frequently on questions of policy, the clubs network gathered momentum, and a sense began to develop of the role a vital, activist but non-aligned socialist current might play in British politics. *New Left Review*, then, was conceived as an opportunity to give shape and political direction to a promising formation which, without a clearer platform, might easily dissipate. It would formalise the emergence of the New Left as a distinctive strand on the British political scene, act as an organising pivot for the clubs and other initiatives, and would be the locus for continued discussion of theoretical and practical problems. A position paper by Thompson set out a breathtakingly ambitious agenda for this new formation: it would 'counter the philistine materialism and anti-intellectualism of the Old Left by appealing to the totality of human interest and poten-tialities'; and promote 'in the great centres of working class life, a richer sense of community -- a socialist youth movement (semi-autonomous, if need be), rank and file international contacts, and social activities'. He was clear that it would not be 'an alternative organisation to those already in the field'. Rather it would offer 'two things to those within and without the existing organisations – a specific propaganda of ideas, and certain practical services (journals, clubs, schools etc)'. It would therefore be distinguished by 'its rupture with inner-party factionalism and its renewal of the tradition of open association'. 'The 'bureaucracy will hold the machine' he predicted, 'but the New Left will hold the passes between it and the younger generation.'[55]

Against such lofty ideals, the reality could hardly fail to disappoint. This early model of NLR was indeed the locus for some brilliant and pioneering intellectual work, its spin-off activities enjoyed notable successes, its critiques of contemporary society attracted wide notice, and for a time it exerted some influence on the Labour left. But the milieu was beset by problems of organisation and strategy, its core team were hopelessly overworked, and its mobilising ambitions proved impossible to sustain.[56] Tensions within the over-large New Left board, especially between Thompson and the managing team around Stuart Hall, were debilitating. Despite his published hopes for the New Left, Thompson had serious misgivings about NLR from the start. Even before the launch, he criticised the new team as 'slack and irresponsible', remarking: 'I have never seen a journal less likely to get off the ground than NLR'.[57] Relations between Thompson as chair of the board and Hall as editor quickly deteriorated. In all this Saville appears to have acted, despite his own reservations about the new project, as a mediating force, attempting to cultivate good relations with Hall's team. He found Thompson's attitude unacceptable, on one occasion telling him angrily 'it would be helpful if you started practising some of that socialist humanism you write about so eloquently' and suggesting that he should 'stop acting high drama and work on the assumption that we are all going to be around for a long time.'[58]

Saville's published contribution to the new journal consisted of three pieces: two book reviews on Chartism, and a short article 'Apathy into politics'. The last expressed his conviction that while for the present the New Left was right not to 'restrict political activity to stereotyped forms or organisations', developments in the labour movement were the key to real progress. For him a shift 'out of apathy' must be a shift '*into politics*: the political definition and organisation of the ideas of the Left in the months to come'.[59] In keeping with this view, his main contribution to the activist agenda of NLR was to try to forge links with the trade union movement via a New Left industrial bulletin 'Searchlight' (which ran for only four issues), and formation of a northern industrial committee.[60] These efforts sat rather uncomfortably within the broad, eclectic agenda of the early New Left; they were, in any case, rapidly overtaken by the crisis that enveloped the movement and forced its fragmentation and reorientation.

CONCLUDING THOUGHTS: SAVILLE, THOMPSON AND THE NEW LEFT

The period between 1956 and 1963 saw Saville give up his organisational allegiance to communism and play a major role in the founding of a New Left. Yet his own intellectual and political preoccupations remained substantially unchanged. Saville in fact retained more traditional concerns than many in the New Left, both substantively, in regard to questions of organisation, and in his focus on concepts of class and state, and stylistically, in his preference for a plain-speaking and accessible idiom, as opposed to the rather self-conscious complexity adopted by the new NLR, whose project Saville nevertheless respected. By the end of the lifespan of the *New Reasoner*, he was intellectually closer to Miliband, who opposed the merger with ULR, than to his former communist comrade Thompson. Had the NR continued, it is possible that the latter's evolution away from Marxism and growing distrust for traditional forms of political organisation could have widened their differences and proved disruptive to a joint project. It is also clear that despite the great personal and intellectual regard Saville had for Thompson, their collaboration was sometimes difficult. Where Thompson was inclined to extremes of both optimism and pessimism about the NR's role and prospects, Saville took a more practical and prosaic approach, and this steadiness of purpose had certainly helped keep that 'most remarkable' publication afloat. It would also prove critical to the success of the subsequent collaboration that Saville embarked on with Miliband in the *Socialist Register*, a journal which in many ways can be regarded as a direct successor to the project of the *New Reasoner*.

Notes

1. All issues of the *New Reasoner* are available to read at www.amielandmelburn.org.uk/collections/nr/index_frame.htm.
2. For accounts of the emergence of the New Left see Michael Kenny, *The First New Left*, Lawrence & Wishart, 1995, Lin Chun, *The British New Left*, Edinburgh University Press, 1993, Madeleine Davis 'The origins of the British New Left' in M. Klimke and J. Scharloth, eds, *1968 in Europe*, London, Palgrave, 2008.
3. A problem noted by Michael Kenny, 'First New Left in Britain 1956-64', Manchester, PhD, 1991, introduction. Kenny's own treatment is appropriately sympathetic to the complexities, despite his use of the term 'first' New Left.
4. John Saville, *Memoirs from the Left*, Merlin, 2003, p104.
5. Thompson to Saville, 4 April 1956, cited Saville, *Memoirs*, p105.
6. *Labour Monthly*, May, 1956.
7. 'Why we are publishing', *Reasoner* 1 July 1956.
8. 'Why we are publishing', p3.
9. Saville, *Memoirs*, pp108-9.
10. 'What should we do about the Reasoner?' *The Reasoner*, 2, September 1956.

11. J Lyons, letter, *The Reasoner*, 2, September 1956.
12. Editorial, *The Reasoner*, 2, September 1956, p5.
13. 'Statement by the editors', *The Reasoner*, 3, November 1956.
14. Editorial, Sunday 4 November, 1956, *The Reasoner*, 3, November 1956.
15. EP Thompson, 'Through the smoke of Budapest', *The Reasoner*, 3, Novermber 1956, p6.
16. Alasdair MacIntyre, *After Virtue*, Duckworth, 1981, preface pvii.
17. Bryan D Palmer, 'Reasoning rebellion: EP Thompson, British Marxist historians, and the making of dissident political mobilisation', *Labour/Le Travail*, 50, 2002. Palmer's own assessment is a notable exception.
18. Saville papers, Hull History Centre, Thompson to Saville, n.d. but probably January 1957.
19. Saville papers, Thompson to Saville, 9 January 1957.
20. Saville, *Memoirs*, p115.
21. Palmer, 'Reasoning rebellion', p10.
22. Palmer's treatment identifies similar themes but also includes 'social science in the service of social transformation', p10.
23. Thompson, 'Socialist humanism: an epistle to the philistines', *New Reasoner*, 1, summer 1957, p109
24. Thompson, 'Socialist humanism', p125.
25. C Taylor 'Marxism and humanism', *New Reasoner*, 2 autumn 1957, p98.
26. H Hanson, 'An open letter to Thompson', *New Reasoner*, 2 autumn 1957, p92.
27. Alasdair MacIntyre, 'Notes from the moral wilderness', *New Reasoner*, 7, winter 1958-9, *New Reasoner*, 8, spring 1959.
28. Thompson, 'Agency and choice 1', *New Reasoner*, 5, summer 1958, p91. A planned second instalment never appeared.
29. Thompson, 'Agency and choice', p96.
30. Saville papers, Thompson to Saville, 7 May 1958.
31. Editorial 'Can we have a neutral Britain', *New Reasoner*, 4, spring 1957, p10.
32. Michael Barratt Brown, 'Positive neutralism then and now' in Robin Archer et al, eds, *Out of Apathy: Voices of the New Left thirty years on* , Verso, 1989, p82.
33. Peter Worsley, 'Non-alignment and the New Left', in Archer, *Out of Apathy*, p89.
34. Thompson, 'Where are we now?', undated editorial circular.
35. Saville, 'Critical friend', *Socialist Review* 177, July/August, 1994.
36. Saville, *Memoirs*, pp109-10.
37. Victor Kiernan 'Culture and society', *New Reasoner*, 9, summer 1959.
38. Thompson, 'The Long Revolution', *New Left Review*, 9, May/June 1961; 10 July/August 1961.
39. Palmer, 'Reasoning rebellion', p35. A third possibility was briefly raised by Saville and Thompson's decision to support Lawrence Daly as an independent socialist candidate for West Fife in the 1959 election. Saville

pointed out that there were special circumstances in the Daly case and that no general principle was being established, but at the same time did not rule out similar moves in the future: no socialist, he said, should promise unconditional loyalty to 'a Labour Party dominated by Mr Gaitskell' (Saville, 'A note on West Fife', NR, 10, autumn 1959).

40. Mike Newman, *Ralph Miliband and the Politics of the New Left*, Merlin, 2002, p92.
41. Saville papers ,Thompson to Saville, 31 March 1958.
42. Saville papers, Thompson to Saville, 2 January 1958.
43. Saville to Miliband, 8 July 1958, quoted Newman, *Ralph Miliband*, p95.
44. Miliband, 'The transition to the transition', *New Reasoner*, 6, autumn 1958, p38.
45. Saville, 'The welfare state: an historical analysis', *New Reasoner*, 3, winter 1957, p14.
46. Saville papers, Thompson to Saville, n.d.
47. D. Thompson, 'The welfare state: discussion', *New Reasoner*, 4, spring 1958.
48. See Newman, *Ralph Miliband*, pp95-8.
49. Miliband, 'Transition', p48.
50. Thompson, 'Revolution', in NLB, *Out of Apathy*, Stevens & Sons, 1960, pp303-5.
51. Savillle papers, Thompson to Saville, 31 December 1957.
52. Saville papers, editorial circular, n.d, but probably early 1958.
53. Saville papers, Saville to Thompson, n.d. but probably April 1958.
54. Saville papers, Saville to Thompson, 15 June 1959.
55. Thompson, 'The New Left', *New Reasoner*, 9, Summer 1959, pp16-17.
56. See Kenny, *First New Left*, pp23-44.
57. Saville papers,Thompson to Saville, n.d., but probably late 1959.
58. Saville papers,, Saville to Thompson, n.d. but probably October/.November, 1959.
59. Saville, 'Apathy into Politics, *New Left Review* 1: 4, July/August 1960.
60. See Kenny, *First New Left*, pp45-6.

'Honest socialists': John Saville and the *Socialist Register*

Colin Leys

The *Socialist Register*, the annual collection of political essays which John Saville founded with Ralph Miliband in 1963, has survived the three decades of the ascendancy of neoliberalism with a strong international reputation and a wide readership. Of all the surviving initiatives of the original 'New Left' in Britain the *Register* has probably stayed closest to its original aims, linking critical analysis with left activism, and especially leading the way in analysing globalisation as it accelerated through the 1990s, and US imperialism as it bombed and blundered its way through the 2000s. The chronicle of its contributors reads like a *Who's Who* of the left's best brains and writers over the four and a half decades of its existence. By any standards, making this happen was a considerable achievement.

Yet in his *Memoirs from the Left* Saville devoted exactly two paragraphs to his work on the *Register*. Did this mean that he thought it unimportant? That seems unlikely, since producing it was demanding work and he stuck to it for almost twenty years. But he was nonetheless glad to hand it over to others while he devoted himself more and more to his work as a labour historian. For Miliband, who continued to edit it until his death in 1994, the *Register* was something more – a way of linking political theory with practice, and potentially developing a 'line' that would give his own work and that of like-minded socialists some influence over current political developments. Saville did not see any prospect of doing that. He had, he said, never thought that socialism was on the agenda for Britain.[1] For him the *Register* was fulfilling its purpose if it maintained a principled critique of capitalist society and provided a forum in which democratic socialists could work out their political positions.

In retrospect neither view seems quite right. The *Socialist Register* did gradually develop something like a distinctive 'line', particularly after the emergence of neoliberalism. It was a line of analysis not policy, but its consistency and quality earned the *Register* a reputation that enabled it to survive the eclipse of the left in party-political terms and offer a serious basis for the political regroupings which began in Europe at the end of the 1990s, and which seem bound to occur more widely in the future. And this owed a lot more to Saville than his own minimalist account suggests.

A word on the background is needed to make clear what the *Register* was intended to do.[2] Following the revelations in Khrushchev's secret speech to the CPSU Twentieth Congress in February 1956 and the repression in Hungary in the same year, Saville and Edward Thompson resigned from the British Communist Party (CPGB) and founded the *New Reasoner*, a quarterly.[3] Their aim was to provide a forum for the kind of debate among party members and ex-members that the party leadership had refused to allow, publishing 'material of three kinds: theoretical and analytical articles, documents and commentary on the international scene, and "a wide range of creative writing – short stories, polemic, satire, reportage, poetry, and occasional historical articles – which contribute to the rediscovery of our traditions, the affirmation of socialist values, and the undogmatic perception of social reality"'.[4]

In 1958 they invited Miliband, a lecturer in political science at the London School of Economics, to join the editorial board – the only member of it who had never been a communist. As a Marxist at the LSE during the cold war years Miliband had become more and more isolated, socially as well as intellectually. His lectures and seminars on socialism drew large audiences but they all had to be given outside the regular curriculum. Working with Saville and Thompson broke his isolation. He felt at home with these dissident communists – more than with the editors of the other 'new left' journal, the student-led *Universities and Left Review* (ULR), launched in the same year (1957) as the *New Reasoner*, although he collaborated with them too. When in 1959 the two journals were merged to form the *New Left Review* (NLR), it was over his strong opposition, but he nonetheless joined the merged board along with Thompson and Saville, who chaired it. In April 1963, after the differences between the two currents of socialism represented by the ULR and the NR had finally proved irreconcilable, and the three of them had left the board, Miliband proposed a new publication – an annual – with three editors – Thompson, Saville and himself – to resume, in effect, the work of the *New Reasoner*.

Thompson declined. He had found editorial work on the *New Reasoner* a burden and was not anxious to return to it, even for an annual. He also had political differences with Miliband: over the USSR, which Miliband at this time was still inclined to think might evolve away from Stalinism; and over the Marxism of Perry Anderson and his colleagues on the NLR. While Miliband persisted in recognising the importance of some of the latter's analyses, Thompson more or less indiscriminately rejected them. In any case, Thompson was anything but a 'team player'. Miliband's biographer Michael Newman rightly remarks that '... while [Thompson's] brilliance and flair could have added a great deal to the *Socialist Register*, it is highly unlikely the publication could have withstood the inevitable clashes between himself and Miliband that would have occurred'.[5]

But Saville was keen to be involved, and luckily for the *Register* he was ideally suited by temperament and political formation to be Miliband's collaborator. He was now politically homeless, and not yet as heavily involved in university work as he would later become, as head of a growing department and in researching his magnum opus, the *Dictionary of Labour Biography*. Saville admired Miliband's intellectual rigour and independence of mind, and shared his political outlook. An annual promised to be less demanding to produce than a quarterly, and less apt to require the editors to take up immediate positions on current developments, which Saville saw had often become hard to interpret.[6] They were very different people, from very different backgrounds, yet during the roughly twenty years in which they worked together as editors they had no major ideological or political disagreements.[7] The fact that Miliband greatly respected Saville's scholarship and sharp mind helped, as did the fact that the whole point of the *New Reasoner*, whose tradition the *Register* was meant to carry forward, had been not to be dogmatic or sectarian. The aim of the *Register* was, Miliband later wrote, to publish 'work that would fall within the broad Marxist tradition to which we both belonged'.[8]

But in practice Miliband was far from relaxed when it came to deciding whether work fell within this tradition, and apt to become very obstinate and worked up about it, and even critical of Saville, when he was less inclined to be so choosy, for not being sufficiently committed to the project. Saville, I think, simply saw the *Register* as a political project that needed to succeed and behaved accordingly. 'It was undoubtedly Saville's ability generally to cultivate "a duck's back" and absorb Miliband's periodic outbursts which enabled the collaboration to survive and the SR succeed.'[9] It seems unlikely that this came naturally to him, as he held strong views and was perfectly capable of expressing himself forcefully. It seems more likely that it reflected his twenty-two years of disciplined political activity within the Communist Party.

Personal feelings were also involved. Saville had become good friends with Miliband and was 'a sort of best man' at his wedding, in 1961, to Marion Kozak. He became a close family friend of the Milibands, and Marion later became one of his favourite graduate students.[10] Editing the *Register* meant that he travelled to London every two months or so – Miliband hardly ever went to Hull – and often stayed with the family, which he enjoyed very much. London also afforded him other opportunities, including buying books and papers for the Hull University library (with the encouragement of Philip Larkin) and, from the mid-1970s onwards, doing research in the Public Record Office at Kew.

So starting in 1963 he and Miliband would meet every year to plan the next volume, and then share out the work of writing the letters to prospective authors. They both read and commented on all the manuscripts as they came in, and shared the work of making them ready for publication. Miliband did most of the work of editing drafts by the many foreign authors who constituted a major strength of the *Register*, most of whom he had recruited; and of correcting translations, which he invariably found fault with. 'He didn't do the translations but he would look at the translations and say "this is terrible", and go bananas about it', Marion Kozak remembers; 'nobody was good enough'. He also told Saville that his editing was too lenient, and would complain to Marion that John was 'too sloppy'. In reality, as Newman points out, Miliband's standards were impossibly – ridiculously – high. Volumes of the *Register* that contained essays by writers such as Isaac Deutscher, Ernest Mandel, André Gorz, Hamza Alavi, Victor Kiernan, EP Thompson and Georg Lukacs – essays which have passed into the canon of left literature – he rated, in a typical letter to Saville, as 'not good enough, mate'.[11] Saville tolerated his friend's hyper-perfectionism, no doubt recognising that, irritating as it was, it produced remarkable results.

The title of the *Register* was suggested by Martin Eve, who had founded the Merlin Press in 1956 and was a friend of Thompson's from their time as students at Cambridge. Eve also offered to publish the *Register* if Saville and Miliband would put up £150 to get it started. They were delighted both with this offer and with the title, which was, as Eve said, 'borrowed of course from Cobbett'.[12] Cobbett's *Political Register* looked like an attractive model, its broadsheet version having at one time (1816-17) had a circulation of 200,000 copies and an enormous influence on public opinion.[13] On the other hand, as Thompson pointed out in *The Making of the English Working Class*, 'Cobbett … helped to create and nourish an anti-intellectualism, and the theoretical opportunism (masked as "practical" empiricism) which remained an important characteristic of the British labour movement'.[14] This was one of the things that Saville and Miliband, almost as much as Anderson and Nairn in the NLR, wanted to combat. Yet in another way Cobbett's example was apt: he had addressed himself to ordinary people, not to the educated class. This was, as Thompson said, 'a matter of tone'. The *Socialist Register* could not emulate Cobbett's tone. Its contributors were largely university-based experts, and few had a common touch. But the readers whom the editors always had in mind were the activist intelligentsia, not academics. Miliband used to say that the *Register* should be hard to read, but this was a call for theoretical and analytic rigour, not scholastic obscurity. Making it readable was (and still is) an important editorial aim.

In his *Memoirs* Saville remarked that: 'I have written a fair number of articles for the *Register* but most of my energies in this context have naturally been on the editorial side'.[15] Yet between 1964 and 1995 he contributed nineteen essays, not counting one co-written with Miliband in the first volume – certainly a 'fair' number. So besides doing his share of the editing tasks, and giving Miliband the intellectual companionship and support he needed, and periodically preventing him from giving up, Saville's contribution to the *Register* also consisted to a considerable extent in writing frequently – and always reliably – for it.

THE *REGISTER* ESSAYS

In any case his *Register* essays make very interesting reading. From the late 1960s he became involved in a wide range of other activities, on top of his teaching and research. Among much else, these included the Oral History Society, the Society for the Study of Labour History, the Council for Academic Freedom and Democracy, speaking classes for trade unionists, assessing postgraduate programmes for the SSRC. Saville could thus have been forgiven if his contributions had been occasionally rushed and relatively lightweight and he did sometimes appear to use something drawn from his current historical work that had no great current significance. On the whole, however, his essays were substantial, pertinent to current politics, and often powerful. The topics covered fall into five relatively distinct categories: critiques of right and left ideologies, represented respectively by *Encounter* and *Marxism Today* (two essays); labour or left historiography (four);[16] the end of the British Communist Party, and of communism (three); socialist strategy and the Labour Party (eight); and analyses of major issues in British politics in the 1980s (two).

Saville's prose was workmanlike rather than elegant. At its best it displayed an 'unsectarian fluency of style and content', though spiced with an occasional barb.[17] His caustic demolition of the 'liberal' (read, anti-communist) magazine *Encounter* in the first volume of the *Register* in 1964 – several years before it was revealed that *Encounter* was funded by the CIA – contained various examples of the latter characteristic: for instance, its editor's mission to 'deepen and maintain the gulf between East and West', Saville wrote, was 'a task which called for a fine sense of imbalance in the editorial make-up of each number'. The 'stale prejudices of the English middle class' shown by some *Encounter* authors – for instance Cyril Connolly complaining of 'the endless grinding cancer of the income tax' – provoked his particular contempt:

> Some of those among the middle classes with a claim to progressive thinking found their liberal pretensions crumbling before the difficulties of obtaining domestic help and the growing conviction, which had no basis in fact, that their living standards were being sacrificed to the 'vast redistribution of incomes' in favour of the working class ...[18]

The editors of *Marxism Today* – which at the end of the 1980s still called itself 'the theoretical journal of the Communist Party' – were by then evangelists of 'post-fordism' and post-modernism, without any real political ties, which upset Saville even more. Their dismissal of earlier Marxist thought as 'reductionist' had, he thought, left them close to celebrating what they thought they had identified as a new era of capitalism, instead of seeking to assist popular struggles against it:

> There is almost certainly no doubt of the theoretical inadequacies or the dogmatism of those who led the Long March; or of those German Communists whose record in concentration camps was so astounding and heroic; or of the 70,000 French communists who were killed in the Resistance movement; or of the guerrillas in El Salvador today and their nearby comrades in Nicaragua. The latter, undoubtedly, would be in better theoretical shape if only they had access to *MT*'s elaboration of the 'New Times' we now live in.[19]

He was bluntly intolerant of compromises with power of whatever nature, especially when they were accompanied by poor scholarship. This was a central theme of his historiographical essays, which were mainly concerned with critiquing the growing output of 'revisionist' labour history. A notable example was the attempt by John Stevenson and Chris Cook to show that the 1930s slump had not been as bad as generally supposed. Saville (writing with Alun Howkins) showed that they had misused some sources and ignored others that contradicted their thesis, such as newly available data on unemployment, or individual accounts of the tyrannical working conditions of Welsh mineworkers who had been forced to leave their families and take non-unionised jobs in the new motor industry.[20]

He did the same for the introduction by Valentine Cunningham, an Oxford English don, to a 1980 Penguin anthology of poetry from the Spanish Civil War. This traduced the motives of many British volunteers who fought on the Republican side, and those of the leaders of the CPGB, to which many British volunteers had belonged. Saville was very well read in the copious literature on the civil war and had no illusions about the sectarianism and power-plays that did so much damage to the republican cause. But nothing aroused his fury so much as the kind of sneering denigration of the struggle for socialism, based on cheap innuendo and ignorance of the facts, that Cunningham's essay indulged in. It provoked an exceptionally passionate concluding statement of his own political outlook that is worth quoting at some length:

In the past quarter of a century we have begun to set the agonies of the war, its nobility, its lies, its betrayals, into a more truthful historical perspective. The adjustments have been painful and often very difficult to absorb and appreciate, but if we now see the Civil War in Spain in its international perspectives with clearer eyes, nothing has taken away from the people of the Republic the heroism of their struggle against Franco, and nothing has diminished the bravery and commitment of those who went to Spain to assist in that struggle. If Manchuria in 1931 was the first shot in the Second World War, Spain was its first major battle; and the six years of war against international fascism that followed, with its heroism, cruelties, betrayals and tragedies, all on a vastly greater scale than in Spain, culminated in a major victory for the peoples of the world: a victory within which there remained fundamental contradictions and future conflicts... Spain was but a moment in the history of human emancipation, and the bitter struggles of the Spanish Republicans against their militarists and landlords, lay and clerical, have become part of the larger struggles that are yet to come.

'These', he added, 'are not the political perspectives that Cunningham understands, let alone appreciates; his essay, an unedifying exhibition of inaccurate scholarship, misleadingly and inexpertly arranged, is a disgrace to his publishers.'[21]

Saville's first *Register* essay on communism and the CPGB was occasioned by the twentieth anniversary of the CPSU Twentieth Congress, which, along with the subsequent suppression of the Hungarian uprising by the Red Army, had led him and Thompson and thousands of other British communists to leave the party. The key question for him and Thompson in 1956, he wrote in 1976, had been the need to restore the credibility of the party by undertaking a full and open self-examination after Khrushchev's secret speech had revealed the brutality and lies of Stalinism; it was the failure of the leadership to do so that had precipitated their resignations.[22] John Gollan, who had taken over as the party's general secretary in 1956 and remained in the job until 1975, had also written a retrospective article earlier in 1976. In Saville's view, it showed how little the leadership had really learned from the debacle. Gollan, he maintained, was still suppressing 'unpleasant facts and episodes' in the British party's history, but above all he had not dealt seriously with 'the

central problems that emerged from the Khrushchev revelations.
These are the nature and character of socialist democracy, its forms
and institutions, and above all the ways in which freedom, democracy
and socialism can be realised, and then maintained, as integral and
living processes of social life.'[23]

A second essay on this topic was published in 1991 as a response to
the democratic revolutions in Eastern Europe in 1989-90. What he
now had to add was a sombre declaration. He quoted Engels's statement that Marx and he had called themselves 'Communists' rather
than 'Socialists' because 'Communists' was what the revolutionary
element of the working class called themselves at that time; and,
Engels added, it was a label they had never wished to repudiate. But,
said Saville, the time had now come to do just that:

> The period of Communism, centred upon the history of the Soviet
> Union since 1917, and the countries of Eastern Europe since the late
> 1940s, which gave inspiration and hope to millions of people all over
> the world, has now ended in discredit and dishonour ... in Europe
> especially the name and the organisation are synonymous with
> economic incompetence and material ineptitude of a massive kind,
> together with the bitter political regimes of Stalinism.[24]

What had happened in 1990 was 'a major defeat of the socialist idea
and ideal'. But he looked at this in the long perspective of history:

> To suggest, however, that the Communist experience has been a
> folly is seriously to misunderstand – indeed fundamentally to misun-
> derstand – what it meant in global political terms, in the national
> politics of individual countries and within the individuals themselves
> who played their minor parts in the historical experience. We have
> all begun to understand, much more clearly than before, what the
> radicals of the early nineteenth [century] felt when they remembered
> the wonderful hopes they had all experienced with the Revolution in
> France, and witnessed its descent into Bonapartism thereafter.
> William Hazlitt is once again required reading.[25]

The rest of Saville's 1991 reflections on communism were devoted to
what being a party member had meant to him personally and, he
thought, to most other party members too. For him it was not a sect,

or a substitute for a family, as described by Raphael Samuel, for example, and by some commentators outside the party, but simply a rationally chosen way of working for socialism, along with the discipline that this called for.[26] But the CPGB no longer represented such a way. The need was therefore to create new means of socialist education, new forms of engagement with the unions, and ultimately something like a new party. Only in this way might the inequality, violence and corruption of modern capitalism be – eventually ('within two or three centuries') – transcended.[27]

In the 1960s and 1970s Saville wrote several commentaries on the state of the British left and the prospects for socialism. Here his ideas converged closely with Miliband's, whose classic text, *Parliamentary Socialism*, had appeared in 1961; and also, to a considerable extent, with those of Anderson and Nairn in their equally classic 1964 analyses in the NLR of the historical origins of Britain's failure to produce a strong revolutionary left. In the 1965 *Register* Saville underscored the extent to which the Labour leadership had seized on the fallacious idea, strongly promoted by the *Economist* and the Conservatives, that income distribution had been made so much more equal in the immediately post-war years that it would be rash to push it any further, for fear of alienating the middle classes. He reproached Labour intellectuals for their uncritical endorsement of this view, which he saw as a major factor in demobilising the party and the unions, and disillusioning their supporters. In 1967 he went much deeper, offering an extended critique of the Wilson government, then in its second term after securing a real majority in 1966. In his view it was simply a bourgeois government with socialist rhetoric. 'How it comes about', he observed, 'that those who win elections with socialist phrases on their lips – and most are not conscious hypocrites – then proceed to administer a capitalist society, which they have previously denounced, in as efficient a way as possible, is one of the central ironies of modern British history. For socialists who have struggled to put their leaders in power, it is tragedy.'[28] The illusions of parliamentary socialism that Miliband had anatomised – the belief in the neutrality of the state, and the ability of parliament to secure a transition to socialism merely by legislating it – had deep historical origins:

> There is, indeed, a general law of social change which can be applied to social and political reform measures in Britain. It is a law of delay,

for to the conservative interests in society delay means life and an abundance of opportunities to trim, modify and limit reforming measures as they continue their long journey through political life. It is the density and tenacity of conservative institutions in Britain that defeats the genuine reformer and when reform is finally granted, after many years of weary struggle, its significance is usually exaggerated. The Labour leaders are inhibited in a fundamental way by their parliamentarism: by their unshakeable belief that all the British are gentlemen and will play the Parliamentary game according to its rules.

'They have, it must be admitted', Saville added in one of his characteristic mordant remarks, 'good reason for these beliefs since nothing has ever been done by the Labour leadership to cause the gentlemen of England to abandon their acceptance of the rules ...'[29] His view of the Labour left was almost equally biting. In general he was gentle with them, deploring the tendency among socialists to engage in mutually wounding exchanges; but he saw them as serving essentially to protect the Labour right, and in a review of the prospects for the 1970s he didn't pull any punches:

> If the Labour Party is a massive institutional obstacle to the achievement of socialism in Britain, then the Parliamentary Left and their many supporters outside the Commons, storing up as they do the greater part of the reserves of the Left within the labour movement as a whole, are the major stumbling block in the way of a serious reassessment of the means towards a socialist future. So long as the Parliamentary Left proceed along their present paths they will continue to encapsulate a large number of socialists within the politics of frenzied impotence; and the fetish of parliamentarism, the belief that socialism as well as social reform can come through a bourgeois Parliament, will exercise in the future as in the past its paralysing fascination over the minds of the majority of British socialists.[30]

The need, he said, was to wean the working class from the Labour Party as it had previously, over the course of a hundred years, been weaned from the Liberal Party. But whereas the break with the Liberal Party had been achieved at the cost of adopting 'the same types of activity but with different labels' and of getting the labour movement 'in all its aspects ... increasingly enmeshed within the state apparatus', a different kind of break must now be attempted:

> What we need now are new styles of work as socialists: new methods
> of organization: new forms of socialist agitation; but how and in
> what ways the old techniques and organizational forms can be
> supplanted are not easy questions to answer. [31]

Responsibility for trying to answer these questions rested with left intellectuals. There was also an educational and media vacuum to fill. There was a lack of 'hard line theoreticians capable of confronting bourgeois ideas' – but without doing so in the kind of 'unreadable jargon' that, he complained, afflicted so many of the articles in the *New Left Review*, which he otherwise complimented for its theoretical efforts. It was also necessary for left intellectuals to recapture the vigour and liveliness of earlier, if cruder, formulations ('today the tone is too often muted and all too gentlemanly') and to accept a new degree of collective commitment and discipline: 'Most socialist intellectuals at the present time do not appear to work in conditions that demand any kind of self-discipline and personal commitment to a common cause: their socialism is still too much in terms of a narrow personal discretion rather than a firm social enfranchisement ' – such as he and other communist intellectuals had known. More yet: a new socialist party was required, which could not emerge unless a 'practical demonstration of a viable alternative' convinced 'large numbers of people of the possibilities of supplanting the Labour Party'. And while revolutionary events elsewhere might affect the odds on this, the real change needed to occur in Britain. Therefore, he concluded:

> The likelihood of achieving socialism in Britain in the next two or
> three decades is remote, and many of us will have to accept, what
> nineteenth century revolutionaries so often emphasised, that the
> fundamental changes they were working for would not come about
> in their lifetime.[32]

Which did not stop Saville working as hard as ever for socialism for as long as his health and energy permitted, over more than three further decades.

Three essays on socialism and the Labour Party were prompted by

biographies of Attlee, Bevin and Gaitskell, all published in the 1980s
as Thatcherism was unfolding. Two themes in particular stand out in
these assessments – the role of social class in the Labour leadership,
and the impact of Britain's 'special relationship' with the US.

Saville's attitude to class reflected his childhood experience of
moving between the working class and the lower middle class, and his
encounters with the officer class in the army during the war. He
acknowledged that someone from an upper-class background, like
Attlee, could shed their upper-class prejudices and identify with
working-class values through long involvement in the Labour Party.
But he thought that Attlee's public school background had eventually
made him ready to think that welfare and full employment, and state
ownership of the means of production without popular control, were
more or less equivalent to socialism. The reality, Saville pointed out,
was that without popular control 'it could only be a matter of time,
given the inherent tendency of capitalist society to generate
inequality, for the momentum of change to be reversed'.[33]

Gaitskell, Attlee's successor as Labour leader, was an even clearer
case in point: 'one of the more extreme examples of a Labour politi-
cian whose origins were far removed from the working people his
party was in existence to represent'. Beatrice Webb had rightly judged
him 'a comfortable middle class young man', and his subsequent
contact with workers as a WEA lecturer was very brief and patron-
ising. Saville's final judgment was that Gaitskell belonged to the
ruling class and thought like it:

> the fundamental consensus with the Tories that Gaitskell
> bequeathed to those who followed him became deeply embedded in
> Labour Party thinking and practice; and the logic of that kind of
> accommodation, when set against the background of worsening
> crisis, led inexorably to the revisionism of the radical Right which
> the Thatcher government represents.[34]

Bevin represented a different aspect of class: the deep conservatism
and visceral anti-communism of some working class trade union
leaders.[35] Unlike his middle and upper-class colleagues in the Labour
leadership Bevin felt no need to clothe his labourism in socialist rhetoric and saw communism as a greater threat than capitalism. More
than anyone else he was responsible, as foreign secretary in the post-

war Attlee government, for creating the 'special relationship' with the US that became the one constant in economic and social policy under all later Labour governments. Harold Wilson, Saville had remarked in 1965, was 'not known as a man either of principle or consistency, but in this matter of allegiance to the State Department he has shown a remarkable firmness of purpose and resolution of will' – words that could have been applied just as accurately to Tony Blair thirty-odd years later.[36]

The subordination of Britain's foreign relations to Washington was a recurrent theme. In 1987, following the American attempt to kill Libya's President Gaddafi using, with Thatcher's approval, aircraft based in Britain, Saville wrote what is in my opinion one of the best two essays of his entire *Register* output: 'The Price of Alliance: American Bases in Britain'. He pointed out that the bombing of Libya could have been done far more easily from American aircraft carriers in the Mediterranean: so why was it done from bases in Britain, with Mrs Thatcher's public consent? To answer this question it was first necessary to establish how the US had come to have no fewer than twenty-five operational bases in Britain, including some armed with nuclear weapons (and most of them deliberately disguised as RAF bases), plus another thirty-five minor or reserve bases; and on what terms they were there. For this Saville dug deep into post-war history, using an impressively wide range of official sources, memoirs and histories. What emerged was a catalogue of secrecy and deception calculated to conceal – from parliament, and even from the cabinet – the reality that US forces in Britain operated entirely independently of British control. The belief, assiduously fostered by successive prime ministers and foreign secretaries, that they could be used only with British consent, was (and is) a fiction. The real motive for attacking Libya using US airplanes based in Britain, Saville concluded, was to associate Britain publicly with a flagrant international crime. For him, the most dangerous implication of all this was that the US felt entirely free to use nuclear weapons based in Britain with at most 'consultation' – in reality, entirely as they chose. For us today what perhaps stands out as most significant is the precedent the episode set for securing British complicity in subsequent international crimes.

Saville's other truly outstanding essay (he himself considered it 'one of his better pieces on contemporary politics'[37]) was on a topic even closer to his heart – the miners' strike of 1984-5. For an analysis written so soon after the event – it was dated 'July-August 1985' – it was impressively researched, realistic and coherent.[38] It showed how the Conservative Party in opposition after 1974 had drawn the lessons of the Heath government's defeat by the miners and had prepared a detailed plan to take them on again and reverse the outcome when they were next in power. The Ridley report which contained this plan was leaked to the *Economist*, which published it in full in 1978. The National Union of Mineworkers (NUM) and the Labour leadership ignored it, but in 1984 the Thatcher government followed its recommendations to the letter. Once the strike was in progress Saville's main complaint was that both the NUM and the Labour leadership had failed to research and present the miners' case well enough. Critiques of the National Coal Board's case that were, belatedly, made available to them, were ignored, just as the Ridley report had been. The Labour leadership, he wrote, had still not grasped that the postwar consensus was over.

THE VOICE OF A NEW ALIGNMENT?

These two essays were, in fact, models of the kind of 'intervention' in contemporary politics that both Miliband and Saville always wanted the *Register* to make, and which the left badly needs and too seldom gets. Well-researched, objective, politically committed and explicit, they focused on crucial events that disclose the whole system of class forces at work; and the fact that the *Register* has always emphasised work of this kind has, arguably, always been its greatest strength. For a long time, however, Miliband went further and dreamed of the *Register* becoming the 'voice' of a new alignment of political forces such as he had originally hoped the *New Reasoner* might be. In 1979 he wrote:

> the *New Reasoner* 'rebellion' should have been followed by a sustained and systematic attempt to regroup whoever was willing into a socialist association, league or party, of which the journal might have been the voice ... The main reason why the *New Reasoner* was not kept going is that there was no adequate perception that a socialist organisation was needed, and when there was some kind of perception of it, there was no clear view as to what it should specifically stand for, in programmatic and organisational as well as in theoretical terms.[39]

It was because he could not at first give up all hope that the *Register* might fulfil this role that Miliband periodically expressed the wish that it should take more of a 'line'. In 1970 he went so far as to propose setting up a small group of advisers to assist him and Saville in doing that. Saville's response was to urge him to go ahead, but without him. He had had enough of editorial boards. In his view the need was not for a more defined 'line' but for more of what the *Register* already did, providing analysis and a forum for debate. In any case, he wrote, 'I am not sure you are right to suggest that our line has been all over the place ... I should have thought that our place in the spectrum is fairly well defined ...'. Miliband backed away immediately, saying that 'I have no wish to carry on the *Register* without you.'[40] Miliband imagined, perhaps, that the *Register* might play the sort of role in a new socialist movement that the Left Book Club, which was highly programmatic as well as analytic and theoretical, was seen as having played in the socialist movement in Britain in the 1930s.[41] Saville doubted whether the new left – and certainly whether any publication, however excellent – had the potential to convert the working class to socialism. His long years as an active party member had made him very much a realist. He had rejected the CPGB but retained a clear conception of the essential requirements of a serious socialist party, and the various new left initiatives (most notably, the Socialist Society) that tended to attract Miliband did not seem to him likely to measure up to them.[42]

On the other hand he saw the struggle for socialism as one lasting centuries, and his political convictions meant that it must never be abandoned. Writing to Edward and Dorothy Thompson in September 1956 he said he thought there were thousands of members still in the Communist Party who were 'honest socialists' and who could be rallied to a new, independent socialist initiative.[43] Whether or not this was so, the phrase perfectly described himself, and the duty of an honest socialist was to do whatever he could to sustain the struggle; the *Register* was part of that struggle and must survive. His characteristic political attitude was always 'matter of fact, well-tempered and hard-headed, measured and reasonable'.[44] At the same time he was tough; he remarked of himself that he had the 'physical and psychological armour-plating of a sergeant-major'. But as Miliband well recognised, sergeant-majors also 'have a sense of organisation, of being part of a purpose larger than themselves, of professional work that needs to be done efficiently, properly and without fuss'.[45] All of this Saville brought to the *Register*, and communicated by example to his editorial successors. As Miliband made clear, the project would not have outlived its early years without him. It was no small achievement.

Notes

1. Saville, 'The Communist experience: a personal appraisal' in Ralph Miliband and Leo Panitch, eds, *Communist Regimes: the Aftermath, Socialist Register 1991*, Merlin, 1991, p14.
2. The story of the founding of the *Register* has been well told by both Marion Kozak, Ralph Miliband's widow, writing soon after his death in 1994 ('How it all began; a footnote to history' in Leo Panitch, ed., *Why Not Capitalism? Socialist Register 1995*, Merlin, 1995, pp264-85) and by Michael Newman in *Ralph Miliband and the Politics of the New Left*, Merlin 2002, especially pp113-25. I have relied heavily on these accounts, and on an interview kindly given me by Marion Kozak on 17 December 2009.
3. See the chapter in this collection by Madeleine Davis.
4. John Saville, *Memoirs from the Left*, Merlin, 2003, p115, quoting from the editors' introduction to the *New Reasoner*'s first issue.
5. Newman, *Ralph Miliband*, p120.
6. Ralph Miliband, 'John Saville: a presentation', in David E Martin and David Rubinstein, eds, *Ideology and the Labour Movement: Essays Presented to John Saville*, Croom Helm 1979, pp27-8.
7. Saville, *Memoirs*, p160; Miliband, 'Thirty years of *The Socialist Register*' in Ralph Miliband and Leo Panitch, eds, *Between Globalism and Nationalism, Socialist Register 1994*, Merlin, 1994, p2. In 1982 Miliband and Saville felt tired and took a year off, leaving that year's volume to be edited by their publisher at the Merlin Press, Martin Eve, and his colleague David Musson. Over the next several years Saville wanted to retire but Miliband begged him to stay on. Saville's share of the editorial work was, however, increasingly taken over by Leo Panitch, who joined Miliband and Saville as a co-editor from 1985-6. Saville's last year as a co-editor was 1989, although he continued to write for it down to 1995.
8. Miliband, 'Thirty Years', p2.
9. Newman, *Ralph Miliband*, p121.
10. Saville, *Memoirs*, p159.
11. Kozak interview; Newman, *Ralph Miliband*, p123.
12. Martin Eve, 'Merlin Press: early years', in Walter Kelmsley, ed, *Martin Eve Remembered*, Rendlesham: Merlin, p39.
13. Richard Ingrams, *The Life and Adventures of William Cobbett*, HarperCollins, 2005, p304.

14. E P Thompson, *The Making of the English Working Class*, Penguin Books 1988 edn, p830.
15. Saville, *Memoirs*, p159-60.
16. An essay in the 1982 volume, although called 'Reflections on recent labour historiography', was really an analysis of the state of the socialist project in the UK, and so is included in the next category.
17. Miliband, 'John Saville', p24.
18. John Saville, 'The politics of *Encounter*', Ralph Miliband and John Saville, eds, *The Socialist Register 1964*, Merlin, 1964, pp192 and 200.
19. '*Marxism Today*: an anatomy' in Ralph Miliband, Leo Panitch and John Saville, eds, *The Retreat of the Intellectuals: The Socialist Register 1990*, Merlin, 1990, pp51-2.
20. Alun Howkins and John Saville, 'The nineteen thirties: a revisionist history' in Ralph Miliband and John Saville, eds, *The Socialist Register 1979*, Merlin, 1979, pp89-100.
21. 'Valentine Cunningham and the poetry of the Spanish Civil War', Ralph Miliband and John Saville, eds, *The Socialist Register 1981*, Merlin, 1981, p283.
22. Saville's third essay on this topic, in the 1994 *Socialist Register*, was occasioned by Thompson's death the previous year. It elaborated the account of their response to Khrushchev's speech given in Saville's 1976 essay, citing correspondence with Thompson with whom the 1976 essay was originally meant to have been co-written.
23. 'The 20th Congress and the British Communist Party' in Ralph Miliband and John Saville, eds, *The Socialist Register 1976*, Merlin, 1976, p23.
24. 'The communist experience', p1.
25. Ibid, pp7-8.
26. Much of this material was repeated in Saville's *Memoirs from the Left*. Samuel's account, which originally appeared in instalments in NLR, has recently been reissued in book form: Samuel, *The Lost World of British Communism*, Verso, 2006.
27. 'The Communist experience', p25.
28. 'Labourism and the Labour government', Ralph Miliband and John Saville, eds, *Socialist Register 1967*, Merlin, 1967, p53.
29. Ibid, p57.
30. 'Britain: prospects for the seventies', Ralph Miliband and John Saville, eds, *The Socialist Register 1970*, Merlin, p210.
31. Ibid, p210.
32. Ibid, p212.
33. Saville, 'C R Attlee: an assessment' in Ralph Miliband and John Saville, eds, *The Socialist Register 1983*, Merlin, p150.
34. Saville, 'Hugh Gaitskell: an assessment', Ralph Miliband and John Saville, eds, *The Socialist Register 1980*, Merlin, 1980, p168.
35. Saville, 'Ernest Bevin and the Cold War 1945-1950', Ralph Miliband and

John Saville, eds, *The Socialist Register 1984*, Merlin, 1984, pp68-100.
36. 'Labourism and the Labour government', p63. Wilson, however, did not accede to American pressure to join in the war in Vietnam.
37. Saville, *Memoirs*, p177.
38. Saville, 'An open conspiracy: Conservative politics and the miners' strike 1984-5', Ralph Miliband, John Saville, Marcel Liebman and Leo Panitch, eds, *The Socialist Register 1985/86: Social Democracy and After*, Merlin, 1986, pp295-329.
39. Miliband, 'John Saville', p26-27.
40. Kozak, 'How it all began', pp283-4. See also Saville, *Memoirs*, p160.
41. Kozak interview.
42. The Socialist Society (1981-86) sought to bring together socialists inside and outside the Labour Party with activists in the new social movements (especially feminism), with a view to making a socialist intervention in British politics (see Newman, *Ralph Miliband*, pp270-8).
43. Saville, 'Edward Thompson, The Communist Party and 1956' in Ralph Miliband, Leo Panitch and John Saville, eds, *Between Globalism and Nationalism: Socialist Register 1994*, Merlin, 1994, p30.
44. Miliband, 'John Saville', p25.
45. Ibid, pp29-30.

PART TWO

Themes

The first casualty of a socialist foreign policy? Greece and Britain in the 1940s

John Sakkas

The occupation of Greece by the Axis forces in 1941-4 created extraordinary conditions never before seen by Greek society. The old political system collapsed and the Greek people experienced repression, hardship and mass violence unprecedented in degree and scale. In response to fascist occupation, a broad-based national resistance movement developed in 1941, led by the small Greek Communist Party (KKE) but including a wide variety of anti-fascist, republican forces. The National Liberation Front (EAM) and its armed force, the National Popular Liberation Army (ELAS), became the most significant opponent of the Germans and the most powerful political force inside Greece. By the end of the war EAM/ELAS controlled most rural areas of Greece and seemed determined to reshape the country according to its own revolutionary political vision.[1]

The vexed issue of communist intentions in Greece during the occupation and after has been the focus of historical debate since the early stages of the Cold War. The conventional view is that there were 'three rounds' to the Greek civil war between October 1943 and 1949 and that the KKE was engaged over this period in attempting to seize power on the instructions of Moscow. In 1989-92 I wrote my PhD thesis 'Greece and the British public opinion, 1944-49' under John Saville's supervision. Discussing with him the British intervention in Greece in December 1944, I agreed with him at that time that the communist-led resistance forces would have followed the Yugoslav road to socialism had it not been for British intervention. More recent, well-researched studies, however, show that although the December events were not a deliberate communist attempt to seize power, the KKE had every intention of employing all available means, including armed force, to impose a communist regime in Greece. Had the KKE prevailed in 1944-5, Greece would sooner or later have become a Soviet satellite, like Czechoslovakia, because of its Stalinist leadership.[2]

In Saville's analysis Churchill emerges as the catalyst for the fighting in Athens. The British prime minister, 'dominated by his vivid imperialist sense of history... had been preparing the counter-revolution in Greece from at least 1943'.[3] His objectives in Greece were 'to contain and if possible to eliminate the resistance movement, to restore the Greek monarchy backed by a right-wing government, and thereby to safeguard what was still considered to be a major strategic life-line to the oilfields of the Middle East and to India'.[4] The contrast with his attitude towards Yugoslavia, a country with much less strategic importance for Britain, is illuminating. 'He muted his anti-communism in respect of Yugoslavia while allowing it full play in the case of Greece.' As a result the Foreign Office deprecated the importance of the Greek resistance, which was beyond the control of the monarchists, and there developed in consequence a bitter conflict between the Foreign Office in London with its long-range political goal – preventing the growth of communist power – and the Special Operations Executive (SOE) in Cairo, with its short-run military goal of building up resistance to Nazism.[5]

By the summer of 1944 Churchill was becoming seriously concerned with the advance of the victorious Red Army in the direction of Greece and with what was likely to follow in Greece after a German collapse. It was essential, Churchill wrote in his memoirs, 'that there should be no political vacuum in Greece. As I minuted on August 29 "it is most desirable to strike out of the blue without any preliminary crisis. It is the best way to forestall the EAM".'[6] At the same time, the Foreign Office approached the Soviet government and proposed an Anglo-Soviet division of responsibility in the Balkans, thus setting in motion the diplomatic process that resulted in the much-debated 'spheres of influence' agreement of October 1944, by which Greece fell to the British sphere. Stalin accepted British supremacy in Greece as part of the price to be paid for communist dominance elsewhere in Eastern Europe. During the crisis in Athens two months later he remained silent, allowing the British a free hand. But as Saville rightly observed:

> it is improbable that the Kremlin did not take full note of the ruthlessness of British actions, and appreciate their implications for their own position in Eastern Europe. It is necessary to underline the point which is mostly forgotten in the analysis of post-war Europe that the British were the first to engage in clearly defined self-interested military action in a country that had been occupied by the Germans; and this before the war with the Nazis was over.[7]

Following the arrival in Athens in October of a coalition government established with London's blessing under the liberal George Papandreou, along with its British military escort, the internal situation steadily deteriorated. EAM/ELAS were determined to resist any attempt to disarm them while their opponents still bore arms. The British suspected that the communists were planning to seize power by force and impose their will on the country. In a minute to Eden of 7 November, Churchill wrote that 'in my opinion having paid the price we have to Russia for freedom of action in Greece we should not hesitate to use British troops to support the Royal Hellenic Government under Mr. Papandreou ... I fully expect a clash with EAM, and we must not shrink from it provided the ground is well chosen.'[8]

In early December the EAM members of the Papandreou government resigned and an EAM demonstration in the centre of Athens was fired upon by the police. In London, Churchill intervened directly with orders to the British commander, General Ronald Scobie 'to act as if you were in a conquered city where a local rebellion is in progress ... We have to hold and dominate Athens. It would be a great thing for you to succeed in this without bloodshed if possible, but also with bloodshed if necessary.' Churchill treated Greece like a colony. 'I had in my mind', he wrote, after giving the full text of his telegram to Scobie, 'Arthur Balfour's celebrated telegram in the eighties to the British authorities in Ireland: Don't hesitate to shoot'.[9] The bitter fighting that followed between ELAS units and British forces lasted a few weeks and was brought to an uneasy end only when Churchill conceded the one point on which he had remained intransigent throughout the crisis – the need for a plebiscite on the monarchy.

The Labour government that came to power in mid-1945 continued the wartime coalition's foreign policy. Saville pointed out emphatically that 'there was no Labour foreign policy, there was a British policy which continued that which had been elaborated by Churchill and agreed by his colleagues in the War Cabinet'.[10] In this well-researched study, Saville set events in Greece into the broader framework of Labour's axioms of foreign policy. The first of these was the implacable hostility towards communism in all its forms. In the inter-war years Bevin, as a right-wing leader of the Transport and General Workers' Union, fought passionately against communist rivals and became deeply suspicious of Soviet intentions. When he was appointed Foreign Secretary in 1945 he did not modify his vigorous anti-communism, but steadfastly pursued a policy of opposition towards the USSR and to all those radical movements in Europe and elsewhere in which communists played, or were thought to be playing, an important part.

The second axiom equally shared by the Foreign Office, the cabinet and the chiefs of staff was that Britain remained a great power alongside the United States and the Soviet Union and that the British empire contributed to the political status of Britain as a world power. Greece was an essential part of Labour's dominant imperial assumptions in military and political planning for the post-war era; and it became part of the 'vacuum theory' that was developed within the Foreign Office in the last year of the war; namely, that if for any reason Britain moved out of a given area or region, Russia would take its place. In a paper circulated to the cabinet dated 11 August 1945, Bevin insisted that 'we must maintain our position in Greece as a part of our Middle East policy, and that unless it is asserted and settled it may have a bad effect on the whole of our Middle East position'.[11] Obsessed with the spectre of Soviet involvement in the region, the British found themselves unable to rein in the Greek right. A 'white terror' and domestic political polarisation led to an atmosphere of increasing violence in the provinces and eventually to the civil war of 1946-9. Saville accepted the revisionist view that in post-liberation Greece leftists fled to the mountains not to foment revolution but to escape right-wing persecution, and that they resorted to insurrection only when their persistent efforts at political compromise and national reconciliation were rejected by their domestic opponents with British and American support.[12] It was in this sense that he described Greece as 'the first casualty of what many at the time of the 1945 general election thought would be a "socialist" foreign policy'.[13]

PUBLIC REACTION TO BRITISH INTERVENTION IN GREECE IN DECEMBER 1944

The military intervention in Greece generated a notable opposition among wide sections of opinion in Britain. Most of the British war correspondents to Greece, and leader writers and columnists in Britain, felt sympathetic to the European anti-fascist movements and suspicious of the conservative aims that Churchill was relentlessly pursuing in states like Greece. Strongly condemning the intervention, they argued that instead of trying to preserve as much as possible of Britain's traditional imperial position, Churchill should seek to co-operate with the other great powers and with the new social movements of Europe in establishing a reborn world where international disputes would be decided on their merits and not by the disposition of military power. EH Carr and Donald Tyerman in *The Times*, AJ Cummings in the *News Chronicle*, Michael Foot in the *Daily Herald*, Kingsley Martin in the *New Statesman*, and Malcolm MacEwen in the *Daily Worker* were among the most implacable of the Fleet Street critics of British intervention in Greece.[14] But Churchill was particularly enraged at *The Times*'s criticism.[15] Speaking in the House of Commons on 18 January 1945 he left no doubt about which paper he meant by 'important organs of the press', when he accused them of maligning and traducing the government's motives and of 'gay, reckless, unbridled partisanship' unleashed on those who bore the burdens of power.[16]

Churchill also was subjected to severe criticism in parliament. Two general assumptions appeared to command widespread support from his opponents during the course of the debates. The first viewpoint, commonly expressed in the speeches of various MPs, was that the Greek crisis could have been avoided had Churchill not insisted on the restoration of the monarchy at the moment of liberation and before a free plebiscite could be held. A second assumption was that the resistance movements in Europe, like EAM/ELAS, were genuine mass popular movements which Britain should support to establish socialist regimes in their liberated countries. In the heated debates on Greece many Labour MPs, not just left-wingers, but pacifists, ethical socialists and those in a radical Liberal tradition, made common cause with the communist William Gallacher, Common Wealth MPs like Richard Acland and Hugh Lawson, and the independent socialist Tom Driberg. Even the Labour peers put forward a motion in the House of Lords on 21 December condemning 'military action against our Greek allies' as 'shameful'.[17]

The wider public had severe misgivings about what was going on in Greece, and the idea that Britain was supporting reactionaries everywhere cropped up repeatedly. During the crisis in Athens many constituency and city Labour parties and trade unions passed resolutions critical of British policy in Greece.[18] On 17 December a crowd of about 15,000 marched to Trafalgar Square in London for a 'Hands off Greece' demonstration organized by the Fire Brigades Union and addressed by members of left-wing parties. The protesters paraded with banners proclaiming 'Let the Greeks alone' and 'The British troops for Greek fascism'. It was the biggest demonstration of Londoners since the days when they had gathered to demand the opening of the second front. Next day thousands of engineering and shipbuilding workers in Glasgow stopped work at 4 pm. Then, their representatives went to a big meeting in St Andrew's Hall and passed a resolution demanding that Churchill withdraw British troops and allow the Greek people to form a democratic government.[19] On 29 December, John Bailey of the Co-operative Party declared that 'its London headquarters received more resolutions on this than on almost any other issue which had arisen during the war'.[20]

The degree of excitement of British public opinion over Greece can also be gauged through the letters to the press and the opinion polls. About two fifths of the correspondence received by *The Times* endorsed the editorial line which was critical of Churchill's Greek policy. AJ Cummings reminded readers that only once in his long experience could he recall receipt of a larger postbag on a single issue and that this was overwhelmingly supportive of the line adopted by the *News Chronicle* on Greece.[21] In January 1945, when the Greek crisis was at its height, forty-three per cent of the British people approved of Churchill's attitude on the Greek question, thirty-eight per cent disapproved, while nineteen per cent expressed no opinion. These figures suggest that in a period when Churchill's personal popularity was impressively high as a result of his war record, his policy in Greece and his general attitude towards the resistance movements in Europe were questioned by a large part of the population.[22] And there is no doubt that public opinion played a major role in the modification of his initially rigid course in Greece, which eventually, though unfortunately temporarily, led to pacification.

Official Labour responses to the events in Greece were, however, in a very different key, regulated by the character of a leadership pushed on by mass emotion rather than eager to arouse it. On the trade-union flank, Walter Citrine, the TUC general secretary, accepted the British official version of the events uncritically when, in January 1945, at Churchill's instigation, he led a TUC delegation to Greece to investigate the situation on the spot.[23] On the political side, the Labour members in the war cabinet, as Saville observed, not only refrained from criticising the policy followed in Greece; they even claimed for themselves individually and for the cabinet collectively participation in and foreknowledge of all policy decisions over Greece. 'At all points there was unequivocal support for Churchill's approach.'[24]

At the Labour Party Conference, which met in mid-December, an anodyne resolution on Greece was devised by the National Executive Committee (NEC), calling for 'an armistice without delay' and 'the resumption of conversations between all sections of the people who had resisted the Nazi invaders, with a view to the establishment of a provisional national government'. Much stiffer emergency resolutions which had been submitted by the Railwaymen, the Miners, and other trade unionists, expressing deep concern at the action of the British government, were ruled out by the conference arrangements committee.[25] Bevin, then Minister of Labour, 'hunching his shoulders and sticking his hands in the pocket of his jacket' rose 'to face the concentrated hostility of the audience crowding Central Hall'.[26] He first made it clear to his comrades that 'we cannot govern this world by emotionalism', and then took responsibility, as a member of the war cabinet, for the government's policy. Although he neither supported nor condemned the resolution, he gave the fullest and most unqualified support to Churchill. Like the prime minister, Bevin believed that Greece was just one of the countries which should remain 'safe', that is non-communist, because 'the British Empire could not abandon its position in the Mediterranean'.[27] Despite his powerful performance, Bevin failed to convince the audience. Aneurin Bevan, who had the previous day been elected as a constituency party representative to the NEC, described Bevin's account of events in Greece as 'garbled and inaccurate when it was not unveracious', and made the much-quoted comment that the Labour Minister had lined up with the only three bodies in the world to have supported Britain's actions, 'namely Fascist Spain, Fascist Portugal and the majority of Tories in the House of Commons'.[28] Saville pointed out correctly that 'Bevin's account was certainly garbled, but it was an approach that he continued without any alteration when he became Foreign Secretary'.[29]

OPPOSITION TO BEVIN

In July 1945, the election of Britain's first majority Labour government raised high hopes of a radical change in British foreign policy. There still echoed in the ears of many Labour supporters the words of Denis Healey, soon to be appointed Labour's international secretary, at the Labour Party Conference in May, that Britain's principal task in foreign affairs should be to 'protect and assist the socialist revolution that had already begun in Europe'.[30] 'In no circumstances', Harold Laski declared in August 1945, 'would a Labour government help to uphold royalist or other regimes that did not enjoy the support of the people'.[31] Michael Foot was also optimistic about the government's socialist intentions and its desire to alter Churchill's Greek policy. 'The foreign affairs of this country', he stated in the House of Commons the same month, 'were no longer conducted by persons who had a vested interest in securing the return to his throne of King George'.[32]

The Labour leaders, however, did not seem to share these expectations. Continuity in foreign policy was not to be disputed. In his first Commons statement as Foreign Secretary, on 20 August 1945, Bevin pointed out that 'the basis of the Government's policy is in keeping with that marked out by the coalition government'. His Tory counterpart, Anthony Eden, intervened with a long speech in the debate that followed and remarked that in the war cabinet 'there were no differences on any important issue of foreign policy'.[33] Saville rightly suggested that the Greek issue remained controversial and that 'for the first two years of Bevin's tenure as Foreign Secretary Greece was the main target of criticism in foreign affairs from within the British Labour movement'.[34] Already in the debate following Bevin's speech, a number of Labour backbenchers spoke on the Greek question and almost all of them asked for a drastic change in British policy.[35] Two days later, Seymour Cocks, chairman of the Labour Party's external affairs group, asked Bevin in the Commons about the falsification of the electoral lists in Greece, and whether the Yalta formula, providing for the formation in all liberated countries of provisional representative governments based on all democratic elements, was to be applied to that country.[36] On the same day, Donald Bruce, Bevan's parliamentary private secretary, expressed at the Parliamentary Labour Party's (PLP) second meeting since Labour's electoral victory his concern with Bevin's statement on foreign policy, particularly in regard to Greece, Spain and Bulgaria.[37] During the following months many local Labour parties and trade union branches joined the MPs in placing on record their growing anxiety about the government's Greek policy and their disappointment with the lack of any reversal in foreign policy.[38] In February 1946, a note to Attlee by Konni Zilliacus, a former League of Nations official with a remarkable understanding of the realities of world politics, echoed the suspicions by Bevin of the party rank and file:

> In December 1944, Mr Bevin told the Labour Conference that we had gone into Greece because the British Empire could not abandon its position in the Mediterranean. To put it concretely the admiralty have insisted from the Cairo days onward that we should install a Greek government that would allow us to build a bigger and better Malta on Greek territory in order to keep the Russians out of the Mediterranean.

That, along with British policy in the Middle East and elsewhere, was 'the traditional language of power politics and these are the traditional aims of British imperialism since the nineteenth century'. Attlee dismissed the note as 'based on an astonishing lack of understanding of the facts'.[39]

At the Labour Party conference in June 1946, of sixty-nine submitted resolutions concerning foreign policy, sixty-four were critical. The government was condemned for failing to recruit socialists to the Foreign Office, for its policy in Greece, Spain and Palestine, and for its intimate relationship with the United States. The general feeling in the conference was summed up by a constituency delegate: 'Up and down the country, in workshops, in trade union branches, in local Labour parties, and so forth, two questions are being asked: is there a difference between the policy of the Labour government and of former governments, and is the policy sufficiently socialist?'.[40] Bevin defended his policies strongly and all resolutions he opposed were either withdrawn or defeated on a show of hands. As *Tribune* bitterly commented, only a year after Labour had taken power 'the delegates had assembled with the firm intention of praising Caesar and the whole Senate'.[41] A few weeks later, Foot, in the same journal, criticised the government's failure to adhere to its socialist principles in the field of foreign policy. Although he was wholly out of sympathy with the 'Soviet belligerence', he thought that the hostility which the Soviet Union exhibited towards Britain was 'not a reason for abandoning our socialist objectives; it is rather a reason for pursuing them all the more boldly'.[42]

In the following months opposition to Bevin's foreign policy came to a climax. In late October twenty-one backbenchers wrote to Attlee to protest against the government's foreign policy, particularly with regard to Greece and Spain, and argue for a 'third way' – an alternative to American capitalism and Soviet communism based on British social democracy.[43] The demand for a decisive change in foreign policy was repeated the following month, when a considerable number of Labour MPs signed an amendment to the government's opening address to parliament. The government put on a three-line whip, but in the subsequent vote about 120 Labour MPs chose to abstain rather than support their leaders. Within a few months the Keep Left group was formed with the aim of working for a third force independent of both blocs. In its pamphlet, published in May 1947, it stressed that the division of the world into two hostile blocs had squeezed democracy in Europe:

> The most tragic example is Greece. Our feeble attempts to create a democratic socialist regime in Athens failed miserably; and the Greeks are now divided into a Right ready to accept American money and a Left which intends to impose a communist-controlled regime.[44]

The 1947 conference at Margate 'was the last time an effective opposition to Bevin came from the floor of the conference'.[45] The Foreign
Secretary made clear he would not tolerate an alternative foreign
policy nor backstabbing from middle-class 'comrades'. 'If you are to
expect loyalty from ministers', he declared, 'the ministers – however
much they may make mistakes – have a right to expect loyalty in
return. I grew up in the trade union, you see, and I have never been
used to this sort of thing.' With this appeal to working-class solidarity
and with the major trade unions standing firmly with the government
Bevin had no difficulty in securing a general endorsement for his policies.[46] An attack on policy in Greece, demanding withdrawal of
British troops, was rejected without a card vote, while references to
'subservience to capitalist America' were swept aside.[47]

THE TRIUMPH OF 'BEVINISM'

By that time opposition to 'Bevinism' had begun to disintegrate and
the Third Force movement was soon to succumb to cold war tensions
and split into hostile factions. According to Saville, there were two
factors that contributed to this development. One was the Marshall
Plan, which 'gave the United States political leverage within western
Europe'. About a quarter of all Marshall Aid-financed imports went
to Britain, 'but there were political consequences … the way was eased
for the permanent establishment of American air forces in the United
Kingdom, and it was understood that Britain would increase its
defence expenditure'.[48] The Marshall Plan inspired the moderate left
in the Labour Party to undertake a re-evaluation of American policy.
RHS Crossman, formerly the leading opponent of the Anglo-
American alliance, was one of the first to announce in the House of
Commons in January 1948 his conversion to pro-Americanism.[49]
Like Crossman, most critics accepted, albeit often reluctantly, that
some kind of alliance with the United States was inevitable. The
Soviet Union's increasingly ruthless control of Eastern Europe obvi-
ously intensified this sense of inevitability, and 'Harry Truman began
to be seen as a leader with whom Labour Britain could co-operate. His
re-election in the autumn of the year was greeted by many of the
Labour Left with enthusiasm.'[50]

   The second factor contributing to the collapse of the opposition
to Bevin's policy, and to the support of his vigorous anti-commu-

nism, was the 'rapid decline of sympathy, especially among the working class, with the Soviet Union and its post-war attitudes and policies'. Moscow was overwhelmingly concerned with the problems of security in Eastern Europe against a background of massive physical and human destruction, unparalleled anywhere else in Europe. But, as Saville allowed, in its foreign policy it 'exhibited – certainly under great provocation from the West – some monumental stupidities, and cruelties, in matters of foreign policy, of which the communist takeover in Czechoslovakia and the break with Yugoslavia were among the most influential in their impact upon world opinion'.[51] Foot, one of the foremost campaigners for a Third Force, had chosen sides much earlier. He was particularly angered by the Soviet criticism of Labour's Greek policy at the UN Security Council in January 1946, and the establishment of totalitarian regimes in Eastern Europe.[52] By 1948, when he took over the editorship of *Tribune*, he was convinced that the Soviet Union was an enemy and that there was no real alternative to Western European Union and the American alliance: 'The policy of neutrality was fantasy.'[53] At the end of 1949 the signatories of the pamphlet *Keeping Left*, which was published in the run-up to the February 1950 election, acknowledged the destruction of the foreign policy advocated in *Keep Left*: 'the foreign policy in which we believed in 1945 had to be scrapped'.[54]

Cold war developments also had their negative effect upon the trade union movement. In the immediate post-war period dissatisfaction with the government's Greek policy was vigorous and widespread among trade union activists. The 1945 TUC voiced its disquiet at the handling of Greek affairs, principally on trade union questions. At the next TUC left-wing delegates attacked the Greek government and the British support for it. 'Is it the job of our movement to provide the beds which will make the chains of reaction on the Greek people a little less burdensome', one trade unionist asked, 'or is it not the job of our people to smash those chains entirely?'. When a delegate of the Boot and Shoe Operatives asked the audience to support Bevin's Greek policy, he was answered by LC White of the Civil Service Clerical Association (CSCA): 'I am all for loyalty to Mr. Bevin and for not embarrassing the government, but the government must not embarrass us.'[55] In 1948 the TUC again demanded an end to 'persecution' in Greece and asked the government to help restore

democracy there, although it rejected demands for withdrawal of
British troops. [56]

The concern amongst many trade unionists at the course of Bevin's
foreign policy was also manifested in individual unions in which the
left-wing popular front was still strong. In 1946, the national
committee of the Amalgamated Engineers (AEU) carried the
following resolution by thirty votes to twenty-two:

> This national committee views with alarm and apprehension the
> foreign policy of the Labour government in relation to the British
> armed forces in Greece and Indonesia ... [and] the maintenance of
> diplomatic and trading relationships with the fascist dictatorships of
> Spain and Portugal. It therefore calls upon the government to
> formulate its foreign policy more in keeping with the aims and aspi-
> rations of the Labour movement.

The Shop, Distributive and Allied Workers (USDAW) also passed a
motion condemning British policy in Greece and Indonesia by 391
votes to three, despite the warning of Evelyn Walkden that it
possessed 'a communist sting in the tail'. Although the Scottish
Miners, at their own annual conference, failed to adopt a resolution
of condemnation by seventy-one votes to sixty-one, the size of the
minority suggested considerable misgivings. [57] The 1946 conference
of the CSCA 'deplored the continuation of the Tory line' in
bolstering 'near fascist' governments in Greece, Persia and Indonesia,
and demanded a 'complete revision of British foreign policy'. [58] In
1947 the AEU national committee carried a motion supporting the
policy laid down at the Margate conference of the Labour Party by a
majority of only two; and at the USDAW conference a resolution
expressing alarm at the continuation of foreign policy, and warning
against the dangers of a tie-up with capitalist America, was narrowly
rejected by an amendment which urged the government to strive for
'a democratic socialist alternative'. [59]

As in parliament, so in the trade union movement the volume of
opposition to Bevin's policies began to diminish fast after the announce-
ment of the Marshall Plan. This process was accelerated when the
Labour government's anti-communist campaign got under way in the
winter of 1947-8. The close co-operation that was established between
the Foreign Office and leading personalities of the TUC general council

produced a 'manufactured consensus' of anti-Soviet ideas and attitudes.[60] Even trade unionists who had once been advocates of
'progressive' unity and the Third Force, such as William Lawther, the
Miners' president, Jack Tanner, the AEU president, and Walter Padley,
the USDAW president, offered their support to Bevin. Non-communist
left-wing organisations, such as the League for Democracy in Greece,
also suffered from cold war tensions.[61] This organization was founded in
October 1945 to campaign for a change in British policy and for the
Greek left-wing resistance. Its president was the author and philhellene
Compton Mackenzie, and its executive committee included many
Liberal, Labour and Independent MPs as well as trade unionists and
other personalities. In March 1948, Lyall Wilkes, who had served in
Greece during the last months of the occupation and had been particularly energetic and active on issues relating to trials of former resistance
fighters, withdrew his support from the League. In a letter to its secretary, he explained the reason for his decision:

> I doubt if all LDG members care very much for democracy, since it
> seems to me to be rather a League for Communism in Greece. I do
> suggest to you that what is required is an organization led and
> controlled by people who really do care for Democracy in Greece,
> and elsewhere, instead of by persons who are only too anxious to
> support executions and repression in Eastern Europe whilst fighting
> the same evils in Greece ... It is this entirely one-sided attitude
> which, I believe, will lead to the League for Democracy in Greece
> fast losing support. I do, therefore, hope that you will reconstitute
> your Society on a proper basis before it suffers too drastically from a
> falling off in support. Until that is done, and re-organisation of some
> sort takes place, I do not wish to be associated in any way with the
> activities of the present League.

Almost a year later, the Labour MP George Thomas resigned his position as vice-chairman of the League. The LDG, he claimed in his own
letter to the secretary, supported the guerrillas' army 'which was
dominated by communists who pursued the Cominform line'.[62]
Compton Mackenzie, who also had doubts about the LDG's political
orientation and its attitude towards the civil war, retained his presi-
dency because, as he explained in his ten-volume autobiography, 'men
with Liberal ideas should have the courage to express them without

being afraid of being smeared with red paint by unintelligent political fossils'.[63] When in 1949, Pat Sloan, the director of the Greek news agency, sent a letter to the editor of the monthly progressive review, *Greek Outlook*, stating 'with the fullest knowledge that the Provisional Democratic Government of Greece [KKE's government in the civil war] ... continued to strive for a peaceful settlement if this is humanly possible', Mackenzie replied as follows:

> My reasoning is crystal. What I want to know is whether the Provisional Democratic Government of Free Greece proposes to be both democratic and free, or whether it proposes to follow in the wake of Poland, Bulgaria, Romania, Hungary and Czechoslovakia. An unequivocal answer to this question is required. It is essential for those of us who are not communists and yet deplore the present state of affairs in Athens to know where we stand and to what we are committed.

By 1949 the co-operation of communist and non-communist leftists in the labour movement, upon which left-wing strength and effectiveness depended, had ended, and opposition to 'Bevinism' had largely disappeared. There were occasional nostalgic demands for a 'socialist foreign policy', criticism of the government's handling of relatively narrow questions, like that of Palestine, and sporadic calls for a revision of Britain's attitude towards the eastern Bloc, but they hardly constituted a serious challenge. Greece was now an issue of minority concern, especially associated with a handful of irreconcilables on the Labour left and with the Communist Party.

Notes

1. On the German occupation see especially Mark Mazower, *Inside Hitler's Greece: The Experience of Occupation, 1941-44*, Princeton University Press, 1993.
2. John Iatrides, 'Revolution or self-defense? Communist goals, strategy, and tactics in the Greek civil war', *Journal of Cold War Studies*, 7, 3, 2005, pp9, 16.
3. John Saville, 'Ernest Bevin and the Cold War', J. Saville and R. Miliband, eds, *The Socialist Register 1984*, Merlin, 1984, pp81, 83.
4. John Saville, *The Labour Movement in Britain*, Faber and Faber, 1988, pp89-90.

5. John Saville, 'Ernest Bevin', p82.
6. Winston S. Churchill, *The Second World War*, vol. VI, *Triumph and Tragedy*, Houghton Mifflin, 1953 edn, p284.
7. Saville, 'Ernest Bevin', p85.
8. Winston S. Churchill, *Triumph and Tragedy*, pp286-7.
9. Ibid., p289.
10. Saville, 'Ernest Bevin', p90. See also *The Politics of Continuity: British Foreign Policy and the Labour Government 1945-46*, Verso, 1993; for an extended commentary on this book and on Labour attitudes to the Cold War, see John Callaghan's chapter in this book.
11. Alan Bullock, *Ernest Bevin: Foreign Secretary, 1945-51*, Heinemann, 1983, p160. The Middle East was of cardinal importance to Britain, both strategically and economically (a focal point of communications, a source of oil, a shield to Africa and the Indian Ocean, an irreplaceable offensive base).
12. Saville, 'Ernest Bevin', p87.
13. Saville, *Labour Movement in Britain*, p91.
14. Alan J Foster, 'The politicians, public opinion, and the press: The storm over British military intervention in Greece in December 1944', *Journal of Contemporary History*, 19, 1984, pp453-94.
15. EH Carr, 'A tragedy of errors', *Times*, 5 December 1944; Carr, 'Next steps in Greece', *Times*, 29 December 1944. In the latter, Carr wrote that there was 'no ground for pride or satisfaction in the knowledge that British troops have been engaged in house-to-house fighting in a working-class suburb of Athens … British troops were fighting against forces representing what is according to all evidence the largest organized party, or group of parties, in Greece.'
16. *Hansard*, vol 407, col 400, 18 January 1945.
17. *Hansard*, House of Lords, vol 134, cols 500-10, 518-28, 21 December 1945.
18. Andrew Thorpe, '"In a rather emotional state"? The Labour Party and British intervention in Greece, 1944-5', *English Historical Review*, 71, 2006, pp1075-1105.
19. *Daily Worker* 18 and 19 December 1944; *Daily Herald*, 18 December 1944.
20. *Daily Worker*, 30 December 1944.
21. *News Chronicle*, 12 December 1944; National Archives (NA) FO 371/43717 (file comprising letters and press clippings on the Greek crisis).
22. The opinion polls were organized by the British Gallup Institute and were published in the *News Chronicle*. Extracted from *Gallup International Public Opinion Polls: Great Britain, 1937-1975*, Random, 1976.
23. *What we Saw in Greece: Report of the TUC Delegation*, London, 1945.
24. Saville, 'Ernest Bevin', p86.

25. Michael Foot, *Aneurin Bevan. A Biography*, vol.1, 1897-1945; MacGibbon and Kee, 1962, p486.
26. Alan Bullock, *The Life and Times of Ernest Bevin, Volume 2: Minister of Labour*, Heinemann, 1967, pp343-4.
27. *Labour Party Annual Conference (LPAC)*, 1944, pp145-7. A measure of Churchill's gratitude for Bevin's speech is the handsome tribute he was to pay him in his memoirs (vol.6, p299 – 'with characteristic loyalty and courage he defended and vindicated our policy in Greece').
28. *LPAC*, 1944, p148.
29. Saville, 'Ernest Bevin', p86.
30. *LPAC*, 1945, p114.
31. Laski's interview during the thirty-seventh national congress of the French socialist party, *Times*, 13 August 1945.
32. *Hansard*, vol 413, cols 337-8, 20 August 1945.
33. John Saville, *The Politics of Continuity*, p93.
34. John Saville, *The Labour Movement in Britain*, p91.
35. *Hansard* , vol 413, cols 283-300, 385-7, 337-8, 20 August 1945.
36. Ibid., vol 413, cols 588-90, 22 August 1945.
37. Labour History Archive and Study Centre, Manchester, PLP minutes, 22 August 1945.
38. FO 371/48325 'British policy in Greece, reactions'.
39. Attlee papers, Bodleian Library, Oxford, box 31, ff 166-74: Zilliacus to Attlee, 11 February 1946; Box 31, Folios 242: Attlee to Zilliacus, 17 Feb.1946.
40. *LPAC*, 1946, p151.
41. *Tribune*, 14 June 1946.
42. Ibid, 7 July 1946.
43. *Manchester Guardian*, 16 November 1946.
44. *Keep Left*, p34.
45. John Saville, *The Politics of Continuity*, p61.
46. These unions were the Transport and General Workers, the National Union of General and Municipal Workers, and the National Union of Mineworkers. Their loyalty was fuelled not just by support for government policies, but by a strong sense of solidarity to a Foreign Secretary who symbolised the union presence at the highest level of government.
47. *LPAC*, 1947, pp141-2, 160, 179.
48. Saville, *Labour Movement in Britain*, p101.
49. *Hansard*, vol 446, col 566, 23 January 1948.
50. Saville, 'Ernest Bevin', pp95-6; Saville, *Labour Movement in Britain*, p102.
51. Saville, *Labour Movement in Britain*, pp102-3.
52. *Tribune*, 1 March 1946.
53. *Tribune*, 18 March 1949.
54. *Keeping Left*, pp16, 27.

55. TUC report, 1946, pp439, 473-4.
56. TUC report, 1948, pp451, 455-61.
57. AEU, *Records and Proceedings*, 1946, p247; *New Dawn*, 11 May 1946; *Daily Worker*, 14 June 1946.
58. *Red Tape*, July 1946, p274.
59. AEU, *Records and Proceedings*, 1947, p235; *New Dawn*, 12 April 1947.
60. Peter Weiler, *British Labour and the Cold War*, Stanford University Press, 1988, esp. ch. 6. Weiler's work is a major contribution to the ongoing reassessment of Britain's role in the origins of the Cold War.
61. John Sakkas, 'The League for Democracy in Greece and the Greek civil war, 1946-49', *Thetis* 3, 1996, pp243-54. In 1977 the executive committee of the LDG gave the archives to the Department of Byzantine and Modern Greek Studies at King's College London.
62. Modern Greek Archive (King's College), Corresp. VII, 'Lyall Wilkes', Wilkes to Pym, 15 March 1948; Corresp. VI, 'George Thomas', 6 April 1949.
63. Compton Mackenzie, *My Life and Times*, IX, 1946-53, Chatto & Windus, 1970, pp213-14.

Islam and the religious Cold War

Dianne Kirby

John Saville is mostly remembered as a socialist economic and
social historian, but his wide interests also embraced international affairs, not least the Cold War, which framed his political life
and his career as a historian. John agreed with Stuart Hall's maxim
on the need to 'Submit everything to the discipline of present
reality, to our understanding of the forces which are really shaping
and changing our world'.[1] The reality confronting him was, in his
own words, that 'the world has been a bitter and bloody planet ever
since the end of World War II'. The onus of responsibility for this
state of affairs was directed toward the United States, the centre of
world reaction, whose enormous resources were committed to
crushing, curbing and containing democratic and progressive
movements in all continents. However, despite leaving 'a wide trail
of devastation round the world', and being 'stained with the blood
of the millions of Third World citizens who have been butchered
to keep the world safe for the property owners of the world',
American actions, as Saville's meticulous research revealed, were
supported and facilitated by a diverse variety of allies.[2] Saville's
penetrating gaze was directed particularly toward Britain, especially
its post-war Labour government.

In an article published in the 1984 *Socialist Register*, Saville
addressed the roles of Ernest Bevin and Clement Attlee as pacesetters
in the Cold War, the extent to which the 1945 Labour government
continued the policies of Churchill's coalition government, and the
remarkable degree of British subservience toward the US.[3]
Elaborating on these important themes in what was to be his magnum
opus in the field of foreign affairs, *The Politics of Continuity* (1993),
Saville opened new avenues in post-war diplomatic history, showing

how the US was actively supported by its allies among the advanced capitalist countries, and Britain above all.[4]

Unsurprisingly, Saville paid substantive attention to the Middle East, strategically crucial and resource rich, and a major area of instability with unpalatable regimes supported by the West. John's research cogently identified the continuities in policy between the pre-cold war period and the cold war era itself, well aware of the extent to which the same policies and attitudes exacted a terrible price and continued to plague the post-cold war world, long after the collapse of the Soviet Union. In tribute to Saville's prescience, the following chapter deals with continuities and legacies, as it reveals how the religious dimension of American cold war policies helped facilitate the rise of militant Islam, with, of course, British support.

The British were adept at using religion, and did so in more subtle and covert ways than their American counterparts. As early as April 1948 there were discussions within the Foreign Office Research Department (FORD) about the potential of Islam to resist or oppose Soviet influence. When in the 1950s the Americans began to promote Islam as a counter to the left and to the spread of Soviet influence in the Middle East, Britain's well-established contacts and still considerable influence throughout the region were put at the disposal of their US ally in accordance with Foreign Office policy. In early 1950 an Anglo-American information committee had been established to co-ordinate British and American propaganda, meaning, as the Foreign Office remarked, 'In all information work we and the Americans now operate very much as one team …'.[5] Unfortunately, the team gave insufficient consideration to the dangers of playing the Islamic card.

In the immediate aftermath of the Cold War, the scholarly tendency was to approach religion as either an obstacle to secular democracy or as evidence of embedded cultural and civilisational differences.[6] Subsequently, the secularisation hypothesis, with its teleology of modernity, was challenged by what seemed a 'resurgence' of religion to those who had neglected to notice the important role it had been accorded in the Cold War as a means of emphasising the shared values of the non-communist world. In the fundamental reappraisal of previous paradigms now taking place, some suggest the relationship was not, as once thought, between secularisation and modernisation, but between modernisation and religious pluralism.[7] As these deliberations progress and twentieth-century history is reassessed, the significance of what can be termed the 'religious cold war' must be considered, particularly in the context of Thomas Friedman's observation of the post-1989 international system, that whilst the Cold War didn't shape everything, it shaped many things.[8]

RELIGION IN THE COLD WAR

Despite the widespread separation of religion from the ensemble of political institutions that constitute the modern national state and geopolitical system, it still performed a significant political role in the constitution of the world order. The Cold War presented the world with two competing models of modernisation: the communist-socialist, represented by the Soviet Union, versus the liberal-capitalist, represented by the US. In the cold war battle for hearts and minds, each of these supposedly secular models used religion – a reliable source of emotion, ready-made symbols and rituals – to enhance the appeal of their competing political and economic models, particularly in the developing world and within traditional societies where religion remained important.

Western policy-makers saw Marxist atheism as the window of vulnerability through which to attack the Soviet experiment and curtail its potential appeal. Whilst the Soviet Union was never able to use religion as effectively as its American rival, it also deployed its religious resources, endowing East-West rivalry with a religious dimension that was to have global implications, not least in the Muslim world. The support accorded the Taliban in Afghanistan by the USA in the final years of the Cold War is well-documented. Less known is its promotion of the most conservative and militant interpretations of Islam in the early years of the Cold War as a means of consolidating its hold on the strategically important, oil-rich Middle East, aided and abetted by its British ally. Presidents Truman and subsequently Eisenhower both believed that religion gave the US and its western allies a crucial advantage in this Muslim-dominated region. This was largely owing to the critical importance of faith; the usual emphasis on democracy and freedom characteristic of American anti-communist propaganda was clearly problematic, owing to alliances with the region's autocratic leaders. The emphasis on religion was intended to encourage a belief in shared western-Muslim values.

The claim advanced was that the Christian West and the Muslim East confronted a common global foe that required a common global bond in defence of religious faith. In Iran, for example, in order to convey the sense of a 'common moral front', the American embassy distributed a brochure entitled *The Voices of God*. Intended to suggest a nexus between various faiths and American values, the brochure, with a mosque on its cover, contained quotations from the Koran, Muslim poetry, Jesus Christ, Isaiah, Chinese philosophy, the Buddha, the Sanskrit Bhagavad Gita, Abraham Lincoln and Mahatma Gandhi.[9] An alliance with Islam conformed to a cold war narrative in which the distinction drawn between the godly US and the godless USSR affirmed the value of religion itself more than that of any particular form.[10] During the 1950s a 'Christian amendment' to the American Constitution was easily defeated. In line with Harry Truman's vision of a united, anti-communist religious front: 'Adhesional religious symbolism was what Congress wanted, not invidious distinctions among the God-fearing'.[11] The same sentiment permeated the Supreme Court, which in 1931 had used the word *Christian* to describe the nation, but by 1952 was using the term *religious*: 'We are a religious people whose institutions presuppose a Supreme Being.'[12]

An international united front of the world's religious and moral leaders was part of Truman's evolving containment strategy.[13] With strategically placed spies, the Kremlin was well aware of the intent to rally the religious for a global anti-Soviet crusade. The Second World War had already demonstrated that significant numbers of Soviet citizens would respond to religious appeals and turn against the regime.[14] With religion a natural focus for dissent, Stalin's inherent suspicion about the subversive potential of religion was inevitably exacerbated.

The Soviet leadership could not revert to the sort of historical alliance that existed between the church and regimes from which the communist revolution was meant to be a radical departure. Communism had its own internal legitimation that would be called into question should it seem to be seeking 'sacralisation'. An alliance with religion risked alienating communist adherents for whom religion remained a reactionary and anti-progressive force from which the masses had to be liberated. Rather than eradicate religion, however, Soviet efforts were directed toward controlling and domesticating it within its own sphere, and rallying believers with socialist sympathies everywhere in its defence. Nonetheless, even if subdued or subservient, religion retained the potential to undermine, or at least compromise, communist power. The result was vacillating and contradictory policies toward religion throughout the Soviet era.

Although as early as the March 1919 Communist Party programme warnings were offered against offending religious sentiments in order not to strengthen religious fanaticism, religious harassment and persecution, however ad hoc and inconsistent, had marked the history of the post-revolutionary years. Stalin's more militant anti-religious policies meant an alienated population and a weaker state, which was to have significant repercussions in the confrontation with Hitler. Notably, the Russian Orthodox Patriarch's voice was the first to rally the people against the Nazis;[15] and religion subsequently became a crucial consideration in defeating Hitler, maintaining the wartime alliance, securing the territories newly incorporated into the Soviet sphere and strategically spreading Soviet influence. Stalin had had emphatically impressed upon him the extent to which authoritative cultural and religious systems of belief and practice were powerful determinants that he could neither ignore nor overcome, but which he could use to his advantage. Throughout the Soviet bloc, the nexus between religion and national identity, and the congruence, at times, of church-state interests, not to mention the importance of religion in the rest of the world, meant that it had to be given consideration by Soviet policy-makers.

In the post-war period, Stalin's need to reduce anti-Soviet hostility within and without the communist bloc, as well as his desire to improve his regime's image abroad, militated against the violent and crude anti-religious policies that had previously helped the West promote a negative, indeed demonic, image of communism and the Soviet leadership. Indeed, evidence indicates that during the war both Roosevelt and Stalin considered religion a potential bridge that would help ease the wartime alliance into post-war co-operation.[16] At home, Stalin implemented links and structures intended to secure compliant religious institutions responsive to top-down authoritarian policies. Soviet generals and local communist leaders honoured Greek Orthodox clergy in the Balkans and courted Roman Catholic clergy in Poland. Religion might have provided Stalin with a ready and relatively easy means of reducing the gulf that remained between him and his allies during the war, but neither he nor they could sway the Vatican.

Seemingly worried that the crucible of war might merge the Orthodox conception of a messianic Russia with the Marxist conception of a messianic proletariat, the Vatican would not risk any seeming legitimisation of Soviet power. Notable British and American leaders shared Vatican fears as they observed a world disillusioned with and critically questioning the system that had delivered slump, fascism and war. Adding to concerns that Stalin might not remain content with his allotted 'security zone', were worries about the appeal of a creed that promised 'from each according to his ability, to each according to his need', particularly should it be complemented by a religious dimension.

American diplomats scrutinised religious activity in the Soviet bloc. Stalin's effective use of religious leaders of all persuasions to support what the West referred to as the 'Soviet-inspired peace campaign', caused grave concern that the Soviets too could derive some benefit from appearing to support religion. For example, reporting a little publicised visit of a Muslim delegation from Albania to the USSR, the Moscow embassy told the State Department:

> Visit, of course, constitutes renewed evidence of present Soviet policy of utilising religious bodies in interests Soviet imperialism. Despite slight publicity given this visit, presumably it may be brought to attention world's Muslims as indicative Soviet religious tolerance, particularly in NEA [Near East and Africa] area.[17]

THE POLITICS OF ISLAM

In the immediate post-war period, American officials tended in a general sense to see Islam outside of the Soviet Union as a bulwark against the spread of communism and key to engendering pro-western attitudes and cooperation.[18] Within the British Foreign Office Research Department, there were some reservations. FORD warned that Muslims were becoming more susceptible to communism owing to the encroachment of western materialism. When western propagandists insisted that communism and religion were incompatible, FORD pointed out that this was not necessarily true, and certainly not for Islam. FORD considered that the Islamic revivalist movements, vaguely directed against Europe and Christianity, should oppose communism much more forcefully; but, it advised, this would not mean or lead to a genuine rapprochement with other opponents of communism. FORD concluded that Islam 'occupies an intermediate position between western civilisation and communism and the direction in which it moves will not only decide the fate of Islam but will have a profound effect upon western civilisation itself'.[19]

By the 1950s, the US was discernibly worried about the direction of Islam. The rise of anti-Americanism in the region was fuelled by US support for Israel, America's ties with the region's colonial powers, Britain and France, plus the perception that: 'the British tail is all too successfully wagging the American dog'.[20] The principal threat to US interests was seen as 'anti-western' nationalism.[21] Moreover, the currents of neutralism and nationalism sweeping Muslim lands were seen as 'intimately related to Islam'. Nationalism was viewed as having grown with communism, equated as it was with independence, home rule and the evacuation of foreign forces. Violent Muslim opposition to colonialism and foreign influences was not regarded as an indication that 'Muslims prize or even understand freedom as do Westerners', but as an 'outlet for numerous repressions and feelings' and 'a fluctuating and sometimes temporary expedient … to free Muslim nations from colonialism'. Soviet foreign policy was judged to have as at least its minimum target the neutralisation of Arab countries in the Middle East, deemed by US officials as 'comparatively easy because public opinion in the Arab countries is strongly in favour of neutralism'.[22]

As 'a dominant feature of regional culture, society and politics', Islam was naturally of considerable interest to regional specialists focused on America's relations with the Middle East. The tendency was to respond to it as inherently political. The development of political Islam is notably linked to the work of non-clerical political intellectuals such as Muhammad Iqbal and Muhammad Ali Jinnah in colonial India, and Abul A'la Mawdudi, Sayyid Qutb, and Ali Shariati in post-colonial Pakistan, Egypt and Iran respectively.[23] It was the intellectuals not the ulama that pioneered the development of Islamist political movements, concerned with contemporary political and social issues rather than spiritual. Islamist intellectuals encountered both Marxism and western liberalism.[24] Political Islam can be both emancipatory and authoritarian. Moderate political Islam fought for reforms within the system. Radicals sought power, convinced that no meaningful social reform was possible without state control.

Because the radicals were the most virulently anti-communist and anti-Soviet, American support gravitated to right-wing Islamism. It was a tendency that can at least be partially explained by the relative success and mutually beneficial relationships the US enjoyed elsewhere with political religion: in particular, Christian Democracy in Western Europe, which, like political Islam, also held principles at odds with American liberalism. However, as a product of western civilisation, Christian Democracy had none of Islam's anti-western tendencies that concerned some of America's Middle East specialists. An informal network of professional Middle East watchers, derived from government employees in the State Department and CIA, academics in the emerging field of Middle East studies, journalists and people in business, were all trying to understand the region. Despite recognising regional diversity, religious splits and ethnic differences, there was a tendency to see a dominant Islam producing homogeneous Muslim peoples, trapped between tradition and modernity by a religion that was potentially dangerous and confrontational.[25]

There was concern within official circles that Islam was unlikely to prove an effective barrier against communism and that it could well serve to unite Muslims against western interests in the region.[26] Certainly proponents of modernisation and westernisation in the Muslim world saw religion as an obstacle to economic and political development, and to progress.[27] Truman, however, remained committed to the prospect of an international anti-communist religious front. He claimed in his autobiography, *Mr. Citizen*, that 'contact had been made with spiritual authorities in the Moslem world'.[28] In June 1951 the consul general in Dhahran, William A. Eddy, discussed progress toward a 'possible strategy of the Christian democratic West joining with the Muslim world in a common moral front against communism'.[29]

Eddy claimed that in the event of friendly overtures from the Christian West, he had 'new proof that such an alliance would be welcomed by Muslim leaders'. The Secretary-General of the Arab League, Abdul Rahman Pasha, had discussed the idea with high ranking officials of the US Army and Navy in Washington in December 1950. Even more significantly, Azzam Pasha discussed the idea with Pope Pius XII during a private audience. Pius XII had himself suggested a religious front against Soviet communism during a visit to the US in 1936 when he was a cardinal. In the post-war period he worked with Myron C. Taylor, Truman's personal representative at the Vatican, to bring such a scheme to fruition.[30] The pope welcomed Muslim participation, as well as Muslim diplomatic representatives, 'contrary to Vatican policy of the past which required Muslim countries to designate a Christian'.[31]

The idea was also endorsed by Haj Amin al-Husseini, the Grand Mufti of Jerusalem, who, according to Eddy, had 'great influence in Islamic religious circles'. An unrepentant Nazi supporter, he told Eddy he had been vindicated by West German rearmament and was happy to act with Christians to clarify 'that all historic religion will be destroyed if Russia conquers the world'. Eddy, a former intelligence operative for the Office of Strategic Services (OSS) during the Second World War, may well have approached even more extreme elements. In his OSS days he had worked with a Muslim secret society, a member of which was the 'leader of a powerful Muslim brotherhood in northern Morocco'.[32]

Another potential supporter was the profligate King of Saudi Arabia, described by Eddy as 'the most representative and influential Muslim in the world today'. The Saudi leadership, with its system of state Islam as well as its guardianship of Medina and Mecca, was perceived as having the potential to become 'Islam's Vatican'. In 1952 Prince Saud, soon to become king, advised an American diplomat that he had plans for a pan-Islamic movement, and was assured it would be welcomed because such a movement under his leadership 'would be friendly'.[33] Eisenhower assumed office concerned that the Soviet Union might be able to build up Egyptian president Nasser as the 'head of an enormous Moslem confederation'. He explored the possibility of using King Saud as 'a counter weight to Nasser'. Saud's religious position and his 'professed anti-Communism' made him the 'logical choice'.[34] As relations with Egypt worsened during spring 1956, Eisenhower revealed in his diary that he thought the king could be built up as a spiritual leader, after which 'we might begin to urge his right to political leadership'.[35] He put the same proposition to British defence minister Duncan Sandys the following year, subsequently reminding Saud of his 'special position'.[36]

Eisenhower's support for Saud's religious leadership meant support for the excessively conservative Wahhabi pan-Islamic movement. Furthermore, Allen Dulles, head of the CIA, encouraged Saudi Arabia to support the Muslim Brotherhood, widely regarded as a terrorist organisation, fanatically religious, nationalist and anti-western.[37] Nasser largely expelled it from Egypt following its implication in an attempt to assassinate him in November 1954. Founded in 1928, the Muslim Brotherhood was a major source of religio-political radicalism in Egypt. Accused of trying to overthrow the government 'under cover of religion' in 1953, the Muslim Brotherhood had been welcomed to the anti-Nasser struggle by Egypt's communists, who regarded Nasser as an 'Anglo-American stooge', owing to the Anglo-Egyptian agreement.[38] Hence, to concerns amongst some American officials that Islam was reactionary, backward looking, anti-western, anti-democratic and a potential threat to western interests,[39] were added fears that it could ally with Moscow, with local communists, or with both.

Organised Islam had many forms in the Middle East, the most common being traditionalist, clergy-based, with a powerful social impact but lacking a centre of authority and usually not political. More promising from the American perspective were the explicitly conservative political organisations committed to the establishment of an Islamic republic. Despite their deep reservations, American officials were impressed by the capacity of this strand of Islam to counter the left. In Pakistan, for example, the Islamic Student Society (ITJ), influenced by Egypt's Muslim Brotherhood, battled the left relentlessly and effectively, especially on university campuses, an important factor for US officials concerned about the attraction of the left for the Arab intelligentsia.[40]

In the 1950s *The Middle East Journal* reflected the preoccupations of the region's observers. They worried about the appeal of communism to the middle and professional classes, as capitalism and democracy were regarded with suspicion by the very strata of society assumed elsewhere to be its natural constituency.[41] In 1955, Middle East specialist Walter Z. Laqueur explained: 'Capitalism is identified with imperialist rule and democracy is something the imperialist powers allegedly practice at home.'[42] Nor could the West rely on nationalism in the region to obstruct communism: 'On the contrary, at the present time it has paved the way for and occasionally collaborated with it.'[43] Laqueur warned that the attraction of communism as a creed 'should never be underestimated, and it is nowhere so strong as in underdeveloped countries, such as those of the Middle East'. Although suggesting that ignorance of Soviet conditions was a factor,

Laqueur argued that 'the *idea* is the important criterion'.[44] Of paramount importance were 'the religious elements in Communism and its ethics': 'Any attempt to understand or counteract the power of attraction of Communism in the Middle East which disregards the very existence of its moral concepts and the sources of its fervour and ideals is doomed from the outset.'[45]

Still, Laqueur considered that a detailed investigation of whether Islam aided or arrested the growth of communism would be of little practical importance: whilst religion was important to the masses, it was not so to the intelligentsia. Laqueur rather thought 'the decay of Islamic society and its values', combined with the authoritarian character of Middle Eastern regimes, made 'an easy transition to the Communist ideology a possibility and in some cases a probability'.[46] Although Laqueur considered the 'quest for a universal creed' stronger than it had been for many years, he dismissed Islam as a viable counter to communism, seeing it as sterile and losing appeal. Nonetheless, his exegesis still identified the religious hierarchy as the key bulwark against a communist state.

In observations that reflected those of Bernard Lewis,[47] another key Middle East expert, Laqueur stressed that traditional Islamic autocracy rested on three pillars: bureaucracy, the army and the religious hierarchy. In his opinion, only the latter, the religious hierarchy, 'need be changed in order to prepare the way for a Communist state'. Therefore, although insisting that traditional Islam in its current state was not a viable counter to communism, Laqueur still identified the religious hierarchy as the main obstacle to it. Furthermore, Laqueur identified the Muslim Brotherhood as the only party with sufficient militant support to challenge the communists. He observed: 'The decisive issue in the Middle East is that no party in Syria and Lebanon has more than 10,000 militants apart from the Communists, *and only the Muslim Brotherhood has more than the Communists in Egypt.*'[48] The message was mixed, but specific elements of Islam were clearly identified as key to containing communism.

A POLITICAL FOOTBALL

Eisenhower symbolised the generalised religiosity and patriotic moralism characteristic of America's post-war religious revival, crystallised in his 1954 declaration: 'Our government makes no sense unless it is founded on a deeply felt religious faith – and I don't care what it is.'[49] This was an essential distinction if America was to compete effectively for influence with the Soviet Union and China in the non-Christian world. The latter each had sizeable Muslim populations, and evidence gathered by the CIA suggested that religion was a significant consideration in their policies of outreach, both to western audiences and third world peoples. The CIA was wary of the communist bloc's utilisation of its religious leaders and institutions to appeal to their co-religionists in strategic areas, particularly the Middle East.[50] Islamic delegations from communist regimes appeared to validate Sino-Soviet claims of co-existence and co-operation between communism and religion. They were also reminders of the potential for common cause via shared values, such as the Koranic insistence that a Muslim's first duty is to create a just and egalitarian society in which poor people are treated with respect. And indeed there were historical precedents for cooperation between Islamists and communists, intimately connected to the Bolsheviks' support for national rights. As similar demands subsequently fired the Middle East's Muslims, an Islam-communist alliance seemed a possibility to an American administration worried about the relationship between Islam, communism and nationalism.[51]

State Department responses to pan-Islamic unity movements suggested a preference 'to limit Islam as a political force in the early 1950s'.[52] However, Eisenhower, following the same calculations as his predecessor, saw Islam as a counter in the Middle East to Soviet moves, and to the influence of the radical, secular forces aligned with the left. Moreover, in keeping Muslim peoples oriented toward the West, the Islamic right – with its preference for capitalism and its opposition to state ownership, land reform and social welfare programmes – offered significant advantages for US administrations concerned that communist doctrines might otherwise appeal to the Arab masses. With anti-communism the key criteria, the tendency was to ally the US with the most conservative representatives of Islam. Hence, the support of America and its allies in the region, most notably Saudi Arabia, helped create a situation in which otherwise unpopular and unrepresentative versions of Islam were able to secure a power and influence they otherwise would have been unlikely to attain.

The Operations Co-ordinating Board (OCB), composed of key

members of the administration and intended to follow up on all
National Security Council decisions, was concerned that neither
private organisations nor US government agencies interacted with the
Islamic world in a religious sense. Rather, their activities 'tended to
parallel local movements toward the secularisation of society'.
Identifying Islam as crucial to achieving American objectives, OCB
wanted US officials in the field to be trained in Muslim ideology and
culture, with private organisations 'encouraged' to promote Muslim-
Christian cooperation.[53] It named only the Asia Foundation and the
Continuing Committee on Muslim-Christian co-operation as effective organisations in this respect.[54]

In reality, Islam was far from a neglected entity. The CIA engaged
in 'operations with religious leaders and religious groups', as did the
US Information Service (USIS) and the US Information Agency
(USIA). USIS's chief of religious policy, Elton Trueblood, was one of
the promoters of the Foundation for Religious Action in the Social
and Civil Order. Established in 1953, it had two major aims: 'to stress
the importance of religious truth in the preservation and development
of genuine democracy; and to unite all believers in God in the struggle
between the free world and atheistic Communism, which aims to
destroy both religion and liberty'.[55] USIA worked closely with private
American organisations, especially oil companies 'such as Caltex,
Socony and Aramco' to explain 'the American position to Muslim
leaders and believers'.

In addition to its CIA connections, in 1953 USIA incorporated
into its structure the International Information Administration (IIA),
a branch of the State Department with roots in the US intelligence
community. The IIA, responsible for cultural exchange programmes,
funded a Colloquium on Islamic Culture at Princeton University in
September 1953 that was 'expected to bring together persons exerting
great influence in formulating Moslem opinion in fields such as
education, science, law and philosophy and inevitably, therefore, on
politics'.[56] A memorandum on the event prepared for Secretary of
State John Foster Dulles declared: 'Among the various results
expected from the colloquium are the impetus and direction that may
be given to the Renaissance movement within Islam itself.' As a
measure of the colloquium's importance, hopes were expressed to
Dulles that in addition to his own possible participation, he and the
president might 'wish to entertain the delegates'.[57]

These included Said Ramadhan, 'a militant official and ideologue of the Muslim Brotherhood'.[58] His inclusion was supported by the Cairo embassy, which emphasised his position and the undesirability 'of offending this important body'. It also advised of his intent to 'visit Muslim leaders and university faculty members throughout the US' after the Colloquium.[59] The Muslim Brotherhood, the flagship of fundamentalism in the Arab world, was a product of both religious and economic dissent.[60] It had served British imperialism and was similarly to serve the CIA.[61]

The OCB insisted that 'The Communists are exploiting Islam'.[62] The American response to ensure a pro-western Muslim world, in both government and private spheres, was set out in an OCB-compiled inventory.[63] The inventory and its recommendations were referred to OCB working groups concerned with Muslim countries, intended to facilitate 'special operating guidance and courses of action regarding Islam'. The inventory, noting Islam's 'compatible values', presented the 'true division' of the world as 'between a society in which the individual is motivated by spiritual and ethical values and one in which he is the tool of a materialistic state'. However, it insisted, communists had 'far surpassed' America 'in making direct appeals to the Muslims as Muslims'. Unhappy with what it regarded as complacent views of Islam as a natural barrier to communism, OCB argued that the Soviets sold friendship, not communism or atheism.[64]

Positing that Muslims were unaware of the Soviet threat to their religion and society, OCB wanted to see implemented 'a powerful, regionally planned effort, to expose the basic incompatibility between Islam and communism'. OCB claimed that such was not only long overdue, but also 'capable of producing far-reaching results'. OCB recognised that the CIA was already conducting 'operations with religious leaders and religious groups and USIA has shown a real interest, stronger in some countries, in explaining the American position to Muslim leaders and believers'. However, concerns were raised that Chinese communists, not perceived to be as tainted with anti-Muslim tendencies as their Soviet counterparts, were assuming the leading role in cultivating the Muslim world.

Interestingly, OCB conceded that there was no evidence of tangible results from this alleged Sino-Soviet cooperation in the Islamic sphere. Far too cautious to risk the rise of Islam within its own

Muslim republics, Moscow showed little inclination to promote pan-Islamism in the Middle East, in view of the possible attendant risk of it spreading to Central Asia. Certainly Islamic forces within the Soviet republics were both cultivated and coerced as part of communist endeavours to control and domesticate religion. Building relations with Islamic leaders and allowing some Muslims to visit the Holy Shrines was good propaganda. Yet the possibility of Muslim-communist co-operation clearly bothered US policy-makers, and consideration was given not simply to how to impress on Muslim populations that communism was their enemy, but also to the potential of Islam to serve as a fifth column inside the Soviet bloc.[65]

By 1957 Islam was seen as critical to the balance of power in the international arena. Sixteen nations with Muslim majorities acted as a bloc within the UN. With some 366 million adherents covering a vast area that extended from Morocco to Indonesia, including the majority population of five Soviet republics, Islam was 'the fastest growing of the world's great religions'. OCB worried that modernisation would bring secularism that would, in turn, facilitate the spread of communism: 'unless a reconciliation is achieved between Islamic principles and current social and political trends, the spiritual values of Islam will be lost and the swing toward materialism will be hastened'. OCB's concerns embraced areas of instability in the Middle East where 'the populace responds most readily to inflammatory appeals'. Also 'blacker Africa', where 'Islam is spreading like flame and large areas may become increasingly receptive to bold anti-foreign and anti-Western propaganda'.[66]

OCB made positive assumptions about Islam's potential, defining it as a constructive, stabilising force for which movements such as extreme nationalism, pan-Arabism, materialism and downgrading of minority rights were inimical. Islam was presented as a ubiquitous force that permeated every aspect of Muslim existence. OCB argued that as 'religion colors all life in the community', a wide range of organisations involved in a broad band of activities could be classed as Islamic, from youth and women's groups, to health, welfare, cultural and educational. In pursuit of closer and better relations with Islam in the anti-Soviet struggle, OCB's preference was to support reform-minded individuals and groups prepared 'to search for a bridge between traditional Islam and the modern state', but which were also opposed to 'reactionary movements and to communist and extremist propaganda'. But in the cold war context, anti-communism always became the main criterion.

Despite OCB claims that insufficient was being done to promote anti-communism in the Islamic community, the available evidence indicates that much of what it proposed was already being implemented. USIS was notably pro-active. In Indonesia it cooperated with an Indonesian anti-communist group, Front Anti-Komunis (FAK), whose leaders were Muslims identified with the Masjumi party.[67] USIS financed FAK anti-communist publications, including a series on Muslims in China. All publications were attributed to the Muslim Missionary Association. FAK placed five thousand copies of the pamphlet *Communism vs. Islam* aboard a pilgrim ship to Mecca on behalf of USIS. Owing to their 'liaison in the Ministry of Religious Affairs', USIS was able to place its material in the religious schools, and was making a 'concerted effort ... to penetrate Nahdatul Ulama, the rising Orthodox Muslim Party, through the Ulamas and the Madrasahs'.[68]

OCB's directive that to be effective, and to avoid the charge of using religion for political purposes, US programmes and propaganda had to be indirect and unattributable was already established practice. In Iran, unattributable material indicting Soviet designs on Islam were 'distributed through bus companies, airlines, and travel agencies', as well as 'through a Muslim theologian and leading anti-communist, Kalbassi'. Even 'the Mufti of Lebanon has mailed unattributed anti-Communist materials published by USIS'. In Pakistan, 'In the Fall of 1955, USIS indirectly sponsored an all-Pakistan religious conference at Dacca'. Indeed, the papers presented at the conference were published and distributed before OCB's directives requiring anonymity were even in circulation. Although OCB advised against the open use of Islamic organisations for the inculcation of hard-line propaganda, in practice it happened. In Iraq, for example, where occasionally a Mullah used 'a statement prepared by USIS in his Friday sermon ... such messages are "hard-line" propaganda against communism'.[69]

OCB wanted more use of conventional means for promoting positive attitudes toward the US amongst Muslims. Already gauged a dividend-paying success was the Department of State Exchange of Persons Program (IES). Hence recommendations for increased numbers of grants to Muslim leaders for both study in the US and visits to other Muslim countries. IES activities influenced Islamic organisations through contacts with individual leaders in a range of professions, including banking, law, medicine, social welfare, government and, of course, the media. In Ceylon, USIS worked closely with Senator Aziz, a former US grantee and head of the Muslim College in Colombo, as well as one of the pillars of the Ceylon American Society. In Pakistan, the head of the department of Islamic Studies at the University of Punjab was a Foreign Leader grantee and formerly secretary of the Pakistan-American Society of Lahore. Former Fulbright grantee Miss Musharraf Sufi delivered sixty lectures on American education at the behest of USIS in Karachi.[70]

Although it was clearly in US interests to minimise differences and emphasise the fight against their common communist foe, US policies toward Islamic movements and states in the early cold war period reveal a deep residue of ambivalence, scepticism and mistrust. Dispatches from US embassies recorded the extent to which Islam was becoming a political football, creating a situation fraught with potential danger for the countries concerned and for future relations with the West. However, the dangers of playing the Islamic card were subsumed by American administrations lauding their nation's religiosity and fired by a sense of mission. Policy-makers, moreover, failed to understand the complexity and power of Islam. Too many remained wedded to the view that third world nationalism was a Soviet tool, and political Islam an ally to be used against presumed pro-Soviet nationalist leaders such as Nasser in Egypt. The situation was exacerbated by the fact that America's Middle East allies shared assumptions that Islam would provide a local buffer against secular nationalism. Conservative Arab regimes sheltered and aided militant Islamists, whilst Israel was to allow Hamas to operate unhindered during the first intifada.[71]

LEGACY: THE WAR ON TERROR?

For Truman and Eisenhower and their successors, dealing with Islam meant dealing with often oppressive and corrupt regimes that lacked popular support and for whom Islam was as much a tool as it was for the Americans. Consequently, much of America's Middle East cold war agenda was being mediated through regimes and religious movements that would inevitably prioritise their own political agendas.

These were naturally concerned with consolidating and/or extending their own power bases. In addition, US cold war policies that eroded the left and progressive nationalism in the Middle East further helped the rise of right-wing political Islam. By removing what American officialdom regarded as their common foes on the left, the US facilitated political Islam's growing support throughout the region, albeit as a default option. US officials worried by the strength of the anti-western sentiment harboured by some of their Islamist allies possibly drew some reassurance from thinking that the religious extremists lacked a popular base. Most Muslims rejected their ideology and their modes of operating. However, the weakening and discrediting of the left in the Muslim world empowered political Islam, making it the main ideological and organised means through which popular discontent and dissent could be expressed. The lack of progress and reform, and the continuation of oppressive regimes allied with and supported by the West, inflamed anti-western sentiments. In the absence of secular left-liberal alternatives, this further galvanised support for the Islamists as the most ardent opposition to the status quo.[72]

Right-wing Islamism had been an ideological tendency with small and scattered numbers. Out of power, it had neither the aspiration of drawing strength from popular organisation nor the possibility of marshalling strength from any alternative source.[73] This changed following the Soviet military intervention in Afghanistan. National security adviser Zbigniew Brzezinski saw an opportunity to export a composite ideology of nationalism and Islam to the Muslim majority Central Asian republics, with a view to destroying the Soviet system.[74] Little thought was given to how the religious could and would transgress the boundaries between the sacred and profane to assert their own political, social and economic influences. In the portrayal of the Afghan War as an international jihad, bringing together volunteers from Muslim populations all over the world, are resonances of Truman's international anti-communist religious front concept.

The legacy of the religious Cold War lingers around the 'War on Terror', which is presented as a battle against an extremist religious challenge to the legitimacy of the modern international system – a system designated as separate from, and yet the defender of, religion. Understanding the dynamics of the religious Cold War and the legacy it has bequeathed the post-cold war world is even more vital since the 9/11 attacks. The modern nation as an imagined community is mediated through constructed images, and this makes America's failure to engage in a sustained public debate about the significance of the attacks as important as its reversion to its cold war practice of defining itself as 'good' in opposition to its 'evil' enemies at home and abroad.

There is a need to understand more fully how political Islam has attained its present currency, and to question the lamentable tendency of western intellectuals and political leaders to berate the Muslim world for not embracing secularism and modernity and rejecting its violent roots; this would be assisted by attention being directed to the ways in which presidents Truman and Eisenhower invoked the universal tradition of harnessing the power of religion to the policy goals of the state, and to the ways in which the consequences were conditioned by the special religious characters of American and Muslim cultures in the context of the 'religious cold war'.

Notes

1. Stuart Hall, *The Hard Road to Renewal: Thatcherism and the Crisis of the Left*, Verso 1988, p14.
2. John Saville, '*Marxism Today*: an anatomy' in Ralph Miliband, Leo Panitch and John Saville, eds, *The Retreat of the Intellectuals: The Socialist Register 1990*, Merlin, 1990, 35-9.
3. Saville, 'Ernest Bevin and the Cold War', in Saville, Ralph Miliband and Marcel Liebman, eds, *Socialist Register 1984*, Merlin, pp68-100.
4. Saville, *The Politics of Continuity: British Foreign Policy and the Labour Government 1945-6*, Verso, 1993. For extended commentary on this book, see John Callaghan's chapter in this volume; for more on the relationship with Greece, see John Sakkas's chapter.
5. Foreign Office to Colonel AH Read, GPI, 18 July 1950; National Archives (henceforth NA) HO 256 337.
6. For the most famous proponent of the latter, Samuel P. Huntington, secular democracy was deeply rooted in Protestant Christianity, a commonly held assumption amongst America's political elites.
7. See Peter L Berger, *The Desecularization of the World*, Wm. B. Eerdmans, 1999; Berger and Samuel P Huntington, *Many Globalizations: Cultural Diversity in the Contemporary World*, Oxford University Press, 2003.
8. Thomas Friedman, *The Lexus and the Olive Tree*, Anchor Books, 1999, p7.
9. Loy Henderson to State Department, 'Report on the use of anti-Soviet material', 29 May 1953, NARA II, Record Group 59, Decimal Files 1950-54.

10. Michael S Sherry, *In the Shadow of War: The United States Since the 1930s*, Yale University Press, 1995.
11. Mark Silk, *Spiritual Politics: Religion and America Since World War II*, Touchstone, 1988, p107.
12. Fred E Baumann and Kenneth M Jensen, *Religion and Politics*, University Press of Virginia, 1989, p5.
13. Dianne Kirby, 'Harry S. Truman's International Religious Anti-Communist Front, the Archbishop of Canterbury and the 1948 Inaugural Assembly of the World Council of Churches', *Contemporary British History*, 15, 4, 2001.
14. Steven Merritt Miner, *Stalin's Holy War: Religion, Nationalism, and Alliance Politics, 1941-1945*, University of North Carolina Press, 2003.
15. William Van Den Bercken, 'Holy Russia and the Soviet Fatherland', *Religion in Communist Lands*, 15, 3, 1987, pp264- 77.
16. Dianne Kirby, 'Religion' in R Immerman & P Goedde, eds, *The Oxford Handbook of the Cold War*, Oxford University Press, forthcoming 2012.
17. US Embassy, Moscow to State Dept, 26 Aug 1950, NARA II, 867.413/8-2650.
18. US Embassy, Ankara to State Dept, 31 Dec 1946, NARA II, 867.404/12-3146.
19. FORD, 'Islam and Communism', NA FO 371 71707A, April 1948.
20. Stephen Penrose to State Dept, 'The Soviet challenge in the Near East', 2 June 1951; George Cameron to Edward W. Barrett, 'Propaganda Activities in Iraq', 24 Oct 1951, NARA II, RG 59, DF 1950-54; Burton Berry to Henry Byroade, 'Secretary of State's understanding of Middle Eastern problems', 23 July 1953, NARA II, RG 59, Lot File 57 D 298.
21. NSC Executive Secretary Report, 'US Objectives and Policies with Respect to the Arab States and Israel', Annex to NSC 129, 7 April 1952.
22. Laqueur, 'The appeal of Communism in the Middle East', *Middle East Journal*, 9, 1955, p23.
23. Laqueur, 'Appeal' p47.
24. From 1917 to the mid-1920s, the Bolsheviks welcomed practising Muslims into the party and engaged in large-scale united front work with Islamic organisations; see Dave Crouch, 'The Bolsheviks and Islam', *International Socialism*, 110, spring 2006, p38.
25. Paul Kesaris, ed., Office of Intelligence Research, 'Problems and Attitudes in the Arab World: Their implications for US Psychological Strategy', 19 May 1952, OSS/State Department Intelligence and Research Reports, XII: The Middle East, 1950-1961, Microfilm Collection, reel 1, 15; Psychological Strategy Board, 'D-22: Psychological Strategy for the Middle East', Annex B, 'Analysis of the Middle East mind, basic and current attitudes' (6 February 1953), 4, PSB Documents, Box 16, NSC Records 1948-61, White House Office Files, Eisenhower Library, Abilene, Kansas.

26. Laqueur, 'Appeal', pp17-27.
27. Robert Montagne, 'Modern nations and Islam', *Foreign Affairs*, 30, 4, July 1952.
28. Harry S Truman, *Mr. Citizen*, Hutchinson, 1961, p119.
29. Eddy to *New York Herald Tribune* columnist Dorothy Thompson, 7 June 1951, NARA II, RG 59, LF 57 D 28.
30. Kirby, 'Harry Truman's religious legacy: the Holy Alliance, containment and the Cold War', in Kirby, ed. *Religion and the Cold War*, Palgrave Macmillan 2003, pp77-102.
31. Eddy to Thompson, 7 June 1951, National Archives and Records Administrations (NARA) II, RG 59, LF 57 D 28.
32. Robert Dreyfus, *Devil's Game: How the US Helped Unleash Fundamentalist Islam*, Metropolitan Books, 2005, p89.
33. Dreyfus, *Devil's Game*, pp90-1.
34. Dwight Eisenhower, *The White House Years, Vol II: Waging Peace*, Doubleday, 1965.
35. Foreign Relations of the United States (FRUS) 1955-57, XV, Washington 1989, p425.
36. FRUS 1955-57, XIII, Washington 1989, 444-5, pp645-6.
37. Paul Kesaris, ed., *CIA Research Reports: The Middle East, 1946-76*, Microfilm Collection, 7.
38. Malise Ruthven, *Islam in the World*, Oxford University Press, 1984, p33.
39. Philip K. Hitti, 'Current trends in Islam,' in Dorothea Seelye Franck, ed., *Islam in the Modern World*, Middle East Institute, 1951, p5.
40. Seyyed Vali Reza Nasr, *The Vanguard of the Islamic Revolution*, University of California Press, 1994.
41. Reflecting the growth of US interest in the region, the first volume of the *Middle East Journal* appeared in January 1947, reflecting the position of the Middle East Institute, established in 1946 as a conduit of information between Middle East nations and American policy-makers, organisations and public.
42. Laqueur, 'Appeal', p21.
43. Laqueur, 'Appeal', p21.
44. Laqueur, 'Appeal', p25.
45. Laqueur, 'Appeal', pp25-6.
46. Laqueur, 'Appeal', pp18, 26.
47. Bernard Lewis, 'Communism and Islam', *International Affairs*, 30, January 1954, pp1-12.
48. Laqueur, 'Appeal', p22 (emphasis added).
49. *Christian Century*, 71, 1954.
50. 'Islam in Communist China', no date, but can be placed in 1958, NARA II, CIA-RDP78-02646R000400370001-3, 15.
51. 'Inventory', OCB, 3 May 1957, NARA II, RG59, Box 40.
52. Seth Jacobs, 'The perils and problems of Islam: the United States and the

Muslim Middle East in the early Cold War', *Diplomatic History*, 30, 4, 2006, pp705-39.

53. Laqueur, 'Appeal', p23.
54. 'Inventory', OCB, 3 May 1957, NARA II, RG59, Box 40.
55. Silk, *Spiritual Politics*, pp96-7.
56. Wilson S Compton to David KE Bruce, 'Colloquium on Islamic culture', 13 January 1953, NARA II, RG 59, DF 1950-54.
57. 'Colloquium on Islamic culture'.
58. Dreyfus, *Devil's Game*, p72.
59. Caffery to State Dept, 23 June 1953, NARA II, RG 59, DF 1950-54.
60. Milton Viorst, *In the Shadow of the Prophet*, Westview Press, 2001, p53.
61. Samir Amin, 'Political Islam in the service of imperialism', *Monthly Review*, 59, 7, 2007, pp1-19.
62. 'Inventory', OCB, 3 May 1957, NARA II, RG59, Box 40.
63. 'Inventory', OCB, 3 May 1957.
64. 'Inventory', OCB, 3 May 1957. In a contemporary analysis, Eugene Staley argued that in their attempts to influence the peoples of underdeveloped countries, the communists put great emphasis on appeals not to the material wants of man but rather 'to the human desire for status, equality, freedom from domination or oppression, especially by foreigners'; Staley, *The Future of Underdeveloped Countries*, New York: Harper, 1954, 384.
65. Nathan J Citino, *From Arab Nationalism to OPEC*, Bloomington: Indiana University Press, 2002, p96.
66. 'Inventory', OCB, 3 May 1957.
67. In Pakistan USIS, whose mailing list included all known Muslim leaders, plus the student and youth organisation under Jamiat-I-Islami, was accused of supporting the latter because they were anti-communist.
68. 'Inventory', OCB, 3 May 1957.
69. 'Inventory', OCB, 3 May 1957.
70. 'Inventory', OCB, 3 May 1957.
71. Ziad Abu-Amr, *Islamic Fundamentalism in the West Bank and Gaza*, Indiana University Press, 1994, p17; Shaul Mishal and Avraham Sela, *The Palestinian Hamas*, Columbia University Press, 2000, pp17-18.
72. Gilbert Achcar, *The Clash of Barbarisms: September 11 and the making of the New World Disorder*, Paradigm Publishers, 2002.
73. Mahmood Mamdani, *Good Muslim, Bad Muslim*, Three Leaves Press, 2004, pp129-30.
74. Hiro Dilip, *War Without End: The Rise of Islamist Terrorism and Global Response*, New York: Routledge, 2002, p210.

History re-examined: anti-imperialism, the Communist Party of India and international communism

Sobhanlal Datta Gupta

Considering that the communist movement in India was born in the 1920s and that India is the only country in South Asia in which the communist idea continues to survive uninterruptedly through a wide range of communist parties and groups, historically speaking it can perhaps be said that communism in India has come of age. At the same time, its steady erosion and gradual marginalisation over the years is also beyond contestation. One possible reason underlying this incapacity of Indian communism to reach out beyond its own boundaries is that, despite the sustained presence of a communist party, and its persistence since the splits of the 1960s in a series of multiple segments, communism has failed to strike roots in the Indian soil. The explanation is largely historical, to be traced to a flawed theoretical understanding of anti-imperialist struggle in India. This was constituted on the one hand by the historical compulsions of international communism and on the other by a mistaken understanding of the complexities of India's freedom struggle. Both date back to the inter-war period, in the form, first, of the Comintern guidelines, emanating from Moscow, which were transmitted to the leadership of the Communist Party of India (CPI) primarily through the Communist Party of Great Britain (CPGB); and secondly through the formulations of MN Roy when communism in India was virtually in its infancy, even though Roy, ironically, became the *bête noire* of the Comintern and the CPI following his exit from the former in 1929. At the same time there was a complete closure of alternative left viewpoints concerning the understanding of anti-

113

imperialist struggle in India. The present essay provides a historical exploration of what went wrong with Indian communism's apparently quite correct strategy of anti-imperialism, guided as it was by the considerations of international communism.

THE COMINTERN AND THE ROY FACTOR

It has now become customary to hold the Comintern responsible for those failings of communist parties which originated in the inter-war period, the underlying reason being the long shadow of Moscow, which decided everything by ensuring blind loyalty and uncritical support to the Russified Comintern. The Comintern, of course, was a major factor and perhaps ultimately decisive too. Nevertheless, it would be an oversimplification to explain these failings with reference to Moscow's role alone. While the Comintern was hyperactive in controlling the affairs of communist parties in a number of countries, the KPD being one typical instance, there were other instances in which this control was either not feasible or perhaps not necessary. Thus, in the case of India, the Comintern certainly played an important role, especially in its formative years. Even so, it never played any direct pro-active role in controlling the burgeoning communist movement in India, as it was struggling to get a foothold following the CPI's formation in 1925.[1] The puzzling fact is, however, that in course of time the CPI became one of those few communist parties in the colonial world which emerged as Moscow's voice, vigorously implementing Comintern directives to the letter, and thus inviting the charge of turning a blind eye to the realities of anti-imperialist struggle in India. Considering the fact that communism in India was relatively more autonomous in working out a space of its own, wherein lies the explanation of the CPI's inability to negotiate this space?

Examining this question involves a study of the peculiar circumstances in which communism in India was born. It owed its origin to Moscow and the Comintern, the principal architect of this nexus being MN Roy, whose outlook was decisive in shaping the mindset of the scattered communist groups in India, and who played a crucial role in co-ordinating their activities with the object of forming a communist party. Other Indian revolutionary groups were no less active in organising anti-imperialist struggle from abroad, notably from Germany. Historical circumstances, however, favoured Roy's emergence as the Comintern's leading spokesman on the colonial question. These circumstances included his initiation into Marxism in the West, first in Mexico and then in the Soviet Union and western Europe; his authorship of the Supplementary Theses on the Colonial Question, which Lenin allowed him to present parallel to his own theses at the Comintern's Second World Congress in 1920; and, consequently, Roy's meteoric rise in the Comintern hierarchy at a very young age. Understandably, his enormous prestige within the Comintern made him not only its leading exponent of the colonial question, representing the viewpoint of the colonised world, but also the natural and only spokesman of India from the very beginning. Thus Roy's perception of the strategy of anti-imperialist struggle, which grew out of his understanding of the colonial question, also became the theoretical foundation of Indian communism.

Moulded as it was by the dominant understanding prevailing in the Comintern, Roy's outlook was grounded in the belief that nationalism and communism were irreconcilable and that the overriding concern must be with proletarian internationalism. In his understanding of India, he therefore rejected the notion of nationalism; castigated the role of the bourgeoisie and bourgeois nationalist parties in India's anti-imperialist struggle, believing in the accomplishment of a socialist revolution under the leadership of the working class organised by a communist party; and strongly pleaded for the material assistance of the Comintern and Soviet authorities in this venture. The underlying premise, outlined in his Supplementary Theses and elaborated in his *India in Transition* (1922), was that industrialisation had been attained in India under the aegis of British colonial rule with a resulting polarisation of classes within India. With some modifications effected by Lenin, the theses were endorsed by the Comintern's Second World Congress.

Roy's emergence as an authoritative figure on the colonial question in the Comintern, and consequently his lasting influence on Indian communism, can be explained by four main factors. The first, which was widely shared by representatives of the non-European communist parties, was his critique of the Eurocentrism of western communist parties vis-à-vis the colonised countries. This issue became particularly important after the East came to occupy an important place in the Comintern's strategy following the Fourth World Congress in 1922.[2]

The second factor was Roy's characterisation of bourgeois nationalism as a completely spent force, which until the beginning of the 'Third Period' was not exactly the Comintern's position but was largely facilitated by the CPGB's position on the question. Thus, Roy's critique of nationalism, his denunciation of Gandhi and his industrialisation thesis found endorsement in the positions of R Palme Dutt and Ben Bradley, the two most important figures in shaping the CPGB's position on India. Dutt's *Modern India* (1926) was its finest illustration, and Bradley similarly described the Indian National Congress (INC) as a vehicle of 'counterrevolutionary policy' and Gandhi as 'the cleverest stunt worker'.[3]

A third factor underscoring the importance of Roy's Supplementary Theses was the left turn in the Comintern's position on the colonial question that began to be articulated following Stalin's analysis of the Chinese revolution in 1925. That Stalin's position was not in tune with the Comintern's official position and that he favoured a more aggressive stance vis-à-vis nationalism is evident from two documents. The first was a note addressed to Dimitri Manuilsky in July 1924:

> I believe that the time has come to raise the question of the hegemony of the proletariat in the liberation struggle in the colonies such as India, whose bourgeoisie is conciliatory (with British imperialism), and the victory over whom (i.e., over the conciliatory bourgeoisie) is the main condition for liberation from imperialism … It is necessary to smash the conciliatory national bourgeoisie, i.e., to wrest the worker and peasant masses from its influence in order to achieve genuine liberation from imperialism. Without fulfilling this preliminary task it is impossible to achieve victory over British imperialism.[4]

This was followed in 1927 by his justification of Roy's position at the Second World Congress:

> Why were the Supplementary Theses needed? In order to single out from the backward colonial countries which have no industrial proletariat such countries as China and India, of which it cannot be said that they have 'practically no industrial proletariat'. Read the Supplementary Theses, and you will realise they refer chiefly to

China and India ... How could it happen that Roy's special theses were needed to 'supplement' Lenin's theses? The fact is that Lenin's theses had been written and published long before the representatives from the colonial countries had arrived, and prior to the discussion in the special commission of the Second Congress. And since the discussion in the Congress Commission revealed the necessity for singling out from the backward colonies of the East such countries as China and India, the necessity for the 'Supplementary' theses arose.[5]

The underlying premises of Stalin's position were elaborated in a speech he delivered in May 1925 at the Communist University of the Toilers of the East. Here Stalin stated categorically that it was no longer possible to consider the East as a 'homogenous whole'; rather, it was possible to distinguish three categories of countries which constituted the East. Countries like Morocco, which had little or no proletariat were 'undeveloped', while China and Egypt were described as 'under-developed industrially'; but India was listed as 'capitalistically more or less developed'. Therein lies the clue to Stalin's formulation that in countries like India, where capitalism had already developed, the national bourgeoisie had joined the imperialist camp and had turned out to be a counter-revolutionary force. This called for the formation of independent communist parties in these countries and the freeing of the workers and peasants from bourgeois domination. This was also the line of Roy's position in the Supplementary Theses, which Stalin thus found quite appropriate to justify his own position and subsequent Class Against Class strategy. Ironically, while Roy himself after 1928 began to seriously question this strategy, what the Comintern now endorsed was virtually the position in the Supplementary Theses, whereby the entire nationalist leadership, including Gandhi, Nehru and Subhas Chandra Bose, was branded as the bandwagon of counter-revolution.

A fourth factor in Roy's emergence as the unrivalled spokesman for India in the Comintern was his success in weeding out the challenges posed by a number of Indian revolutionary groups, organisationally as well as ideologically. Roy's rapid rise within the Comintern made it possible for him to project his viewpoint as the sole expression of Indian communism, and declare a closure on alternative positions. This was facilitated by Roy's position as a Comintern insider, and with the opening of the Comintern archives it is now clearly established that he made every effort to prevent such rival groups from receiving the support from Moscow which they sought. Marginalised in this way were the Indian Revolutionary Association (IRA), represented by MBPT Acharya and Abdur Rabb Barq, among others, which was active in Tashkhent even before Roy's entry; and the Berlin group of Indian revolutionaries headed by Virendranath Chattopadhyaya, Pandurang Khankhoje and Bhupendranath Datta. While, organisationally, Roy was not prepared to accept the existence of any alternative leadership which might threaten his own, ideologically too their positions were irreconcilable. To summarise briefly, despite the differences between them, the IRA and the Berlin group, while declaring their faith in socialism and revolution, did not favour the complete rejection of nationalism in working out a strategy of anti-imperialist struggle in India. While their position on the issue of nationalism was relatively positive, they held that the complexities of Indian society could not be grasped simply by reference to class, and that ignoring factors like caste, religion and untouchability meant that the problem of Indian revolution could not be properly grasped.[6] Understandably, this was a position which implicitly questioned Roy's industrialisation and class polarisation thesis. As Roy succeeded in declaring a complete closure on these alternative positions, communist groups operating from India had no access to them. Thanks to their total dependence on Roy for the Comintern's material and moral support, the mindset of Indian communism became grounded in Roy's outlook, especially following the CPI's formation in 1925.

THE CPGB ANGLE

With Roy's exit from the Comintern after 1928, the baton of Indian communism passed into the hands of the CPGB. The rise of the CPGB in shaping the future of Indian communism, as well as the CPI's virtual recognition of the CPGB as its guardian and the spokesman for India in the Comintern, may sound quite intriguing. But the opening of the Comintern and CPGB archives has made it possible to explain the factors that contributed to these developments. Again, at least four such factors can be identified.

First, despite the proximity of the ideological positions of the CPI and the CPGB in regard to the Indian nationalist struggle, Roy from the very beginning considered the CPGB as a threat to his authority in the Comintern. The unswerving loyalty to Moscow of the CPGB, and of Dutt in particular, was especially significant. Apart from the fact that Dutt was the key spokesman on India and the colonial question in the CPGB, for the Comintern leadership the CPGB's perception of the anti-imperialist struggle in India was no less important than Roy's understanding. While this created a kind of organisational rivalry between Roy and the CPGB, there is now every reason to believe that the Comintern quite deliberately projected the CPGB as a counterweight against Roy, as the latter's position began gradually to decline from the mid-1920s as his differences with the Comintern began to surface. Thus Roy was never reconciled to the formation of the Colonial Department under the CPGB's auspices in 1925. At the colonial conference held in Amsterdam in July 1925 he contested the CPGB's understanding that its own colonial committee had the sole right to conduct colonial work in regard to India. This in his view was an imperialist mentality; and the CPGB's jurisdiction should be limited to the training of workers and circulation of propaganda literature.[7]

Apart from Roy there was another towering figure, Virendranath Chattopadhyaya, who was a very active member of the Berlin group of revolutionaries. Quite close to Dimitrov, following its formation in 1927 Virendranath played an important role in the League Against Imperialism (LAI) in association with Willi Münzenberg. After the Nazi seizure of power he then settled in Leningrad as an academic, until his arrest and execution as an 'an enemy of the people' in 1937. Despite his unflinching loyalty to the Comintern and the USSR, Virendranath was nevertheless unable to step into Roy's position as spokesman for Indian communism, and correspondence between the two shows that Roy used his position of pre-eminence to scuttle Virendranath's entry into the Comintern apparatus, which permanently sealed his fate.[8] The resulting vacuum was thus a second factor facilitating the CPGB's entry in place of Roy. This was starkly manifested in Manuilsky's pronouncement at the Tenth ECCI Plenum in July 1929:

> If the British Party does not help the splintered unorganised Indian communists now, who will then help them? Other than the British

Communist Party, the Communist International possesses no lever which might act upon the Indian revolutionary movement. The Plenum now has to demand of the British Party that it has to guide the emergent Indian Communist Party by providing active support through labour, spread of agitation and application of all remaining methods.[9]

A further factor was the CPGB's intervention which saved the situation in 1936 after the emergent Indian communist movement had become disorganised, shattered and embroiled in factional conflicts following the Meerut arrests and the impact of the Comintern's Sixth World Congress of 1928. The new CPI general secretary was PC Joshi, a young and vibrant figure with tremendous organisational skills.[10] Joshi was to hold the position until 1948, having effectively been stripped of his powers in June 1947 on account of his alleged 'revisionism'. His appointment, together with the Dutt-Bradley theses of 1936, which was instrumental in effecting the CPI's shift from Class Against Class to the united-front strategy, virtually set the new line for the CPI following the Comintern's Seventh World Congress of July–August 1935. Dutt's testimony is quite revealing of the CPGB's role:

> The decisions of the 7th Congress were attempted to be applied to India in a document prepared by Bradley and myself, which was essentially an application of the United Front tactics to the Indian situation. The Communists in India at that time were split into quarrelling groups. It was decided to put up Joshi as the General Secretary as a representative of the younger comrades who were outside the factional groupings.[11]

In this way the CPGB's position in relation to the CPI was further legitimised and vindicated.

A fourth factor in the CPGB's sustained presence in relation to Indian communism was the role it played in shaping the minds of a group of young men and women who went to Britain from India to study for professional degrees. They returned to India transformed as Marxists, most of them joining the CPI, where they rapidly attained positions in the party leadership. They included figures like Mohan Kumaramangalam, Indrajit Gupta, Hiren Mukherjee, Bhupesh

Gupta, Mohit Sen, NK Krishnan, Nikhil Chakravartty, Romesh Chandra and Arun Bose, to name a few, who became the intellectual face of the Communist Party. Needless to say, for them as well as for the CPI, the CPGB thereby became a sort of mentor, and it was through the lens of the CPGB that the CPI viewed international communism. Here again Palme Dutt's role was crucial, his *India Today* (1940) having attained the status of the Bible of Indian communism. Following Roy's exit the Comintern consequently required no direct control over the CPI, since it was through the CPGB that the international line was carried out in India, following periodic shifts. The CPI, therefore, was quite reconciled to the situation that, instead of anyone from the CPI itself, Ben Bradley was put in charge of India within the ECCI until the time of the Second World War;[12] quite apart from the fact that at the Seventh World Congress the report on India was presented by Bradley under the alias of Tambe. This was of enormous significance for the future of Indian communism, since, as Peter Huber's findings indicate, within the central apparatus of the Comintern the communist parties of China, Argentina, Cuba, Philippines, Indo-China, Brazil, Chile, Japan and Syria all had their representatives stationed in Moscow. From MN Roy to RP Dutt, it was thus a smooth shift that registered a notion of continuity for Indian communism.

The CPI's total dependence on the CPGB for guidance had significant implications for the future of communism in India. In the first place, at every critical moment in the CPI's history, the CPGB was looked upon as its saviour, organisationally as well as ideologically. Secondly, the CPGB connection quickly elevated quite a good number of party members to top positions in the CPI at the cost of other members who were much better organisers. Thus, a veteran Indian communist recalls how Arun Bose, who went to England for higher studies and returned to India in 1940 as a communist, was immediately inducted into the central committee; elsewhere he observes that the CPI was characterised by a kind of colonial mentality which has persisted throughout its history.[13] Thirdly, the kind of Marxism that the CPI imbibed was marked by a strange dualism. At one level, the CPI was heavily influenced by the CPGB's intellectual climate. This meant not simply the influence of Dutt but also that of Eric Hobsbawm, Christopher Hill, V Gordon Childe, Joseph Needham and other outstanding figures who nourished the

CPGB in the 1930s – a group which, of course, also included John Saville, already a leading communist student at the LSE and later a close associate of Hobsbawm and Hill in the party's Historians' Group. Thus, within the CPI there was a stream of enlightened Marxism, shared at least by some of the prominent figures, which presented the 'liberal', intellectual face of Indian communism. This is clearly evident in the reminiscences of notable Indian communists like Mohit Sen, in recalling his Cambridge days of the 1930s, and is corroborated by Hobsbawm too.[14] At another level, however, the overdetermining factor was the unilinear understanding of international communism, which was reminiscent of faith in the Soviet Union and the line it laid down for all communist parties through its auxiliary, the Comintern. This message was largely transmitted through the CPGB to the CPI, which consequently introduced a spirit of dogmatism into the party. In the conflict between reason and faith, the latter, and thereby the party line, always and necessarily had the final say. This, by contrast, presented the authoritarian, political face of the CPI.

POINTS OF TENSION

Despite the CPI's overwhelmingly friendly relationship with the CPGB, there were at certain moments zones of difference and discontent between the two parties on questions concerning the anti-imperialist struggle in India, although this was not reflected in official documents, and nor did it give rise to any major acrimony. Two such key issues can broadly be identified since the opening of the archives.

The first such situation arose in the 1920s and early 1930s, following the allegation that the CPGB was acting like a 'boss' vis-à-vis the group of Indian communists stationed in Britain that included NJ Upadhyaya, AC Banerjee and PC Nandi, in addition to Dutt's brother CP Dutt. In a report from March 1927 prepared by CP Dutt and Muhammad Ali the allegation of 'bossing' was thus practically accepted, and attributed to the CPGB leader JR Campbell, whose conditions were summarised as follows:

1) That the CPI [*the London unit of the CPI hitherto largely controlled by Roy – SDG*] should cut off all direct communication with Roy and his group. 2) That all correspondence for Roy should pass

through his hands. 3) That he should be sole controlling man for all the activities. 4) That the Workers' and Peasants' Party should be affiliated to the British C.P.

The report went on to note a 'feeling of suspicion on the part of the CPI towards the British comrades', adding: 'They suspect a conspiracy against them to take away their Party and to drive them into a British organisation.'[15]

Apart from this big-brotherly attitude, the situation became particularly complicated in the inability of the CPGB to mobilise the ordinary British worker in the anti-colonial struggle. The main reason for this was a mindset coloured by 'empire consciousness', and thereby passivity in regard to India and the colonial question. This admission was made repeatedly by the leading lights of the CPGB, including among others Willie Gallacher, R Page Arnot, Idris Cox, Willie Allan and R Palme Dutt.[16] On the occasion of the Sixth CPGB Congress in 1927 Dutt described it as 'a shame'.[17] Cox, at the CPGB central committee in January 1930, severely reprimanded the party:

Many comrades of the colonial committee have taken up colonial work as an interesting pastime, and they do not realise the significance of the events in India. We must have comrades who do understand the significance of these events, comrades who have contacts in the factories who can drive home to the workers what the Indian revolution means to the workers here.[18]

That, even after the Meerut arrests, the CPGB as a party did not appreciate the role of the communists in India's anti-imperialist struggle came out in Gallacher's speech to the central committee meeting of June 1933:

I want to say that the campaign in connection with Meerut is a disgrace to the Party, that time and again there has been a situation where there had been the greatest possible opportunity of arousing the masses on this question, but it has been allowed to die away. Nothing has been done. Never anything in the nature of a real effective agitation. Never the sensing of any things which arise at any particular moment in order to put their attention on the Meerut prisoners.[19]

In a note prepared by Saklatvala while on a visit to the Soviet Union in 1934, the complexity of the colonial question as encountered by the CPGB was again made clear:

> In Britain there are two real difficulties. One is the lingering heritage of some sort of pride and satisfaction of being the owners of the Great empire, and an Empire that feeds them and clothes them, and without which there would be a shortage of food within two or three months. The second difficulty is the general mentality of the people as a self-centred insular people, who have no contact within their border with life conditions of peoples other than themselves ... The work of the British Party in such conditions is really difficult ... There is a tendency to treat the colonial problem as a mere side issue and as nobody's business in particular. There are no special funds allocated for expenditure for work among the colonial students or workers in Great Britain.[20]

While the CPGB leadership was quite aware of the importance of the anti-imperialist struggle in which the Indian communists were deeply involved, documents such as this suggest that this spirit was not widely shared within the ranks of the party. Figures like Bradley and Spratt travelled to India, courted arrest, underwent sufferings and participated most actively in organising the embryonic Indian communist movement.[21] For the average Indian communist, on the other hand, this show of great solidarity was not reflective of the CPGB as a whole but of certain leaders only. On particular occasions, this perhaps facilitated the levelling of charges of 'bossing' against the CPGB, the 'bosses' being identified with the leaders.

The second issue centres on the differences between the CPGB and the CPI regarding the characterisation of the war as a 'People's War' after 22 June 1941, and the consequent line of extending co-operation to British India's war efforts. The CPI was apprised of the shift in the Comintern's position through Achhar Singh, alias Larkin, a Moscow trained Indian émigré, and the CPGB. In December 1941 the CPI politbureau adopted a resolution stating that in its original under-standing immediately after 22 June 1941 the party had erred by adopting the policy of 'conditional support' for the war effort. This, it said, amounted to 'bourgeois nationalism' and the abandonment of internationalism, the latter signifying the priority to be given to the defence of the Soviet Union against the fascist offensive. The resolution, however, was not easy to adopt; although there was complete unanimity on the question of supporting the Soviet Union, the party was sharply divided on the issue of extending co-operation to the British war effort, and of how to convince the people that this would advance the cause of India's independence. Disillusioned as they were with Gandhi's pacifism and the compromising stance of the Indian National Congress, India's communists had found it logical after the Sixth World Congress to adopt the left-sectarian position of the Comintern on the colonial question. On the other hand, the switch to the popular front/united front strategy and subsequent call for defence of the Soviet Union were more difficult to fathom, for the reason that the phenomenon of fascism was quite alien to the Indian communists except in theoretical terms. The confusion was made worse for them, following the Comintern's shift from all-out opposition to Britain in the phase of 'imperialist war' before June 1941, to total support of British war efforts after that date, in the name of proletarian internationalism and the common fight against the menace of fascism.

Such a development contained very little logic which would convince the Indian communists. As one veteran recalled, for some the war provided an opportunity to launch a full-scale offensive against British rule, while others believed that strengthening the hands of the Soviet Union in the fight against fascism had to be given priority. Eventually what emerged from these conflicting positions was that support for the war must be presented to the masses solely from the viewpoint of India's independence and not from that of protecting the interests of the USSR.[22] The situation was further complicated for the CPI by the INC's adoption of the 'Quit India' resolution of August 1942, which the party felt it must oppose since participation in the Quit India movement would stand in the way of supporting British war efforts. The consequences were disastrous. Besides serious differences within the party, the CPI became isolated from the national mainstream as it invited the charge of having betrayed the freedom struggle.[23]

EXPLORING THE ALTERNATIVES

The tragedy of the communist movement in India has been that, historically, there were certain possibilities which, if recognised, could have introduced an alternative left perspective into the anti-imperialist struggle. Roy's virtual declaration of closure on these alternatives decided the destiny of communism in India, as the CPI's understanding of India's history and society became anchored in his positions from its very birth. This was quite candidly acknowledged by Joshi in later life.[24] One gets a sense of these alternative positions in the documents of the Berlin Committee, some of which could be communicated to Lenin and the Comintern but could not be officially placed on the agenda for discussion. What also remained unknown for decades was what transpired in the very brief meetings between this Berlin group of revolutionaries and Lenin. While many of these young revolutionaries were greatly inspired by the October Revolution and looked upon the October model to be replicated in India, Lenin had no such illusion. In a document sent him by Bhupendranath Datta on the occasion of the Third World Congress in 1921, the accent was on the organisation of communist groups in India for the accomplishment of socialism through a social revolution after the victory of political revolution against British imperialism. Lenin's reply, published only many years later, was that instead of discussing social classes what was necessary was to gather 'statistical facts about Peasant leagues if any exist[ed] in India'.[25] In recalling this comment Datta later admitted that Lenin's recognition of the importance of the peasant question for the first time made him aware of the role of the peasantry in India's anti-imperialist struggle.[26] However, the death of Lenin, together with Roy's industrialisation thesis, completely obscured the importance of the peasantry and the agrarian question in the CPI's perception of the anti-imperialist struggle. Precisely this space was appropriated by Gandhi, and the communists' traditional tirade against Gandhi is therefore self-explanatory.

Then there was the 'Thesis on India and the World Revolution', prepared for the Third World Congress by Virendranath, Luhani and Khankhoje but never discussed there. The understanding of anti-imperialist struggle in India in this document was very different from Roy's unilinear understanding of India in terms of a single category, namely, class. Instead the document highlighted three distinct issues: first, that India was to be regarded as a basically agrarian country with a feudal structure; secondly, that Indian society was believed to be divided not just vertically along class lines but also horizontally along the lines of religion and caste; and thirdly, though without mentioning Roy's name, that the argument was hardly tenable that the Comintern's assistance to bourgeois-democratic and national-revolutionary movements would prove counterproductive.[27] That carrying out a revolution in India involved a proper understanding of its cultural pluralities and social complexities such as caste and religion, and that this required a different kind of strategy which recognised its agrarian character, was what differentiated the position of the Berlin group from that of Roy. Khankhoje, for instance, states in his memoirs that he felt that the plurality of religions, languages and cultures that characterised India could not be simply swept aside, since these had struck deeply into the consciousness of the masses.[28] Again, while the Berlin group was in favour of building up contacts between the Comintern and the national-revolutionary elements in India, Roy was strongly opposed to it. However, it was Roy's position that ultimately prevailed and the Berlin group of Indian revolutionaries effectively came to be considered as persona non grata by the Comintern.[29] The Berlin group had no moorings among the Indian masses and its activities were primarily confined to Indian revolutionaries fighting against British imperialism from European soil. Following the Comintern's refusal to recognise it, it more or less fell apart.

It is therefore unsurprising that a strong undercurrent of left-extremism, dismissive of nationalism and intolerant of categories other than class, characterised the mindset of Indian communism from the very beginning. The consequences were disastrous: following its characterisation of nationalism and the nationalist leaders as counter-revolutionary, the CPI burnt its boats, became completely isolated from the anti-imperialist struggle, and in the wake of the Sixth World Congress embraced the self-destructive line of left-adventurism. After the Seventh World Congress and the publication of the Dutt-Bradley thesis, it became an almost insurmountable problem for the CPI to convince its ranks of the justification of the shift towards the united-front strategy, and the idea of an alliance with bourgeois nationalism in the shape of the Indian National Congress. The problem became particularly complicated in the subsequent period of the CPI's alliance with the Congress Socialist Party (CSP). While the CSP had within it quite a number of elements who were opposed to communism, the CPI too was heavily dominated by a trend which was sharply sceptical of this alliance with the CSP. Bouts of sectarianism and left-adventurism, which have plagued the CPI on repeated occasions since its birth, have been the logical culmination of a flawed understanding of anti-imperialist struggle. The call for establishment of a 'Soviet republic' in the early 1930s was followed in 1948-50 by successive calls for armed proletarian revolution and agrarian revolution, drawing inspiration from the Russian and the Chinese path respectively. The results were disastrous. The splits within the CPI in 1964 and 1969, primarily between the 'right', the 'left' and the 'extreme left', and the consequent weakening of the Marxist left in India, have been the symptoms of an organic crisis of Indian communism. This crisis has been one of orientation, and a mindset typically steeped in dogmatism, which has gripped the communist movement in India from within, since its very birth. Its roots are essentially historical, to be explained by the peculiar circumstances in which communism in India was born.

Notes

1. There were parallels with the CPGB, which for long periods had no permanent Comintern representative stationed in the country. However, while in the CPGB's case there was the factor of the graduates trained at the International Lenin School in Moscow, who acted as the Comintern's voice in the CPGB, often creating tensions, in the case of India there was no such pressure. A large number of Indians, most of whom belonged to the Gadr Party and the Kirti Kishan Party, and other communist groups, active in the North West provinces of British India, were trained in Moscow at the Communist University of the Toilers of the East (KUTV) and other Comintern-sponsored institutions in the 1920s and 1930s. These however had practically no say in shaping the policy and programme of the CPI.
2. For details see Sobhanlal Datta Gupta, *Comintern and the Destiny of Communism in India 1919-1943. Dialectics of Real and a Possible History*, Seribaan, 2006, pp87-94.
3. For Bradley's understanding of India's nationalist struggle, which he ridiculed in choicest phrases, see Labour History Archives and Study Centre, Manchester (LHASC), CPGB archives, CP/Ind/Brad/1/3, Bradley to Len Bradley, 5 February 1931; CP/Ind/Brad/1/4, Bradley to Percy Glading, 16 September 1932; also CP/Ind/Brad/7/1 for Bradley's undated autobiographical note. An entry on Bradley by Jean Jones appeared in *DLB* vol. 8, pp22-7.
4. Cited in AB Reznikov, 'The strategy and tactics of the Communist International in the national and colonial question', in RA Ulyanovsky,

Orestes Stamatopoulos, John Saville's father, in Greek army uniform in 1917, on the Greek front.

With his daughter Jane Saville, on the doorstep at 152 Westbourne Avenue, 1956.

John Saville in army uniform in second world war circa 1941

With Alec Horsley, head of Northern Dairies (later Northern Foods) in 1956. Horsley was a member of the Committee of 100, and provided financial support for a variety of Quaker groups and charities, and also for the Reasoner and CND

With Bryan Dyson, Hull University archivist, 2000

With Roy Hattersley at a fund-raising event organised by the Ferrens Society in Hull in aid of university funds, circa 1999

With Martin Eve, founder of Merlin Press

With Ralph Miliband, 1986. Edward Thompson can just be seen behind the bannisters

With medical soci ologist Margo Jefferys and Eric Hobsbawm, 1986

With Alec Horsley, University of Hull, 1982

Three editors of Socialist Register at the twenty-fifth anniversary celebration: from left to right, Leo Panitch, John Saville, Ralph Miliband

With David Miliband and Constance in 2001.

ed., *The Comintern and the East. The Struggle for the Leninist Strategy and Tactics in the National Liberation Movement*, Progress Publishers, 1979, p170. Unfortunately, Reznikov does not provide any clue to this very important archival reference.

5. JV Stalin, 'Concerning Questions of the Chinese Revolution. Reply to Comrade Marchulin', in *Works*, vol. 9, Foreign Languages Publishing House, 1954, p238.

6. For details of these differences between Roy, the IRA and the Berlin group, see Datta Gupta, *Comintern and the Destiny of Communism*, pp238-64.

7. *Communist Papers. Documents selected from those obtained on the arrest of the Communist leaders on the 14th and 21st October, 1925*, HMSO: Cmd 2682, 1926, pp87-8.

8. I have discussed this issue in detail in Datta Gupta, *Comintern and the Destiny of Communism*, pp260-4. A letter from Virendranath to Dimitrov dated 9 April 1935 provides further confirmation of the kind of situation that he had to encounter: 'Unfortunately, for three years I have been kept away from active work in Comintern. Had there been a serious desire to know the reasons behind it, I would have the occasion to submit certain facts. I am not giving up the hope that the ECCI can and will use me, especially now. I request you, concerning the reorganization of the Indian Department, to take into consideration the question of my use for organizational or other work in an appropriate colony ...'. The document is reproduced in Purabi Roy et al, eds, *Indo-Russian Relations 1917-1947: Select Documents from the Archives of the Russian Federation*, part II: 1929-1947, Asiatic Society, 2000, pp232-3.

9. *Protokoll: 10 Plenum des Exekutivkomitees der Kommunistischen Internationale, Moskau, 3 Juli 1929 bis 19 Juli, 1929*, CH Nachf, 1929, p592.

10. John Saville, when he first met Joshi during his war service in India, described him as having 'a mass of black hair and tremendous energy and bounce. You feel it when you meet'. Saville, *Memoirs from the Left*, Merlin, 2003, p60.

11. LHASC, CPGB archives, CP/Ind/Dutt/12/1, 'Information document no 10 dt. 12.2.51. marked Confidential. Talks with Comrade R Palme Dutt with other impressions gained abroad by Deven and Bal Krishna'.

12. Vilem Kahan, 'The Communist International, 1919-1943: the personnel of its highest bodies', *International Review of Social History*, 21, 1976, pp178, 180.

13. Jolly Mohan Kaul, *In Search of a Better World. Memoirs*, Samya, 2010, pp20, 69. This is further confirmed by an undated letter to Dutt (in CP/Ind/Dutt/12/1) in which Maurice Dobb recorded his impressions of a visit to India in 1951: '*much* too much reliance was placed on any

"word from abroad" if this carried a smell of authority ... this being used as an escape from and, substitute for working out a political line of one's own. This, for example, caused absurdly exaggerated importance to be attached (despite repeated disclaimers) to any comment from me.'

14. See Mohit Sen, *A Traveller and the Road. The Journey of an Indian Communist*, Rupa, 2003, ch. 3; Eric Hobsbawm, *Interesting Times. A Twentieth Century Life*: Abacus edn, 2003, pp112-13, 364-6.

15. Document in Roy et al, *Indo-Russian Relations 1917-1947*, pp234-35.

16. LHASC, CPGB archives, CP/Ind/Klug/4/5, James Klugmann's handwritten notes from Comintern archives.

17. LHASC, CPGB archives, CP/Cent/Cong/1/6, handwritten note of Dutt.

18. LHASC, CPGB archives, microfilm CI 1, CPGB central committee 12 January 1930, discussion on colonial situation.

19. LHASC, CPGB archives, CP/Ind/Klug/6/4, Klugmann's handwritten notes from Comintern archives; microfilm CI 4, CPGB central committee 18 June 1933.

20. LHASC, CPGB archives, CP/Ind/Misc/22/3. 'A Few Thoughts on Party Work', 22 June 1934 (photocopied document; original in Comintern archives). I am grateful to Marika Sherwood who first drew my attention to this document.

21. Deeply affected by his own wartime contacts with the CPI, John Saville was powerfully impressed by the example of such figures, and through essays in the *Dictionary of Labour Biography* and the preservation of his archives at Hull played a particular role in documenting the activities within the LAI of the Comintern supporter Reginald Bridgeman.

22. See Putchalapalli Sundarrayya, *An Autobiography*, National Book Trust, India, 2009, pp164-7. The aforesaid resolution was preceded by two inner-party documents, namely, 'Our new line on war – British comrades correct us!', and the 'Jail Document' emanating from the Deoli Jail. For the texts of these two documents see Subodh Roy, ed., *Communism in India: Unpublished Documents 1935-1945*, National Book Agency, 1976, pp267-324.

23. I have examined this issue in detail in Datta Gupta, *Comintern and the Destiny of Communism*, pp207-21.

24. LHASC, CPGB archives, CP/Ind/Misc/3/7, 'Indian communism – years of formation: 1917-1925. An outline for discussion by PC Joshi'.

25. For the full text of Lenin's reply see VI Lenin, *Collected Works*, vol .45, Progress Publishers, 1970, p270.

26. Bhupendranath Datta, *Dialectics of Land-Economics of India*, Mohendra Publishing Committee, 1952, piii.

27. 'Thesis on India and the World Revolution. Presented to the ECCI and the Congress Commission on Oriental Questions by V Chattopadhyaya, GAK Luhani and P Khankhoje on the occasion of

Comintern's Third Congress', in Roy et al, *Indo-Russian Relations 1917-1947*, pp116-25.

28. Savitri Sawhney, *I Shall Never Ask for Pardon. A Memoir of Pandurang Khankhoje*, Penguin Books, 2008, p219.

29. Khankhoje has described this in detail in Sawhney, *I Shall Never Ask for Pardon*, pp211-25.

Port workers and politics: religion, casual labour and voting in English docklands, 1900-22

Tony Adams

Traditional accounts of popular politics in the later nineteenth and early twentieth centuries have generally characterised port cities as centres of Conservative strength.[1] A pervasive reliance upon casual work – an endemic feature of dockland labour markets – allegedly engendered a depressed and rootless working class that proved particularly susceptible to Tory populism and its sectarian and racist appeals. Lacking the resources to sustain strong and effective organisations – such as trade unions, cooperatives and friendly societies – port workers were, for a range of economic and cultural reasons, seen as distant from the labour movement. The more secure skilled worker, often held to provide the foundations of Liberal and Labour success elsewhere in urban Britain, was, arguably, a marginal figure in the port city.[2] In recent years this approach has fallen increasingly out of favour: firstly, historians have questioned the existence, at a general level, of any meaningful relationships between occupational experience and party political preference in this period;[3] and, secondly, this traditional view has been forcefully challenged in a detailed case study of London's East End. Here it is argued that the votes of the casual poor did not underpin a dominant 'Slum Conservatism' in the East End before 1914; rather, it was more regularly employed workers – together with the middle class – who secured Conservative success. In the new interpretation, it is suggested that organised religion was a more significant influence on voting behaviour in the East End than either occupation or structural poverty.[4]

The traditional association between concentrations of casual work and Conservative electoral dominance did not rest solely on the single case of London's East End. Popular politics in Liverpool, Britain's second port city, have also been interpreted in much the same way.[5] Less attention has been paid to the voting behaviour of port workers elsewhere; notably in Hull, despite its standing as Britain's third largest port before 1914. This chapter will attempt to broaden our view of port worker politics in a comparative study of Britain's three leading Edwardian ports – London's East End, Hull and Liverpool. In so doing this chapter will revisit the extent to which occupational groups such as dockers and other port workers displayed distinctive political preferences and how far these changed over time. Consideration will also be given to the significance of cultural or other local identities – particularly religious preference – and their impact upon the politics of Britain's principal port communities. It will be argued that Conservatism was particularly strong in port communities containing a preponderance of Anglicans. In both Hull and the East End the Conservative Party was far less robust where there were significant centres of nonconformist activity. In these waterfront areas the Liberal Party enjoyed considerable success. As for Labour, the party's poor performance in Britain's docklands before 1914 suggests that, in this respect at least, the traditional view retains some purchase.

LONDON'S EAST END – THE EPITOME OF 'SLUM CONSERVATISM'?

The widely held view that port workers, mired in poverty and victims of the casual labour system, predominantly voted Conservative had its roots in London's East End.[6] This analysis of East End politics has recently been subjected to sharp criticism in Brodie's detailed and often subtle analysis.[7] Two aspects of this critique are examined here. First, the suggested correlation between the strength of religious affiliation, church activity and voting behaviour at a local level; and second, the apparent absence of any relationship between occupational concentrations – particularly port work – and party political strength. The politics of the two riverside East End districts of Stepney and Poplar are explored below, principally through the borough council elections conducted triennially from 1900. As Brodie observes, these elections provide 'the only useful evidence of the small-scale political variations in the East End in this period'.[8] It might be objected that pre-1918 franchise regulations excluded the poor and irregularly employed, creating, as Brodie suggests, an electorate dominated by the better-off with incomes at least on a par with those of police officers and clerks.[9] This conclusion, based upon detailed research, conflicts with the work of historians, such as Davis and Tanner, who have argued that significant numbers of slum dwellers, including the casual poor, qualified to vote before 1914.[10] Indeed, Brodie's own findings indicate that in wards close to the waterfront, 'labourers' were the largest occupational group within the electorate – constituting almost 30% of the electoral register. It seems unlikely that these were largely permanent hands or 'Royals', as Brodie implies. Moreover, it seems Brodie underestimates the importance of multiple income streams for working-class households, which could allow individuals with relatively low incomes – including the casually employed – access to the vote as 'rate compounded' tenants. Brodie rightly suggests that the East End electorate was more socially varied than historians generally allow, but further research is required before we can conclude that casual workers were a marginal force amongst the electorate in waterside wards before 1914.

Despite traditional depictions of the East End in which churches were seen to have only a tenuous hold on the teeming masses, for Brodie Tory success resulted in large part from the work of Protestant churches in local communities. In a detailed study of church attendance figures and voting patterns in municipal wards, Brodie finds evidence of a positive correlation between active Anglican churches and high levels of support for Conservatism.[11] However, this relationship was far from consistent and Brodie possibly overstates the influence of Anglicanism, particularly in some of the waterfront wards. So, for example, if we were to compare church attendance in the dockland ward of Shadwell – described by Brodie as a Conservative stronghold – with an area of Conservative weakness as exemplified by Bow North – the only ward of the thirty-three in Poplar and Stepney where the Conservatives failed to return a councillor between 1900 and 1912 – we might expect to identify significantly higher levels of Anglican attendance in the former.[12] In fact the opposite was true. The parish church in Shadwell, St Paul's, attracted only sixty-one adults on census day, while at St Mark's in

Bow North adult attendance was over four times higher.[13] Other exceptions include St Mary's in Whitechapel Middle ward – the worst performing ward for the Tories in Stepney borough – which enjoyed the largest adult attendance of all Stepney's Anglican churches. None of this is to suggest that a strong Anglican presence could not be a key factor in Conservative strength in working-class communities, quite the contrary.[14] However, such instances suggest that it is no more straightforward to establish a consistent and meaningful relationship between the strength of the Established Church and Tory voting at local level, than it is to relate voting behaviour to the often maligned use of occupational data.

A more novel aspect of Brodie's argument is the suggestion that nonconformist churches encouraged an array of attitudes and beliefs among the East End working class, which enhanced Conservative electoral strength. A corollary of this argument is that nonconformity did not provide similar sustenance for East End Liberalism.[15] Again there are problems with attempts to demonstrate a robust link between high attendance at nonconformist churches and Conservative dominance – and Liberal, or Progressive, weakness. In part this was because attendees at nonconformist churches lacked Anglicanism's formal ties to the local parish church and were more likely to travel some distance to worship. This was evidently the case at East End preaching centres, where attendances – numbered in thousands – dwarfed all other nonconformist churches.[16] As Brodie suggests, many will have attended such centres from beyond the immediate vicinity of the church. Interestingly, two of the three large preaching centres in Stepney borough in all probability drew much of their audiences from areas of relative Progressive strength in the East End. Thus, Dr Barnardo's Edinburgh Castle Evangelistic Mission, although located in Mile End, was said to attract many worshippers from the nearby Limehouse North and South wards.[17] These two Limehouse wards returned Progressive councillors in unusually high numbers. The Edinburgh Castle Mission was but a few hundred yards further away from Ratcliffe, a waterfront ward which housed Barnardo's first Working & Destitute Lads Home. One indication of Barnardo's local influence here was the renaming of a street after the eponymous Doctor. Ratcliffe ward also contained a Congregational Church which enjoyed a recorded adult attendance six times that of the local Anglican parish church.[18] It seems likely that this extensive nonconformist influence contributed to the Progressives strong showing in the ward.

The only other Stepney ward where Progressives were in a majority – Mile End Old Town South East – was also a locus of considerable nonconformist activity much of which was linked to the evangelical preaching centres. Both Barnardo's famous Copperfield Road Ragged School, and the above-mentioned Edinburgh Castle itself, were located towards the southern end of the ward. Within fifty yards of the ward's northern boundary lay another of Stepney's three large evangelical preaching centres, the Baptist East London Tabernacle. With attendances of over 2000, and social activities which included orphanages, soup kitchens and 1000-strong Saturday afternoon prayer meetings aimed at workers, the Tabernacle was another centre of vibrant nonconformist activism.[19] The two wards where Barnardo's main efforts were concentrated – Ratcliffe and Mile End Old Town South East – were also the sole Progressive islands in a Conservative-dominated borough.[20] It seems that centres of nonconformist activism could, after all, sustain a robust Progressivism, even in Edwardian Stepney.

The most consistent relationship between centres of religious worship and local politics was provided by Catholic churches, which provided focal points for London Irish communities in key concentrations across the East End. Large Roman Catholic congregations and centres of Irish settlement – now often second or third generation – were in almost every case located in wards heavily dominated by the Conservative Party. In the borough of Poplar only three Roman Catholic congregations were recorded in Mudie-Smith's 1904 survey of church attendance. The largest, St Mary and St Joseph's, served the dockworker communities which straddled the East India Road in Poplar East and Poplar West wards. Here Tory councillors outnumbered their Progressive rivals by a factor of six to one. The second largest was further north, away from the river in Bow South ward, where Conservatives swept the board at every election except 1903. The third Catholic congregation in Poplar was in Millwall ward on the Isle of Dogs. Millwall returned more Conservative councillors than any other ward in Poplar borough. The presence of a Catholic Irish community within Millwall was perhaps not the sole factor in local Conservative strength. As Brodie suggests, strong social cohesion and a highly developed 'sense of place' in this isolated community, physically separated from the East End, provided added purchase to the philanthropic efforts of local Tory employers.[21] However, it is worth noting that Millwall shared the relative isolation of the Isle of Dogs with the neighbouring ward of Cubitt Town. Here the Conservatives fared far less well, securing only three of the fifteen seats available between 1900 and 1912. One, possibly key, factor which distinguished Cubitt Town from Millwall was the absence of a sizeable Catholic congregation.[22]

Of course this is not to suggest that the East End Irish were consistent Conservative voters. O'Day and Brodie have established that this vote was generally cohesive and typically supported the Progressive cause.[23] Even in wards where the Irish were most heavily concentrated they remained in the minority. Thus, Conservative strength in these areas of the East End may, in large part, reflect the host majority's hostility to the Irish community. These were often the areas in which conflicts over employment, housing and religious expression were most acute. The strong Conservative performance in those East End wards with a significant Catholic and Irish presence strongly suggests that religious sectarianism and opposition to Irish Home Rule in the imperial capital attracted non-Irish votes to the Conservatives, even at borough elections.[24]

The complexities of local politics in the East End of London generally confound attempts to establish consistent relationships between denomination and party political preferences – with the possible exception of Catholicism. Communities where Anglicanism was strong often generated strong electoral support for local Conservative candidates, but equally the party could dominate in localities where the Established Church was weak. Similarly, centres of nonconformist strength in the East End helped sustain Progressive success; elsewhere – but perhaps less frequently – such centres were located in areas of Conservative success.

Is it possible to discern a relationship between concentrations of port employment and voting preference at ward level in the Edwardian East End? The traditional view, which associates concentrations of port workers with popular Conservatism, has relied largely upon an analysis of parliamentary politics. The scale of East End constituencies meant that generally their boundaries extended beyond communities where port workers predominated. A focus upon ward politics in Stepney and Poplar enables comparisons between political units where port workers clearly predominated, and a range of communities further from the waterfront.

In Poplar, Conservatism dominated three of the borough's four waterfront wards, winning eighty-four per cent of the seats between 1900 and 1912 in Millwall, Poplar East, and Poplar West. Cubitt Town stands out among the waterfront wards; here, over the same period, only twenty per cent of councillors were Conservative. In neighbouring Stepney – where Conservatism was stronger than in Poplar at borough, London County Council and parliamentary levels – the picture was more mixed. In Stepney's five riverside wards sixty-two per cent of councillors were Conservatives. This performance placed the riverside wards ahead of the Conservatives' borough-wide figure of fifty-two per cent of all councillors – but not dramatically so. More significantly, in two of these riverside wards – Limehouse South and Ratcliffe – the Progressives achieved parity or better with the Conservatives. It would seem that in East End port worker communities there was in most cases a strong Conservative vote before 1914. Again, however, as in the case of religion, there were significant exceptions.

One striking feature of the municipal election results for Stepney and Poplar was the persistent failure of Labour in the waterfront wards before 1914. Labour made almost no impact in Stepney. Of the borough's three-hundred pre-war councillors only one was Labour – and moreover this single victory was in a ward away from the waterfront. In Poplar, Labour made some progress in the wake of a *de facto* pact with the Progressives implemented in 1906 which allowed Labour unopposed contests against the Conservatives.[25] However, as in Stepney, Labour achieved scant success on the waterfront. Of Labour's twenty-eight pre-war councillors in Poplar only three represented waterfront wards. Significantly, Labour's pre-war success in Poplar was concentrated overwhelmingly in wards away from the docks, where much of the workforce was employed in manufacturing. Labour success came in wards where a string of mills, factories and gasworks stretched along the banks of the River Lea and the Limehouse Cut, away from the dockside wards.

The other conspicuous feature of Labour performance in municipal elections over this period was the dramatic gains made after the war. In 1919 Labour swept almost all before it in Poplar and Stepney, largely irrespective of local religious or occupational differences. In

Stepney the Labour tide was turned back in 1922. Here the Ratepayers Association, an anti-Labour alliance of Conservatives and former Progressives, had some limited success on the waterfront, principally in what had been Progressive wards before 1914. Elsewhere in Stepney, Labour reverses were concentrated in socially mixed and middle-class wards. This pattern was reflected in Labour's far smaller setback in Poplar, although here the waterfront wards remained solidly Labour. In Stepney and Poplar, post-war Labour had transformed its pre-1914 position wherever manual workers were in a clear majority – whether on the waterfront or in the more industrial wards.[26]

HULL – A HAVEN OF LIBERALISM?

Party politics in Hull has received considerably less attention than in other major port cities.[27] Some historians appear to have found Hull politics somewhat perplexing. Thus Henry Pelling observed: 'It is certainly unusual to find a city where the customary political order of things is reversed, and the working class appears more Conservative than the middle class.' In familiar fashion, Pelling suggested that this apparent working-class Conservatism, and its counterpart, weak independent Labour politics 'was no doubt connected with the fact that the Hull working class consisted so largely of the ill-organised, unskilled labour of the docks and chemical works'.[28] Pelling approached Hull politics through the lens of parliamentary elections. Examined in closer focus, using municipal elections, it is clear that Pelling's assessment of class and politics in Hull was misplaced. The central premise that a highly casualised dock workforce provided the bedrock of Conservative strength in Edwardian Hull cannot be sustained. Analysis of the smaller municipal units suggests a more subtly differentiated occupational, denominational and political geography in early twentieth-century Hull, and one which permits more meaningful comparisons with other port communities, such as London's East End.

Hull Conservatism certainly had a presence in the docklands, but this was confined to a specific and distinctive area in the older central districts of the city. Four city-centre dockside wards – Whitefriars, Drypool, Myton and Paragon – were dominated by the Conservatives throughout the Edwardian period. In addition to their central location and the greater age of much of the housing, a number of features distinguished these Tory wards from the rest of the waterfront. Firstly, the religious preference of the majority here appeared to differ markedly from that of the remaining waterfront wards. These wards were home to the city's largest Anglican parish churches. Whitefriars ward, for example, with a population of only 4694, contained two Anglican churches – Holy Trinity and St Mary's – with sufficient sittings for 3200. Anglicanism's deep roots in the city centre appear to have proved relatively durable. Holy Trinity was the only Anglican church where attendances exceeded 1000 in the *Hull Daily News's* survey of religious attendance conducted in 1903-4; and at considerable cost St Mary's built a new parish hall in 1905 for its Sunday school activities.[29] In contrast, nonconformity in the central districts had been facing difficulty for some time as their congregations migrated to the rapidly expanding suburbs. The two main Methodist chapels in Whitefriars ward experienced declining attendances and in one case it was 'seriously proposed to sell the chapel'.[30] Neighbouring Paragon ward housed the city's main Roman Catholic Church. The juxtaposition of evangelical Anglicans and a minority Irish community in Paragon generated episodes of sectarian violence.[31] In religious terms this was ideal Tory territory.

A second factor that set these central wards apart from the remainder of the waterfront in Hull was that Tory strength here also drew upon the presence of a significant business vote, a topic of repeated complaint in the Liberal press.[32] In wards such as these, with relatively small electorates, the business vote could prove crucial. A third, related, factor was the Conservative allegiance of prominent business figures associated with the locality. While elsewhere along the waterfront Liberal paternalists held sway, in central Hull commercial and shipping interests – as represented by, for example, Sir Walter Herbert Cockerline, Sheriff of Hull, councillor for Whitefriars and owner of a fleet of tramp steamers – were more typically active on behalf of Conservatism. Even in the early twentieth century, personal wealth could be deployed in the attempt to secure favour with the electorate. Corrupt electoral practice was a feature of at least one central Hull Tory grandee's engagement with the local electorate. Sir HS King, MP for Hull Central, a wealthy banker and a founder of Lloyds, was charged with corruption and unseated in 1911, having distributed coal and provided free children's entertainments during the election.[33]

Beyond these four central wards, Hull's waterfront belonged over-whelmingly to the Liberals. The heaviest concentrations of dockers and other port workers were by 1900 to be found to the east of the city in Alexandra and Southcoates wards.[34] Both were strongholds of, by local standards, a progressive Liberalism which was generally at ease when supporting candidates jointly sponsored with the trades council. Anglicanism was relatively weak here. Alexandra and Southcoates formed part of the Drypool parish, which, despite a rela-tively large population of 47,000 in 1914, warranted only a single assistant curate. In contrast, the neighbouring parish of Sculcoates, with a far smaller population of only 16,000, engaged four assistant curates.[35] The Church of England was relatively slow to open new churches in the rapidly expanding port worker suburbs of East Hull. By the time new Anglican churches were consecrated in 1903 (Southcoates) and 1916 (Alexandra), the numerous Wesleyan and Primitive Methodist chapels in the area were well-established.[36]

In west Hull, dockland communities – which included significant numbers from the fishing and rail industries – dominated the water-front wards of Albert, Coltman and South Newington. As in the east, Conservative councillors were an extremely rare breed between 1900 and 1914. In these wards well-attended Wesleyan, Primitive Methodist and Congregationalist chapels were, if anything, more in evidence than in the east of the city.[37] Leading nonconformists, including local pastors, were often also activists in Liberal and Progressive politics in this area.[38] In these western waterfront wards, the Irish – and Catholic – presence was considerably smaller than in the city centre.[39] Coltman Ward, which housed a Catholic and an Anglican church with respectable attendances, provided Conservatives with their best prospects of electoral success in this part of the city. However, outnumbered by nonconformists politicised by the education issue, the Conservatives failed to record a win in Coltman between 1902 and 1913.

The more populous waterfront wards, to both east and west of the city centre, were, then, under Liberal control before 1914. Indeed more broadly, Hull was a port city where, unusually, Liberalism was the dominant political creed. Liberal strength was sustained by the influence of powerful employer and commercial interests. First among these was the Wilson family – owners of the world's largest privately owned shipping line. By the early twentieth century the

Wilson family's investments in Hull included dock construction, stevedoring, fishing, and shipbuilding and engineering.[40] The firm played a leading role in the local economy and the city's politics. The West Hull parliamentary seat had become 'looked upon as a preserve of the Wilson family'. As *The Times* observed, 'the electorate of West Hull is composed in large measure of the waterside labourers and seafaring men, whose livelihood depends in no small measure upon the prosperity of shipping firms such as the Wilson's ... their identity of commercial interest, explains in no small measure the political allegiance of the Humber-side voters ... to the firm which have done so much to develop the resources of the port'.[41] Extensive philanthropic effort further bolstered the Wilson's political influence.[42] Other leading figures in Hull Liberalism – such as TH Ferens, MP for East Hull, Sir James Reckitt, chair of the Hull Liberal Party, and Sir Alfred Gelder – were also feted for their philanthropic zeal.

A second key factor in Liberal success was, as suggested above, strong local adherence to nonconformity. Hull's Liberal grandees were prominent within the city's nonconformist churches, an engagement fully reflected in the wider population. Nineteenth-century censuses of church attendance suggest that Hull's nonconformists outnumbered Anglicans by approximately two to one. By the early twentieth century the gap had apparently widened further, with city-wide attendances at nonconformist churches approaching 25,000, while the Church of England mustered a meagre 6438.[43] Nonconformity's dominance was reflected in elections to school boards during the 1890s, and the firm grip they exercised over the education committee from 1904.[44]

What of Labour fortunes in Hull's waterfront districts? While Labour's relative weakness in the city as a whole before 1914 is well established, it is less clear what part the port worker communities played in this.[45] In the eastern dockland wards of Alexandra and Southcoates, Labour struggled to make an impact. In Southcoates ward Labour confronted a Progressive opponent on three occasions between 1900 and 1914. On each occasion Labour was defeated, its share of the vote falling as war approached. In Alexandra ward an early trial of strength with the Progressives in 1901 resulted in a resounding defeat for Labour – a mistake they were not to repeat before the war.[46] Thereafter, collaboration with the Liberals was the norm. Councillors in Alexandra ward were a combination of

Progressives, Lib-Lab trade unionists or official Labour candidates standing with Liberal support.

There was still less sign of Labour progress in the four city-centre dockside wards. In 1904 Labour put forward a strong candidate for the Drypool ward in RH Farrah, secretary of the Gasworkers' union and the trades council. Farrah had been a city councillor in the 1890s, and later won again comfortably in Alexandra ward, but in Drypool he could muster only thirty-nine per cent of the vote. This was Labour's sole candidacy in the fifty-two elections in these city-centre wards between 1901 and 1914 – this was alien terrain for Labour, dominated, according to Farrah, by 'the forces of reaction'.[47]

Labour's prospects appeared better in the western waterfront wards where Liberalism and nonconformity provided a more sympathetic context. However, South Newington, with its concentration of rail-workers around the engine sheds and coal sidings at Dairycoates Junction, was the only one of the three western waterfront wards which witnessed a challenge from independent Labour before 1914. In the main South Newington was the preserve of Liberals, Lib-Labs and Progressives. Labour first asserted its claims in 1911 and was narrowly defeated on two occasions when facing Progressive or Lib-Lab opposition. This was not a significant rupture in relations between Liberal and Labour in Hull. While there were certainly many in Labour's ranks who wished to break with the Liberals, the great majority continued to view such a step as electoral suicide.[48] Instead new accommodations were being sought and found. In 1913 a local engine driver and member of the Amalgamated Society of Railway Servants won South Newington for Labour by a large majority – with the Liberals and Progressives standing aside.[49] This was independent Labour's sole victory in the western waterfront wards between 1901 and 1913.

Before 1914 Labour's greatest electoral successes in Hull came in wards away from both the waterfront and the city centre. Seed-crushing, grain-milling, and paint and varnish manufacture all expanded considerably in the later nineteenth century, establishing a substantial workforce in mills and factories which stretched out north of the Humber along the banks of the River Hull. By the turn of the century this expansion had produced a significant industrial work-force in three inland wards: East Central, West Central and Beverley. Together these three wards elected four times more Labour councillors between 1901 and 1913 than the remaining thirteen Hull wards combined. While Labour was by no means guaranteed of success here – especially in Beverley ward which was more socially mixed – the Party had established a significant presence.[50]

In Hull – as in London's East End – Labour performance in the dockland areas improved markedly after 1918. This change was less dramatic in Hull. Nonetheless, a series of victories for Labour in waterfront wards after 1918 suggest that the politics of these areas had changed significantly as a result of the experience of war. Between 1919 and 1921 Labour won five of the six contests in the dockland wards of Alexandra and Southcoates. And Albert and Coltman had elected their first Labour councillors by 1920, both waterfront wards where Labour had rarely previously stood, and before 1914 had hardly offered any chance of victory. Less striking progress was made in the old city-centre dockside wards of Drypool, Myton, Paragon and Whitefriars. Again, in either 1919 or 1920 Labour had, for the first time, stood a candidate in each of these wards. All were unsuccessful, although polls in excess of forty per cent in Drypool, Myton and Paragon suggested that the Labour cause was no longer hopeless. Across the various types of waterfront communities in Hull, Labour mounted an unprecedented challenge to the traditional parties between 1918 and 1922. Moreover, after the war Labour support proved at least as strong on the waterfront as in the inland industrial wards.[51]

LIVERPOOL: A NOTE

Space does not permit full discussion of the Liverpudlian case. Britain's second port city already has its historian of port workers and municipal politics in Sam Davies.[52] In many ways Davies' conclusions mirror those outlined above in relation to Hull and London's East End. Religion, as is widely acknowledged, was central to party preference across Liverpool before 1914. In Liverpool conflict between host Protestant communities and the Catholic Liverpool Irish remained the most significant feature of local politics. For the majority of Liverpool's nonconformists, differences with Anglicanism were largely secondary to the greater struggle against Catholics. As a result, in wards where port workers were predominant, municipal elections were largely in the hands of either Irish Nationalist candidates in the

Catholic wards, or the Conservative and Protestant parties in the Protestant districts.[53] The Liberal Party achieved only isolated success in Liverpool's port worker wards, typically in Catholic areas when in alliance with Nationalists encouraged by the Liberal Party's stance on Irish Home Rule. This apart the Liberal Party achieved further limited success in city-centre wards where the business vote held sway, and in middle-class wards, but in both these contexts the Conservatives were generally a stronger force. Liverpool Conservatism, bolstered by Archibald Salvidge's Working Men's Conservative Association, was also the dominant force in Protestant working-class Liverpool before 1914, undoubtedly a result of the city's sectarian politics.

As for the spatial distribution of Liverpool Labour before 1914, there are again similarities with Hull and the East End. As Davies suggests, Labour strength was to be found in areas 'with a relatively high proportion of the male workforce concentrated in permanent-employed and often skilled and semi-skilled occupations ...'. In other words, port workers were not in the majority where Liverpool Labour was strong.[54] There were isolated wins for Labour in several dockside wards in 1911 following the bitterly contested port-wide strike. There was also some Labour strength in St Anne's ward, where co-operation between Catholic, Liberal and labour interests – in the form of James Sexton the dockers' leader – secured a series of wins for Labour before 1914.[55] These were exceptions which served to underline Labour's failure across both the Catholic and Protestant port worker wards. Again, as in other ports, the post-war years witnessed a significant improvement in Labour's performance.[56] Labour won eleven seats in 1919, nine of which lay within a short distance of the docks, and many of which contained a majority Catholic community. Labour fared poorly in 1920 and 1921, but the Party's best performances in both years were again in wards dominated by casual workers.[57] Even in Liverpool then, after 1918 Labour, in contrast to the pre-war experience, secured significant support in areas of the city where port-related casual workers dominated the local labour market.

CONCLUSION

The politics of port communities before 1914 were undoubtedly more complex than any ready association between popular

Conservatism and an electorate defined by poverty and casual work
would suggest. Brodie rightly argues that in many parts of London's
East End Conservative victories were sustained by the votes of groups
other than the casual poor, including the middle class and workers in
regular employment.[58] Moreover, port worker communities also
sustained Liberal, Progressive and Nationalist political cultures.
Nonetheless, this study lends some qualified support to the traditional
view that areas of port cities where casual work predominated were,
most commonly, fertile Conservative terrain before 1914. This association between concentrations of casual work and localised Tory
strength can also be identified in several inland urban centres.[59] That
said, the exceptions are numerous and significant: waterfront districts
in east and west Hull, in Limehouse, and in Liverpool's north end,
were anything but Tory strongholds.

Of course, most, if not all, of the localities studied here contained
electorates with multiple overlapping, and often conflicting, identities. The focus here has been on occupation and religion. For the most
part religious identities trumped occupation in Edwardian ports.
Nonconformity bred Liberal strength across areas of the waterfront in
Hull and the East End; while, for the most part, where Anglicanism
was in the majority Tories predominated. To this extent these findings support the arguments of those, such as Trevor Griffiths, who
have argued that religion 'proved altogether more robust' than class or
occupation in shaping political choices before 1914.[60] In one respect
at least, however, occupation seems to have provided a consistent
indicator of political capacity. Communities where port workers
predominated remained almost impenetrable to Labour before 1914.
Thus, in so far as traditional treatments of port worker politics were
concerned with Labour, their conclusions appear accurate. In the
localities studied here, independent Labour politics began to establish
a foothold in municipal politics in wards where employment was
more regular, at a distance from the more highly casual dockland
labour markets. Thus, the geography of Labour strength was strik-
ingly similar in Hull and London's East End before 1914. In these
two port areas the great preponderance of Labour success in municipal elections was located in wards along the banks of inland
waterways where factory and mill employment had developed – with
only isolated and sporadic victories along the waterfront. In
Liverpool's docklands too, Labour were outsiders before 1914.

The Labour Party's difficulties were undoubtedly in part a result of trade union weakness on the waterfront. While the economic insecurities of the casual labour market were clearly critical, as John Saville pointed out in his pioneering study of 'free labour', human agency – in the form of a vigorous employer counter-offensive in the 1890s – dealt an enduring blow to union organisation in the docklands of Hull, London and Liverpool.[61] Union membership in port communities was largely rebuilt between 1910 and 1914; however, independent Labour politics remained largely on the fringes.[62] Something more than a few years of – still often insecure – union building would be necessary before Labour could establish an enduring foothold in Britain's docklands. The First World War transformed Labour's position in Britain's port cities; thereafter the docks were no longer *terra incognita*. A sharp tightening of the labour market reduced insecurity and encouraged significant growth in trade union membership and local Labour organisation. Casual work, however, remained a defining feature for most port communities after 1918, particularly in the East End, the scene of Labour's most spectacular post-war gains. In war a shared urban experience of food and housing shortages, inflation, profiteering and pervasive state intervention into the economics of working-class everyday life provided Labour with circumstances in which its message gained an unprecedented hearing in both port and non-port areas.[63] After the war the gulf between Labour's poor prospects in the docklands, and the Party's relative success in industrial areas, had been bridged, and the politics of class were more firmly on the agenda than heretofore.

Notes

1. Gareth Stedman Jones, *Outcast London: A Study in the Relationship between Classes in Victorian Society*, Penguin, 1976; Paul Thompson, *Socialists, Liberals and Labour: the Struggle for London, 1885–1914*, Routledge & Kegan Paul, 1967; Henry Pelling, *Social Geography of British Elections 1885-1910*, Gregg Revivals, 1994.

2. Henry Pelling, *Popular Politics and Society in Late Victorian Britain*, St Martin's Press, 1968, p56; Duncan Tanner, *Political Change and the Labour Party 1900-1918*, Cambridge University Press, 1990, pp164-5; Neville Kirk, '"Traditional" working-class culture and "the rise of Labour": some preliminary questions and observations', *Social History*, 16, 2, May 1991, pp203-16.

3. For example, Eugenio Biagini and Alistair Reid, 'Currents of radicalism 1850-1914' in idem, eds, *Currents of Radicalism: Popular radicalism, organised labour and party politics in Britain, 1850-1914*, Cambridge University Press, 1991, pp5-18; Christopher Stevens, 'The electoral sociology of modern Britain reconsidered' in *Contemporary British History*, 13, 1999, pp62–94; Jon Lawrence and Miles Taylor, 'Introduction: electoral sociology and the historian' in Lawrence and Taylor, eds, *Party, State and Society: Electoral Behaviour in Britain since 1820*, Scolar Press, 1997.

4. Marc Brodie, *The Politics of the Poor: The East End of London 1885-1914*, Oxford University Press, 2004. More generally, see Trevor Griffiths, *The Lancashire Working Classes c.1880-1930*, Oxford University Press, 2001, p331.

5. Tanner, *Political Change*, pp130-1; Sam Davies, *Liverpool Labour: Social and Political Influences on the Development of the Labour Party in Liverpool, 1900-1939*, Keele University Press, 1996, pp223-4.

6. Thompson, *Socialists, Liberals and Labour*; Stedman Jones, *Outcast London*, p334; see also, Pelling, *Social Geography*, pp42-8; and Tanner, *Political Change*, pp164-5.

7. See, for example, the introduction to Brodie, *Politics of the Poor*; Marc Brodie, 'Voting in the Victorian and Edwardian East End of London', *Parliamentary History*, 23, 2, 2004, pp225-48.

8. Brodie, *Politics of the Poor*, p90.

9. Brodie, 'Voting', pp233-4.

10. John Davis, 'Slums and the Vote 1867-90', *Historical Research*, 64, 155, 1991, pp375-88; John Davis and Duncan Tanner, 'The Borough Franchise After 1867', *Historical Research*, 69, 170, 1996, pp306-27.

11. Brodie, 'Voting', pp238-40; Marc Brodie, 'Late Victorian and Edwardian "Slum Conservatism": How different were the politics of the London poor?' in M Cragoe and A Taylor, eds, *London Politics, 1760-1914*, Palgrave, 2005, p180.

12. Brodie, *Politics of the Poor*, p112.

13. R Mudie-Smith, ed., *The Religious Life of London*, Hodder and Stoughton, 1904, pp45 & 49; Census of England and Wales 1911, Table 10, p217. Differences in population cannot account for the differential attendances – the population of Bow North was only twenty-two per cent greater than that of Shadwell in 1901. P.P. 1902 CXX, Census of England and Wales, County of London, 1901, Table 9.

14. More generally on the importance of Anglicanism for the Tories, see EHH Green, *The Crisis of Conservatism: the politics, economics and ideology of the British Conservative Party*, Routledge, 1995.

15. Brodie, *Politics of the Poor*, pp179 & 204.

16. Mudie-Smith, *Religious Life*, pp50-1.

17. Brodie, *Politics of the Poor*, p108.

18. Mudie-Smith, *Religious Life*, pp49-50.

19. http://www.eltbaptistchurch.org/Groups/31364/East_London_Tabernacle/ about_us/Our_History/Our_History.aspx (accessed 15 July 2010).
20. These were the only wards in Stepney where a majority of councillors between 1900 and 1912 were Progressives.
21. Brodie, *Politics of the Poor*, pp151-6.
22. Mudie-Smith, *Religious Life*, pp46-7; see also BLPES Booth MSS B346, pp24-5.
23. Alan O'Day, 'Irish influence on parliamentary elections in London, 1885-1914: a simple test' in Roger Swift and Sheridan Gilley, eds, *The Irish in the Victorian City*, Croom Helm, 1985. Brodie, *Politics of the Poor*, pp193-8.
24. On the significance of Irish Home Rule for the Tories in London see, Alex Windscheffel, *Popular Conservatism in Imperial London 1868-1906*, Boydell, 2007, pp56-7, 72-3.
25. There were only four contests that involved Progressive and Labour candidates in forty-two ward elections between 1906 and 1912. In two of these the Progressive challenge was only nominal.
26. Julia Bush, *Behind the Lines: East London Labour 1914-19*, Merlin, 1984, ch. 7; James Gillespie, 'Poplarism and proletarianism: unemployment and Labour politics in London' in David Feldman and Gareth Stedman Jones, eds, *Metropolis London: Histories and Representations since 1800*, Routledge, 1989, pp163-88.
27. For one notable recent exception, see Yann Beliard, 'Imperial internationalism? Hull Labour's support for South African trade-unionism on the eve of the Great War' *Labour History Review*, 74, 3, 2009.
28. Pelling, *Social Geography*, pp295 & 297.
29. *Kelly's Directory of North & East Ridings of Yorkshire, Part 2: York & Hull*, Kelly's Directories Limited, 1913, pp v-vi; Peter Stubley, 'Serious religion and the improvement of public manners: The scope and limitations of evangelicalism in Hull, 1770-1914', PhD, Durham, 1991, p205.
30. *Kelly's Directory of North & East Ridings*, ppvi-vii; T Bulmer, *History, topography, and directory of East Yorkshire with Hull*, T Bulmer & Co, 1892.
31. Edward Gillett and Kenneth MacMahon, *A History of Hull*, Oxford University Press, 1980, pp338-9, 383.
32. For example, *Hull Daily News*, 3 and 6 July 1911. This contemporary view is confirmed by analysis of *Kelly's Directory of Hull*, 1901, 1904 and 1906.
33. *Times*, 3 January, 23 and 24 May and 2 June 1911; *Hansard*, vol. 26, cols 1523-5, 14 June 1911, Kingston-Upon-Hull (Central Division) Petition. These central wards should not be confused with the Central Hull constituency, only three of which (Myton, Paragon and Whitefriars) fell within the latter's boundaries. In 1911 these three wards contained only fifty-four per cent of the constituency's parliamentary electorate.

34. On the development of the Hull waterfront see Keith Nolan, 'Municipal politics and regional monopoly: railways and the port of Hull, 1840-1922', D Phil, York, 2006, pp285-6. Although the boundaries of Southcoates fall short of the waterfront itself, the occupational character of the ward, identified in the censuses of 1901 and 1911, warrants its inclusion among the waterfront wards. This view is confirmed in Sam Davies, 'The history of Hull dockers, c.1870-1960' in Davies et al, eds, *Dock Workers: International Explorations in Comparative Labour History, 1790-1970*, Vol 1, Ashgate, 2000, p201.
35. K J Allison, ed., *A History of the County of York East Riding: Volume 1: The City of Kingston upon Hull*, Oxford University Press, 1969, p277.
36. *Kelly's Directory North & East Ridings*, ppv-vii.
37. For example, Wesleyan Chapels in South Newington and Coltman wards recorded attendances of over a thousand in the *Hull Daily News* Survey of 1903-4; Stubley, 'Serious religion', p12.
38. For example, the account of the Rev JQ Christian's career in the *Eastern Morning News*, 3 November 1904.
39. *Times*, 26 November 1907; Stubley, 'Serious religion', p300.
40. Gillett and MacMahon, *History of Hull*, pp319-20, 348-51; J Bellamy, 'A Hull shipbuilding firm: The History of C. & W. Earle and Earle's Shipbuilding and Engineering Company Ltd', *Business History*, 6, 1, 1963, pp27-47.
41. *Times*, 26 November 1907.
42. G M Attwood, *The Wilsons of Tranby Croft*, Hutton Press, 1988. On the Sailor's Mission Hall and Jubilee Institute at Alexandra Dock, both donated by CH Wilson, see Bulmer, *History, topography, and directory*, part 9.
43. These figures, obtained from the *Hull Daily News* survey of 1903-4, probably underestimate Anglican attendance; Stubley, 'Serious religion', pp198-205.
44. *York Herald*, 23 April 1892; 19 April 1895; 31 January 1899, p3; Gillett and MacMahon, *History of Hull*, pp337-40.
45. Tanner, *Political Change*, pp276-7; Pelling, *Social Geography*, pp294-7; David Howell, *British Workers and the Independent Labour Party 1888-1906*, Manchester University Press, 1983, pp117-20.
46. *Eastern Morning News*, 2 November 1901.
47. *Hull Daily News*, 2 November 1904.
48. See, for example, the meeting in the Hull Trades and Labour Council reported in the *Eastern Morning News*, 4 November 1912, where a move to confront the Liberals across the city was defeated by a margin of fifty-three votes to twenty-eight.
49. *Hull Daily Mail*, 3 November 1908 and 2 November 1912; *Eastern Morning News*, 1 and 2 November 1911; *Hull Daily News*, 3 November 1913.

50. See for example, 'Peter Progress' on Labour's 'splendid body of workers' in Beverley ward; *Hull Times*, 28 October 1911.
51. Davies, 'The history of Hull dockers', p201.
52. Davies, *Liverpool Labour*, pp81-139 & 197-231; Davies, 'The Liverpool Labour Party and the Liverpool working class, 1900-39', *Bulletin of the North West Labour History Society*, 6, 1979-80, pp2–14; Sam Davies and Bob Morley, 'Merseyside Labour: influences on the electoral performance of the Labour Party on Merseyside, 1918-1939', *North-West Labour History*, 31, 2006-7, pp20-31.
53. Davies, *Liverpool Labour*, p224.
54. Ibid.
55. Davies, *Liverpool Labour*, pp208, 309-11; PJ Waller, *Democracy and Sectarianism: A Political and Social History of Liverpool 1868-1939*, Liverpool University Press, pp216-7.
56. *Liverpool Daily Post*, 3 November 1919.
57. *Liverpool Pioneer*, November, 1919; *Liverpool Courier*, 2 November 1920; Davies, *Liverpool Labour*, p225.
58. Brodie, *Politics of the Poor*, pp200-1.
59. Tony Adams, 'Labour vanguard, Tory bastion, or the triumph of new Liberalism? Manchester politics 1900 to 1914 in comparative perspective', *Manchester Regional History Review*, 14, 2000, pp33-4.
60. Griffiths, *Lancashire Working Classes*, p331.
61. John Saville, 'Trade unions and free labour: the background to the Taff Vale decision' in Asa Briggs and John Saville, eds, *Essays in Labour History*, Macmillan, 1967, pp317-50.
62. Ken Coates and Tony Topham, *The History of the Transport and General Workers' Union, Vol. I, Part 1*, Blackwell, 1991, pp247-8, 263-4, 325-7 and 339.
63. Tony Adams, 'Labour and the First World War: economy, politics and the erosion of local peculiarity?', *Journal of Regional and Local History*, 10, 1, 1990, pp23-47.

PART THREE

Interventions

The Chartist movement and 1848

Malcolm Chase

John Saville's contribution to the historiography of Chartism would be recognised as significant, even without his *1848: The British State and the Chartist Movement*, whose publication in 1987 in many ways represented the pinnacle of his career as a historian. Saville's authorial contribution to the *Dictionary of Labour Biography* includes an impressive array of biographical essays on Chartists. To volume six alone he contributed an outstanding entry for the black Londoner, trade unionist and Chartist William Cuffay, plus further fine-grained accounts of Robert Gammage and Thomas Martin Wheeler and, as co-author, of Catherine and John Barmby, Thomas Clark and Arthur O'Neill.[1] Similarly invaluable are the editorial introductions he wrote in the 1960s for four reprints of key Chartist texts: GJ Harney's journal *Red Republican*, Gammage's *History of the Chartist Movement*, and the autobiographies of WE Adams and Thomas Cooper.[2] The cumulative importance of these works is considerable. But the publication of *1848* marked Saville out as a historian of real distinction: it is a book of fundamental importance to understanding not Chartism alone, but the nineteenth century as a whole. Chartism really mattered to John Saville, just as it had mattered to early Victorian government and society.

The weight of biographical studies in any simple numerical tally of Saville's output as a Chartist historian might suggest to the uninitiated that he was concerned primarily with empirical retrieval. However, the power of *1848* as a work of historical scholarship derives not from its author's command of historical detail (great though that was) but his rootedness in the Marxist tradition. It is worth examining the book's gestation in some detail for, despite the late date of its publication, there are good grounds for claiming a place for it as a product of the Historians' Group of the Communist Party, alongside stellar earlier works by, for example, Christopher Hill, Eric Hobsbawm and EP Thompson.[3] In fundamental respects, *1848* expands and explicates attitudes towards its subject that emerged within British communism in the immediate post-war years.

Europe's year of revolutions was not, however, where John Saville's career as historian of Chartism began. He never particularly explained why he chose as the subject of his first substantial publication in 1952 the Chartist leader Ernest Jones. Presumably he assumed that Jones's importance as the labour leader who did most to bridge the Chartist period and the 1850s would speak for itself.[4] Saville began researching Jones's career soon after he was demobilised in April 1946, during his brief career as an economist in the Chief Scientific Division of the Ministry of Works. It was only in September 1947 that he took up the post at Hull which initiated his academic career.[5] The pressure of the early months of his appointment probably explains his otherwise puzzling non-appearance in the 1948 'Chartist Centenary Issue' of the CPGB's cultural journal *Our Time*. To that issue, Dorothy Towers – Dorothy Thompson after her marriage later that year – contributed the first ever scholarly examination of the work of the Chartist poets; while the lead feature on 1848, by the veteran CPGB organiser and orator Tommy Jackson, in some ways anticipates arguments in Saville's subsequent work.[6] Jackson was not only alert to the inspirational impact of continental events on British Chartists but was also mindful of the critical dimension that developments in Ireland added to the government's handling of events in Britain. He also emphasised that the well-known Chartist rally on Kennington Common on 10 April had been 'systematically and persistently made the theme of a whole embroidery of falsification … Actually, Chartism began to grow more formidable after April 10th than it had been before'. Jackson concluded that the Chartist conspiracy that followed in August had entirely 'been worked up by police agents'.[7]

Almost certainly Jackson was drawing from Theodore Rothstein's *From Chartism to Labourism: Historical Sketches of the English Working Class Movement*. This had been published in 1929 as the second item in Martin Lawrence's 'Marxist Library' imprint, following Plekhanov's *Fundamental Problems of Marxism*. In his introduction to the 1983 reprint, Saville commented that *From Chartism to Labourism* had been neither widely reviewed nor especially well-received in 1929;

and he speculated that, long out of print, it was effectively unknown to scholars before the late 1950s.[8] Saville himself, however, had first come across the volume in the 1930s, gaining, he said, a great deal from it; his *Ernest Jones: Chartist* gives some prominence to Rothstein, and its bibliography of recommended modern works on Chartism is confined to him and just two other authors.[9] The recognition of Rothstein's work by both Jackson and Saville contrasts with the neglect of later Chartism in other pre-1950 Marxist scholarship.[10]

None of this early scholarship, even Rothstein's, offered a full evaluation of Chartism after 1848. Non-Marxist historiography offered nothing better.[11] In choosing to study Jones, Saville, by contrast, was able to explore the later phases of Chartism. His book has remained an important source of information on the movement in the 1850s, even as the interpretation of its subject has been superseded. This is partly because its bulk consists of selections from Jones's speeches and writing, with brief editorial introductions. The introduction proper makes a concerted case for taking seriously Jones, and likewise Chartism, during the years it operated as a pressure group rather than a mass movement. The young Saville saw these years as pivotal in the evolution of the labour movement due to its synergies with Marx's influence. That Jones should have accepted, towards the end of his life, a place in the Liberal sun somewhat discomfits this interpretation. Saville did not ignore it, citing Jones's acceptance of 'household suffrage, untrammelled and unfettered' alongside a eulogy to Gladstone and Bright. But to remember Jones in this way, Saville briskly claimed, is to present 'a distorted picture', over-emphasising the 'end product' of a career during 'the greater part of which Jones rejected in uncompromising fashion, middle-class ideals and policies'.[12]

Saville was similarly brisk in addressing the abruptness of Jones's conversion to Chartism. The context, Saville recognised, was the collapse of Jones's finances and his failure to persuade the Anti-Corn Law League to support him in launching a newspaper. But ultimately, Saville thought, '[i]t was not despair born of financial catastrophe that drove him into the Chartist ranks ... the world into which he was jolted by the necessity of having to earn a living was one in which a sensitive nature could not fail to be moved at the suffering and misery of so many of his fellow countrymen'. Even so, the sudden intensity of Jones's acceptance of the politics of class conflict could only 'without exaggeration, be called his conversion'.[13] Perhaps the unself-conscious religiosity of British communism at this time led the avowed atheist historian to believe he could understand Ernest Jones's behaviour. Jones's modern biographer is more cynical.[14]

If *Ernest Jones: Chartist* showed the limitations of Saville's historical method in explaining the intimate and personal, two other works from 1952 reveal the acuity of his approach to broad, structural issues. The first, a review of Cole and Filson's *British Working Class Movements: Select Documents, 1789-1875*, took issue with what Saville perceived as its stale assumptions about the inner life of Chartism and its consequences. Echoing Jones's tribute to O'Connor as the man above all others who had created and organised 'the democratic mind', Saville argued for O'Connor's decisive role in 'buttressing the confidence of the working men in their own power', and for the energising contribution to this of his 'striking, polemical English' oratory and prose. 'The historian must not underestimate the effect of such things upon the morale of a political movement.'[15] Among historians of Chartism at the time Saville was unique, and remained so into the late 1970s, in his emphatic belief that 'it is time that O'Connor, with all his faults and with a proper recognition of his strength, was given careful analysis'.[16]

The review also noted in passing 'a most extraordinary bias and prejudice' on the part of the judiciary against the Chartist prisoners in 1848. Saville had not made this point anything like as forcibly in *Ernest Jones*. However, once he had completed the latter in December 1951, he turned to a major re-evaluation of 1848, the fruit of which was the second of his articles from 1952, appearing in Lawrence & Wishart's *Modern Quarterly*.[17] In this Saville attacked 'a theme which has become a commonplace in historical writing in this country, where the story of Chartism in 1848 is almost always the same account of fiasco and inglorious decline'. Saville's nuanced interpretation was to remain influential for three decades. He emphasised how first the media and then public opinion became fixated with the French Revolution of 1848, so that 'the identification between Chartist, rioter and foreign revolutionary was complete ... Parallel with these developments went the consolidation and deployment of the coercive power of the State.' The leitmotiv of government policy was the avoidance of any precipitate clash which might inflame working-class opinion. In contrast to continental Europe, 'and here was the secret of its stability', the British government cultivated and retained the support of both the propertied classes and many others further down the social scale. In decline since 1842, and with its energies diverted into the Land Plan, Chartism, according to Saville, was 'half paralysed'. O'Connor's increasingly deficient leadership was especially significant here: for the first time since 1838 he unequivocally threw his weight 'upon the side of the right-wing moral force advocates', a development compounded in November by what Saville termed 'a violent swing to the right' which O'Connor warmly welcomed. The reference here was to a policy of concentrating on social rather than political issues, endorsed by an emergency congress in Birmingham, as those leading Chartists not in prison wrestled to get the movement back on course.[18]

Subsequent historians have viewed 'the social turn' adopted at Birmingham more positively.[19] The central thrust of Saville's account of 1848, however, has proved far more enduring. The conclusion 'that Chartism collapsed into insignificance after the defeat of April 10th', he pointed out, 'has no basis in fact'. The late spring and summer of 1848 in Britain was marked by growing unrest, culminating in the exposure of a conspiracy in mid-August. What brought Chartism to a standstill, Saville argued, was extensive government use of spies and *agents provocateurs*, confident in the knowledge that judges and middle-class juries could be relied upon to convict Chartists once in court. Critical here was the Crown and Government Security Act pushed through Parliament after a first reading on the very evening of 10 April. The act created new offences of 'treason felony', for which the penalty was imprisonment or transportation for life, in place of the capital offences set out in the Treason Act of 1795. The latter made martyrs of the convicted, as the Whig government had discovered after the 1839 Newport Rising. Furthermore, the rights of prisoners accused of capital offences were more extensive than those charged only with felonies, and juries were more likely to convict where the death penalty did not apply. No less significantly, speech alone had not been deemed treasonable before the 1848 Act, but was treated as a misdemeanour with relatively modest penalties. However, under the new act it became a 'treason felony' to 'compass, imagine, invent, devise, or intend' to levy war against the Crown, either by word or 'by open and advised Speaking'.[20]

Saville's realisation that the gestation of this act and its application is pivotal to understanding 1848 in Britain was a major development. It is all the more significant when one realises that the standard work on the legal history of the period confidently asserts that 'no one was charged in England' under the legislation.[21] Saville had now arrived, with a degree of rigour and detail unmatched in the earlier interpretations of Jackson and even Rothstein, at the conclusion all his subsequent work on Chartism would reiterate and expand: that 'the working class movement was opposed by a political strategy which combined apparent reasonableness and tact with a ruthlessness whose vigour was matched by an insistence upon victory to be achieved by any and all means possible'.[22]

A problem followed, however, from Saville's choice of a relatively obscure Marxist journal for the publication of this interpretation. Read and Glasgow's biography of O'Connor (1961) was oblivious to it; so too was FC Mather's *Public Order in the Age of the Chartists* (1959), a work Saville nonetheless declared 'invaluable' for its detailed research into authority's handling of Chartism.[23] The contributors to the seminal *Chartist Studies* collection of 1959, which in any case was stronger on earlier than on later Chartism, never cited it. A decade later, at a conference devoted to Chartism, Saville reiterated his interpretation of the movement's decline. He was particularly attacked for claiming 'Chartism was not only physically destroyed' but 'intellectually and spiritually annihilated'. He was reported to have characteristically 'made a spirited and unrepentant reply'. Significantly, however, the essence of his interpretation of 1848 went unchallenged. Indeed he reinforced it by also emphasising the relevance to his argument of economic recovery from late 1848, both as a short-term explanation for the decline of the movement and as the motor for structural social shifts (principally, expansion in the number of skilled workers and the growth of consumer cooperation) that were unconducive to Chartism's recovery.[24]

By the time of that conference Saville had consolidated his reputation as a historian of Chartism with an introductory essay to a new edition of the *History* that the second tier leader Robert Gammage had published in 1854. The essay was a *tour de force* which lay bare the shortcomings of Chartist historiography at the end of the 1960s.[25] On the specific issue of the movement in decline, Saville entered a more measured comment that 'it would not be wrong to speak of the submergence, in the national consciousness, of the Chartist movement' in the second half of the nineteenth century. This perception possibly stemmed from, and was certainly reinforced by, a remark of Engels in 1890 about the 'forty years winter sleep' of the English proletariat.[26]

To a significant extent, the force of Saville's thesis about 1848 at this stage depended upon his assertion concerning this 'submergence'. Yet it is in this very introduction, full of meticulously crafted, detailed footnotes, that the shortcomings of this assertion were perhaps most apparent. Almost every page contains references no serious student of Chartism, even now, can afford to ignore, many of them garnered from the years 1850-90. Footnote seventy-three alone encompasses references to twenty-eight articles in *Newcastle Weekly Chronicle,* and thirteen other publications issued between 1857 and 1887. It is clear that Saville was beginning to rethink aspects of his interpretation of Chartism. He now freely admitted that *Ernest Jones, Chartist* was 'too narrow' in interpreting the decline of Chartism in largely economic terms. He now believed '[t]he explanation of Chartist decline must be sought in the total context of social and economic life'. Three years earlier, introducing the reprinted *Red Republican,* he had commented that '[e]xplanations of political defeat and decline which omit the role of human agency, or ignore the many factors which shape and mould social consciousness, are never likely to offer satisfactory conclusions'.[27]

The introduction to the Gammage reprint is also notable for a remarkably rounded account of the Chartist Land Plan, anticipating the turn in that organisation's historiographical fortunes from the late 1980s.[28] Saville himself had not been exempt from the once customary dismissal of the Land Plan, deeming it 'Utopian' and 'unquestionably reactionary' in 1952.[29] However, 'I have come ... to be more sympathetic to the Land Plan than I was ten years ago', he wrote in a 1961 contribution to the *Bulletin* of the Society for the Study of Labour History. This was a well-informed survey of the 'constant ferment of ideas and discussion about land questions and problems' that had both preceded the plan and survived it, and which helped explain the considerable interest with which the Chartist scheme was received. 'The Land Plan was certainly not bizarre', Saville concluded; 'it was a good deal less utopian than most of the milennial [sic] schemes of these years', and it helped to hold Chartism together in the doldrums years of the mid-1840s – a point he acknowledged had earlier been made by Morton and Tate.[30]

Saville's earlier works had only touched on the land question.[31] However, his considerable command of the subject was again evident twelve months later in a critical bibliography, 'Henry George and the British Labour movement'.[32] These pieces emerged from a larger-scale project which he never brought to fruition. David Martin has explained how, when he was a postgraduate at Hull in the late 1960s, Saville 'passed to me some of his unpublished work on the land question and left the way open to me to follow an avenue of research that he might have taken himself'. From this there emerged both Martin's doctoral thesis and one of the 'Hull Occasional Papers' on Mill and the Land Question.[33] However these treated only a facet (albeit an important one) of a question that preoccupied radicals of all persuasions across the long nineteenth century. Enigmatically, *Strict Settlement: A Guide for Historians*, which Saville co-authored in 1983, remains his most substantial work on the land question. However, on its authors' own admission, it is 'not in any way concerned with its economic, social and political consequences'.[34] One senses that John Saville on the English Land Question was one of the great unwritten volumes of the second half of the twentieth century.[35] Only in 2010 was the subject brought at last into the compass of a single volume (and it took a team of fifteen authors to do it).[36]

In the context of his uncompleted projects it is also worth noting the cumulative significance of Saville's work on Owenism. In addition to providing an introduction to Robert Owen's *New View of Society*, he contributed to an important collection of essays published for Owen's bicentenary what remains the best account of the radical journalist and proto-syndicalist James Elishma Smith. And Saville's 1978 essay on Owenite thought concerning the family and marriage appeared 'ahead of the curve' of feminist historiography, and was published five years before Barbara Taylor's now-standard treatment, *Eve and the New Jerusalem*.[37]

Clearly, by the 1970s John Saville was in a position to publish a major work on Chartism, equipped as he was with both a clear understanding of the trajectory of the movement as a whole, and a deep understanding of important contextual elements such as agrarianism and Owenite socialism. Indeed, in his autobiography he noted that the book was 'ready to put together but this had to wait until my retirement [1982]'. Even then it would be another five years before *1848* was published. What deflected him in between were *Strict*

Settlement and his new edition of Rothstein (both 1983); volumes 7 (1984) and 8 (1988) of the *Dictionary of Labour Biography*, plus the second volume of its French abridgement (1986); and substantial pieces for the *Socialist Register* on Bevin and the Cold War and on the British miners' strike of 1984-5. Having been, as he later recollected, 'much involved in the grassroots politics of this major confrontation', the strike itself cannot but have had a disruptive effect on Saville's academic work.[38] But it arguably also sharpened his perception of the operational realities of how the state handled unrest. As we have seen, he had long been impressed by the combination of apparent reasonableness and ruthlessness in the handling of Chartism in 1848. Reasonableness and tact were hardly the defining features of the response to the miners' strike. The experience of it appears to have sharpened Saville's rueful admiration of the effectiveness of Whig policy in 1848.

One ventures to suggest, therefore, that had it been published in the 1970s, *1848* would have been a very different book and a less powerful intervention in the historiography of either the British labour movement or of nineteenth-century Britain generally. But the events of 1984-5 are not the sole explanation for this. By 1987 the historiography of Chartism had reached something of an impasse. Since 1959, with the publication of the seminal collection *Chartist Studies* edited by Asa Briggs, the movement had been subjected to intense but often locally specific, highly empirical and under-theorised scrutiny. Saville himself summarised the situation thus:

> Too much, I thought, was becoming antiquarian and insufficiently probing of the political structures within which the various social groups were located. In particular, it was the nature and ideology of the different ruling groups that was absent from too many accounts of historical change.[39]

However, three books forced John Saville to re-evaluate his interpretation of 1848. Each was a major addition to the historiography of Chartism and needs individual consideration. Saville declared he was 'especially grateful' for David Goodway's *London Chartism* (1982), which constituted the death-knell for the hoary old interpretation of 10 April and left the way clear for Saville to concentrate upon his broader vision of the significance of 1848.[40] Goodway's meticulous

reconstruction of metropolitan Chartism, which reached its considerable zenith in 1848, also flagged that the threat to the capital provided
an ingredient that had been absent in the earlier crisis years of 1838-
9 and 1842. Implicit, too, in Goodway's narrative was the importance
of political espionage and *agents provocateurs* to the government.

The second key work influencing Saville's outlook was likewise
published in 1982. Saville had not participated in the seminars in
1977 and 1978 that led to James Epstein and Dorothy Thompson's
edited collection *The Chartist Experience*. One way of reading his
1848 is as a critique of the deficiencies of this volume, intended to set
a new paradigm for Chartist studies. An extensive and fully integrated
coverage of Ireland in 1848 is one of the great strengths of Saville's
book. It is noticeable that the interconnectedness of Ireland with the
fortunes of British radicalism in 1848 was not addressed by
Thompson in her own contribution to the volume, despite its title
'Ireland and the Irish in English radicalism before 1850'. Indeed, she
candidly observed, 'the full story of 1848 in England remains to be
told'.[41]

Issues relating to 1848, however, were addressed in two of the
volume's essays. Kate Tiller's case study of Halifax, 1847-58,
confirmed the demoralising impact of 'depleted leadership, threatened reprisals and waning support' by late 1848; but it also illustrated
the frequently vital character of Chartism into the late 1850s at a local
level, albeit within an overall context wherein 'the working-class
movement [had] lost direction and is characterised by increasingly
localised responses to different conditions and a breakdown of wider
links'.[42] John Belchem's essay on 1848 itself leaned heavily on
Saville's *Modern Quarterly* article to establish the over-arching context
of press hostility to Chartism. However, it attacked Saville's argument
that O'Connor's behaviour in 1848 constituted any kind of 'abnega-
tion of leadership': 'Rather, it was the forceful assertion of a
redirection of radical endeavour'. Belchem also took issue with
Saville's claim there had been 'a violent swing to the right' that
November. Rather, the emergency conference in Birmingham anticipated the inclusion of social democratic policies alongside
parliamentary reform by the National Charter Association in 1851,
and was an important stage in the evolution of 'mid-Victorian
"consensus and cohesion"'. Belchem also emphasised the continuing
importance of O'Connor, who 'remained the cynosure of the move-

ment'. Although Belchem conceded 'the total failure of 1848' and never denied state policy was critical in determining its course, he somewhat diluted this emphasis by referring to 'the percipience' of the Whigs in 'overpowering a somewhat decrepit protest movement'. For Belchem, Chartism collapsed in 1848 because its defining strategy of the mass platform was unsuited to the circumstances of the time.[43]

The impact of Gareth Stedman Jones's contribution to the collection, 'Rethinking Chartism', was primarily felt through the extended version that appeared the next year in Stedman Jones's book *Languages of Class*.[44] This was the last of the trio that helped shape Saville's final appraisal of 1848. There was much about Stedman Jones's seminal study with which Saville doubtless identified. It made a powerful case that the plethora of local studies had atomised understanding of Chartism, obscuring both the movement's strengths and weaknesses; and it convincingly argued that, in the final analysis, Chartism was a political movement that cannot fully be understood or defined in terms of the disaffection of particular social groups. Stedman Jones also placed great emphasis upon the state's agency in containing and defeating Chartism. In the same year as this book appeared, Saville, in his edition of Rothstein's *From Chartism to Labourism*, emphasised the emergence of the state's apparatus to contain proletarian dissent. This was the primary reason, Rothstein had argued, why Chartism took the form of a movement for parliamentary reform. In this Saville saw a strong resonance with Stedman Jones, specifically setting an extended quotation from him in parallel with one from Rothstein.[45]

Saville found in Rothstein an acute appreciation of the importance of state formation and its coercive capabilities, and therefore an informed understanding of the critical importance of 1848. He found historians' failure to develop and extend Rothstein's analysis 'inexplicable'.[46] Despite the acuteness of Stedman Jones's arguments, one looks in vain for any such development or extension there. Saville's *1848* constituted an extended critique of 'Rethinking Chartism'. The most profound feature of 'Rethinking Chartism' was its seemingly authoritative dismissal of class consciousness as having any explanatory traction for the history of early Victorian Britain in general and Chartism in particular.[47] This was achieved by a detailed examination of the language of Chartism, through which Stedman Jones confronted the apparent exceptionalism of Chartism. Chartism certainly appears exceptional, as the one epic and truly national mass agitation for electoral reform in modern Britain. It is questionable if even the early twentieth-century movement for women's suffrage approached Chartism in extent or potency. As Stedman Jones himself pointed out, though he was widely misinterpreted as arguing the opposite: 'Chartism could not have been a movement except of the working class, for the discontents which the movement addressed were overwhelmingly, if not exclusively, those of wage earners, and the solidarities upon which the movement counted were those between wage earners'.[48]

However, in analysing Chartism in relation to class and the languages by which class is understood, 'Rethinking Chartism' focused almost exclusively upon one linguistic trope, 'old corruption'. It therefore underplayed the potency that class analyses brought to the ideology of the movement, especially from 1842 onwards. This flaw was compounded by the relatively narrow range of contemporary references cited in the essay. Significantly more than half of Stedman Jones's citations of historical material *pre-date* 1838, while fewer than fifteen per cent relate to the 1840s. The pivot of Stedman Jones's argument overall, however, was that reforms passed by Peel's government from 1841 fatally undermined the Chartist case for parliamentary reform. They demonstrated that Parliament was capable of passing legislation that was not in the selfish interests of MPs. Once Parliament ceased to behave corruptly, his argument runs, 'old corruption' lost its ideological force as a medium for critically analysing parliamentary politics and seeking reform of the legislature.

Saville emphasised there was little that was novel in the pivotal point of Stedman Jones's overall argument. Not only had Rothstein anticipated Stedman Jones's explanation for why Chartism took the form of a parliamentary reform movement; another British Marxist historian, Paul Richards, had recently argued that government policy in the 1840s marked a fundamental departure from the 'aggressive liberalism' of the previous decade.[49] However, Saville also questioned the efficacy of Richards's and Stedman Jones's explanation for the decline of Chartism by demonstrating that far from having become (as Stedman Jones believed) stale and anachronistic, Chartist rhetoric and the wider movement had recovered sufficiently from the doldrums of the mid-1840s to constitute a serious threat to the authority of the state. Furthermore, in reaffirming the strength of the

Chartists' continuing attachment to parliamentary reform, both as a principled objective and as the political means to socio-economic ends, Saville powerfully argued that the movement was at heart class-conscious. More than that, he also argued that the actions of the state in 1848 exploded Stedman Jones's claims about 'the high moral tone of the proceedings of the government and the effective raising of the state above the dictates of the particular interests – whether landlords, financiers or manufacturers'.[50] In addition, he argued that Stedman Jones had over-estimated the dominance of the ideological trope of 'old corruption' from the start, a failing Saville ascribed to Stedman Jones's not having consulted Noel Thompson's doctoral research on popular political economy.[51]

Saville predictably had little time for claims about 'the high moral tone' of the State in 1848:

> What is missing from Stedman Jones' general thesis is the recognition that coercion is the other side of the government coin marked conciliation. If consent can be obtained without violence, so much the better; and the history of British domestic politics after 1850 is eloquent testimony to the success of hegemony in the sense used by Gramsci. But the 1840s came at the end of half a century of popular discontent and radical agitation … [I]t was not until 1848 itself that there was demonstrated, beyond question and doubt, the complete and solid support of the middling strata to the defence of existing institutions.[52]

Saville's *1848* both consolidated and built on the author's earlier work on Chartism. However, it also emphasised new lines of argument, for example about the potent intersection, in London especially, of British Chartists and Irish Confederates. For Saville, unrest in Ireland in 1848 was far wider and potentially more destabilising than the fracas even he referred to as 'the abortive cabbage-patch rising'.[53] Critical to his interpretation was a perception that British domestic politics in 1848 could be comprehended only within the 'triangle of revolutionary Paris, insurgent Ireland, and a revitalised native Chartist movement in London and the industrial North'.[54] Thanks to Goodway's research, *1848* was stronger on London than it was on the industrial North; and of the Midlands, where the Chartist revival that year was manifestly weaker, the book was largely silent. At least one reviewer took Saville to task for his uneven narrative of Chartism's history in his chosen year. Yet the careful wording of his subtitle indicates the book is not a history of Chartism *per se* but rather an analysis of the British state in and through its treatment of the movement in 1848. Saville was emphatic that the political temperaments of localities and regions moved to their own rhythms, and these he did not pretend to describe, still less explain. He was no less emphatic, though, that Chartism's unique claim on the attention of the historian was that far more than any preceding political movement, 'it had a national leadership, with a national journal, to bind the parts of the movement together'.[55] It was as a threat to national security, not as a chain of localised disturbances, that the state dealt with Chartism in 1848.

It is in this context, especially given his 'visible and powerful' influence upon the movement's great newspaper *Northern Star*, that Feargus O'Connor is central to Saville's interpretation of Chartism. Given the absence in the 1980s of any sustained account of his life beyond 1842, the cumulative argument of *1848* was also important to understanding the strengths and failings of O'Connor. The rehabilitation of his reputation was a defining feature of Epstein's and Dorothy Thompson's work around this time. But O'Connor's influence (for good or ill) upon Chartism in 1848 was an issue evaded by Epstein, whose biography of O'Connor terminated in the early 1840s. And it was only treatable in broad terms by Thompson in her general history of the movement.[56]

Without denying the importance of police agents in securing Chartist prosecutions in 1848, Saville's earlier stress on *agents provocateurs* now diminished, but his emphasis on the malevolent partiality of the legal system was if anything greater, not least because of his careful dissection of treason trials in Ireland. But the final way in which Saville's *1848* differs from the synoptic accounts he offered earlier in his career is in the contextualisation of the state's impact upon working-class culture and politics in a longer perspective. In the book's 'commentary by way of a conclusion', Saville reiterated the longer term significance of economic growth during the 1850s in shaping the political attitudes of working people. He also stressed that '[i]t is not uncommon for radical historians to confuse party, or movement, with class'. Like EP Thompson, on whose 'Peculiarities of the English' his argument lent heavily at this point, Saville stressed the creation of mutual support movements by members of the working class, 'to counter the insecurities, the harshness and the exploitation of the capital order they inhabited'.[57] Saville believed this process was more deeply rooted by 1848 than Thompson (who saw it essentially as a phenomenon of the second half of the century). While it in no way explained Chartism's defeat in 1848, in Saville's view it did help explain 'the apparent smoothness of the transition from the turbulent 1840s to the less disturbed fifties'.[58]

The smoothness of the transition was also assisted negatively, Saville suggested, by the failure of British radicalism to build on the achievements of the 'Smithian socialists' of the 1820s – primarily Thomas Hodgskin and William Thompson – and extend their intellectual challenge to the orthodoxies of industrial capitalism. Saville argued that the steadily narrowing Owenite movement offered little to Chartism, and his interest in James Elishma Smith, already noted, was as a potential heir to Hodgskin and Thompson's mantle. In *1848* he explicitly lamented how Smith 'shrug[ged] off his militant socialism without any apparent emotional or intellectual difficulty'. Later Saville (like Rothstein before him) would point to the need to understand James Bronterre O'Brien as the pivotal figure between the alternative political economy of the 1820s and late Chartism. However, *1848* barely mentions him.[59] Arguably this accurately reflects O'Brien's stature in both the year of revolutions and after. Saville concluded his digression on the cultural and intellectual factors reinforcing the state's victory over Chartism in 1848 with the observation that working-class radicalism after the 1850s lacked 'anything approaching a theory of capitalist exploitation – even something equivalent to the fuzzy analysis that that has served the greater part of the labour movement in the twentieth century'.[60]

That remark is no polemical aside. It underlines that for Saville the defeat of Chartism in 1848 mattered. It mattered not as a simple historical conundrum in need of explication but as a fundamental fracture, a point where history *did* actually turn – to reverse AJP Taylor's dictum about the course of German history in 1848.[61] 'The great Chartist movement', Saville would recapitulate a few years later, 'was the greatest challenge the British state faced throughout the whole of the last two centuries'.[62] He saw its defeat as eclipsing in importance even the accommodation reached between the traditional landed political elite and the industrial and commercial bourgeoisie.

Indeed the spectre of Chartism arguably sealed that accommodation. In Saville as a historian of Chartism we have a remarkable example of a muscular thinker, hammering out the essential framework of his interpretation at an early stage but then refining it over the course of nearly four decades. 'Spirited and unrepentant' in the face of new thinking when he thought it justified to be so, he nonetheless showed a refreshing preparedness to acknowledge where previously he had been mistaken. His approach to Chartism was rooted in his own lived experience as a political actor, and the account he has left is a powerful blend of structural economic and social analysis, with an unusual attentiveness to legal history and a deft deployment of cultural and intellectual insight.

Notes

1. Joyce M Bellamy and John Saville, eds, *Dictionary of Labour Biography* (henceforth *DLB*), vol. 6, Macmillan, 1982. His co-authors were AL Morton (Catherine and John Barmby); Naomi Reid (Thomas Clark); John Rowley and Eric Taylor (Arthur O'Neill).
2. *The Red Republican & The Friend of the People*, Merlin, 1966, introduction, vol. 1, ppi-xv; Robert George Gammage, *History of the Chartist movement, 1837-1854.... Second edition, 1894*, Kelley, 1969, 'Introduction: RG Gammage and the Chartist movement', pp5-65; WE Adams, *Memoirs of a Social Atom*, Kelley, 1968, introduction, pp5-26; Thomas Cooper, *The Life of Thomas Cooper*, University of Leicester Press, 1971, introduction, pp7-33.
3. Eric Hobsbawm, 'The Historians Group of the Communist Party' in Maurice Cornforth, ed., *Rebels and their Causes: Essays in honour of AL Morton*, Lawrence & Wishart, 1978, pp21-48.
4. Saville, *Ernest Jones: Chartist; selections from the writings and speeches of Ernest Jones*, Lawrence & Wishart, 1952.
5. Saville, *Memoirs from the Left*, Merlin, 2003, pp77-8, 86.
6. Dorothy Towers, 'The Chartist poets', and TA Jackson, 'Eighteen forty-eight', both in *Our Time*, April 1948, pp168-9 and 163-6.
7. Curiously the *Our Time* article is missing from the bibliography of Jackson's writings appended to the *DLB* entry Saville co-authored with Jackson's daughter Vivien Morton: *DLB* vol. 4, Macmillan, 1977, pp99-108.
8. Saville, 'Introduction' to Theodore Rothstein, *From Chartism to Labourism: Historical Sketches of the English Working Class Movement* (1929), Lawrence & Wishart, 1983, pxviii.
9. Saville, *Ernest Jones*, p280. The other two were GDH Cole, *Chartist*

Portraits, Macmillan, 1941; and PW Slosson, *The Decline of the Chartist Movement*, Columbia University Press, 1916. For Saville's initial encounter with Rothstein, see his 'The Communist experience: a personal appraisal' in Ralph Miliband and Leo Panitch, eds, *Communist Regimes: the Aftermath, Socialist Register 1991*, Merlin, 1991, p13.

10. Reg Groves, *But We Shall Rise Again: A Narrative History of Chartism*, Secker & Warburg, 1938, pp171ff; AL Morton, *A People's History of England*, Gollancz, 1938, pp425-6; Salme A Dutt, *When England Arose*, Key Books, 1939, and *The Chartist Movement*, Lawrence & Wishart, [1944], pp44-5; Max Morris, 'Chartism and the British working-class movement', *Science & Society*, 12:4, 1948, p415.

11. Edouard Dolléans, *Le Chartisme, 1831-1848*, Floury, 1912, stops abruptly at April 1848; Mark Hovell, *The Chartist Movement*, Manchester University Press, 1918, was completed posthumously by the medievalist TF Tout, and its later chapters are negligible; Julius West, *A History of the Chartist Movement*, Constable, 1920, pp258-93 is descriptive rather than analytical. Even Slosson, *Decline of the Chartist Movement*, by seeing Chartism as essentially doomed from its inception, offers little by way of analysis for the years from 1848.

12. Saville, *Ernest Jones*, pp81-2.

13. Saville, *Ernest Jones*, p17.

14. E.g. Jones 'did not so much cross the Rubicon as wander over the road', Miles Taylor, *Ernest Jones, Chartism, and the Romance of Politics, 1819-1869*, Cambridge University Press, 2003, p77. On the religious overtones of much of the internal life of the CPGB see Raphael Samuel, *The Lost World of British Communism*, Verso, 2006, esp. pp45-68.

15. 'A note on the present position of working-class history', *Yorkshire Bulletin of Economic and Social Research* 4, 1952, p130.

16. Quotation from Saville, 'Labour movement historiography', *Universities and Left Review* 3, winter 1958, p76. A rounded understanding of O'Connor is the hallmark of Dorothy Thompson's work and of those younger historians she influenced, but had to wait until her *The Early Chartists* (1971) for its first iteration. Meanwhile, oblivious to Saville's work, Donald Read and Eric Glasgow produced their truly lamentable *Feargus O'Connor: Irishman and Chartist*, Arnold, 1961.

17. 'Chartism in the year of revolution, 1848', *Modern Quarterly*, winter 1952, pp23-33; also Saville, 'Labour movement historiography', p129; Saville, *Ernest Jones*, p10.

18. 'Chartism in the year of revolution', pp23, 25-6, 32; Saville made the same point in his introduction to *Red Republican*, vol. 1, pix.

19. E.g. John Belchem, '1848: Feargus O'Connor and the collapse of the mass platform', in James Epstein and Dorothy Thompson, eds, *The Chartist Experience: Studies in Working-Class Radicalism and Culture, 1830-1860*, Macmillan, 1982, pp301-2; Malcolm Chase, *Chartism: A*

New History, Manchester University Press, 2007, pp331-2.

20. 'Chartism in the year of revolution, 1848', pp28, 30-31. Treason Felony Act (its modern name) as cited in Leon Radzinowicz, *A History of English Criminal Law and its Administration from 1750: Volume 4, Grappling for Control*, Stevens, 1968, p325.

21. Leon Radzinowicz and Roger Hood, *The Emergence of Penal Policy in Victorian and Edwardian England*, Oxford University Press, 1990, p419, n52. For prosecutions in English courts under the Act see JEP Wallis, *Reports of State Trials. New Series, Volume VII, 1848-50*, HMSO, 1896, cols 381-484, 1110-16 and 1127-30.

22. Saville, 'Chartism in the year of revolution, 1848', p33.

23. Saville, 'Introduction', to *The Red Republican & The Friend of the People*, vol. 1, London, 1966, pix.

24. Saville, 'Some aspects of Chartism in decline', *Bulletin of the Society for the Study of Labour History* (henceforth *BSSLH*), 20, 1970, pp16-18.

25. Saville, 'Introduction' to Gammage, *History*, pp5-65.

26. Saville, 'Introduction' to Gammage, *History*, p30, also pp45 and 47, citing Engels, 'The fourth of May in London' in Donna Torr, ed., *Karl Marx and Friedrich Engels: Correspondence 1846-1895* (1934).

27. Saville, 'Introduction' to Gammage, *History*, pp44-5; *Red Republican*, introduction pxiv.

28. Saville, 'Introduction' to Gammage, *History*, pp48-62. For the later historiography of the Land Plan see especially Malcolm Chase, '"We wish only to work for ourselves": the Chartist Land Plan', in Malcolm Chase and Ian Dyck, eds, *Living and Learning: Essays in Honour of JFC Harrison*, Scolar, 1996, pp133-48; Jamie Bronstein, *Land Reform and Working-class Experience in Britain and the United States, 1800-1862*, Stanford University Press, 1999; Malcolm Chase, '"Wholesome object lessons": the Chartist Land Plan in retrospect', *English Historical Review* 118, 2003, pp59-85.

29. Saville, 'Chartism in the year of revolution', p23; *Ernest Jones*, p24.

30. Saville, 'The Chartist Land Plan', *BSSLH* 3, 1961, pp10-12; AL Morton and George Tate, *The British Labour Movement, 1750-1920*, Lawrence & Wishart, 1956, p95.

31. Saville, *Ernest Jones*, pp45, 152; 'Labour movement historiography', p73.

32. Saville, 'Henry George and the British labour movement: a select bibliography with commentary' *BSSLH* 5, 1962, 18-26.

33. David Martin, *John Stuart Mill and the Land Question*, University of Hull Occasional Papers in Economic and Social History, No. 9, 1981, pi.

34. John Saville and Barbara English, *Strict Settlement: A Guide for Historians*, University of Hull Occasional Papers in Economic and Social History, 9, 1983, p5.

35. For an indication of what might have been, in addition to the *BSSLH* contributions cited above, see Saville's entries on Robert Outhwaite,

William Saunders and Frederick Verinder in *DLB*, vol. 8. With characteristic disregard for his own writing commitments, John set work to one
side on *1848* to write these, to complement the entries by the present
author on earlier land reformers that appear in the same volume.

36. Matthew Cragoe and Paul Readman, eds, *The Land Question in Britain,
1750-1950*, Basingstoke: Macmillan, 2010.

37. Robert Owen, *A New View of Society* ... *with an introduction by John
Saville*, Macmillan, 1972; Saville, 'JE Smith and the Owenite movement,
1833-34' in Sidney Pollard and John Salt, eds, *Robert Owen: Prophet of
the Poor*, Macmillan, 1971, pp115-44; Saville, 'Robert Owen on the
family and the marriage system of the old unmoral world', in Cornforth,
Rebels and their Causes, pp107-21.

38. Saville, *Memoirs from the Left*, pp161 and 175.

39. Saville, *Memoirs from the Left*, p180.

40. David Goodway, *London Chartism: 1838–1848*, Cambridge University
Press, 1982.

41. Epstein and Thompson, *Chartist Experience*; quotation from Thompson,
'Ireland and the Irish in English radicalism before 1850', p142.

42. Kate Tiller, 'Late Chartism: Halifax, 1847-58', *Chartist Experience*, pp317
and 341.

43. Belchem, '1848: Feargus O'Connor and the collapse of the mass platform', *Chartist Experience*, pp275-6, 301, 303 and 280-1.

44. Gareth Stedman Jones, 'The language of Chartism', *Chartist Experience*,
pp1-58; Gareth Stedman Jones, 'Rethinking Chartism', in his *Languages
of Class: Studies in English Working-Class History, 1832-1982*, Cambridge
University Press, 1982, pp90-178.

45. Saville, 'Introduction' to Rothstein, *From Chartism to Labourism*, ppxx-
xxi.

46. Saville, 'Introduction' to Rothstein, pxxiii. Rothstein had devoted a forty-
page appendix to analysing 1848 in England, in addition to the treatment
in his main text.

47. The analysis in this and the following paragraph draws on Malcolm Chase
and Joan Allen, 'Great Britain, 1750-1900' in Joan Allen, Alan Campbell
and John McIlroy, eds, *Histories of Labour: National and Transnational
Perspectives*, Merlin, 2010, pp72-5.

48. Jones, 'Rethinking Chartism', p95.

49. Saville, *1848*, pp217-18, citing Richards, 'State formation and class
struggle, 1832-48', in Philip Corrigan, ed., *Capitalism, State Formation
and Marxist Theory* (1980).

50. Saville, *1848*, p219; and see Stedman Jones, 'Rethinking Chartism',
p177.

51. Saville, *1848*, pp214-15 and 280n7, citing Noel Thompson, *The People's
Science: The Popular Political Economy of Exploitation and Crisis, 1816-34*
(1984).

52. Saville, *1848*, p220.
53. Saville, *1848*, p39.
54. Saville, *1848*, p1.
55. Dorothy Thompson, review in *History Workshop Journal* 28, 1989, pp160-6; Saville, *1848*, p212, cf. 207.
56. James Epstein, *The Lion of Freedom: Feargus O'Connor and the Chartist Movement, 1837-42*, London, 1982 and Dorothy Thompson, *The Chartists: Popular Politics in the Industrial Revolution*, London, 1984. Paul Pickering, *Feargus O'Connor: A Political Life*, Monmouth, 2008, has since gone some way to address the limitations of Epstein's focus on the early years of Chartism.
57. EP Thompson, 'The peculiarities of the English' (1965), revised edition in his *The Poverty of Theory and other Essays*, Woodbridge: Merlin, 1978.
58. Saville, *1848*, p211.
59. See his call for 'a modern analysis of Bronterre O'Brien' in 'The crisis in labour history: a further comment', *Labour History Review* 61: 3, 1996, p327; and compare 'Introduction' to Rothstein, *From Chartism to Labourism*, pxxii, where Saville comments O'Brien was 'Rothstein's especial hero'.
60. Saville, *1848*, p216.
61. AJP Taylor, *The Course of German History*, Routledge, 2001 edn, p67.
62. Saville, *The Consolidation of the Capitalist State, 1800-1850*, Pluto, 1994, p69.

The ideology of labourism

David Howell

The first volume of the *Dictionary of Labour Biography* appeared in 1972. Compared with later volumes many entries were brief. Subsequently there would be a shift to longer and more nuanced essays on fewer subjects. Each volume has tended to emphasise specific themes. In the first volume miners dominated, with seventy entries. Many came from the period when mining trade unionism shifted from zealous advocacy of Liberalism to become the most robust defender of the Labour Party. This prominence within the volume fuelled a typically cautious comment by John Saville on the broader significance of his biographical research agenda:

> It is ... already clear that to collect biographical information on the present scale does offer, if not new perspectives, then at least some new emphases within labour movement historiography. The involvement, for example, of working men and women in the development of more democratic political institutions at the local and county level is most striking; and it provides a new dimension to the analysis of the labourist tradition.[1]

This emphasis had been central to a paper that Saville had given to the Society for the Study of Labour History in 1971. He had utilised the material collected for the Dictionary to illuminate and explain the tenacity of the miners' industrial and political culture, as this had developed in the late nineteenth century and had subsequently helped to shape the labour movement in the twentieth.[2] But for Saville, as the preceding quotation suggests and as the 1971 paper explicitly stated, his intellectual concern was much broader. He wished to understand the 'historical process by which the growing radical consciousness of the 1830s and 1840s was transformed into the ideology of labourism ie into an ideology which looked to parliamentary methods for the redress of grievances and the long term solution to working-class problems'.[3]

This question was addressed directly in another paper, given in a seminar series at Hull in the academic session 1971-2 and published in the resulting collection of essays in 1973. 'The Ideology of Labourism' became widely cited.[4] The paper provided a clear and succinct survey of a historical and political problem and suggested areas for future research. However the piece did not lead to a mono-graph equivalent to that on 1848.[5] *The Politics of Continuity* was not the product of his thoughts on labourism, except for the material on Ernest Bevin, but of his understanding of the British state and the international rivalries of the early and mid 1940s.[6] In conversation John often emphasised the desirability of a book on '1919', a moment when the British state faced both industrial conflict and the Irish war of independence. Perhaps this could have provided an opportunity for an exploration of the themes charted in his 1973 essay.

Saville's argument began with an insistence on 'certain striking political and intellectual contradictions'.[7] The early numerical domi-nation of British society by wage labourers meant a socio-economic structure unique in the nineteenth century. Universal male suffrage would mean an electorate in which the propertied were a minority, a prospect welcomed by Engels and dreaded by Macaulay.[8] The destruction of Chartism and the incremental extension of the suffrage led to what Saville presented as 'the central paradox of domestic poli-tics ... the failure to develop an independent working-class political party'. Rather there developed a 'labourist ideology' which Saville viewed as a significant obstacle to the socialist revival of the 1880s and 1890s.[9]

His characterisation of labourism emphasised its optimism about the feasibility of social change within the existing institutional frame-work. Practical objectives could be secured through parliament; physical force was rejected. This strategy was class-collaborationist, insisting in theory, and usually endorsing in practice, the unity of Capital and Labour. Industrial disputes should be avoided wherever possible through conciliation and arbitration. Yet labourism was also ambiguous. It involved persistent, often keenly contested, attempts to construct an effective workplace trade unionism. Trade union reactions to the Taff Vale judgement and the subsequent cases in other sectors demonstrated the strength of this commitment.[10] Conflict could also arise from disputes not just over wages and hours but increasingly over the introduction of new technology and intrusive managerial practices.[11] Yet this oppositional consciousness typically cohabited with political collaboration. Workers frequently voted for employers or for those who defended employers' interests and prerogatives. Their motivations included religion, ethnicity, neighbourhood, deference and fear.

The miners' industrial and political organisations were viewed by Saville as a paradigmatic example of labourism. By the late nineteenth century, across coalfields that varied in geology and economic position, they had constructed district trade unions. This achievement was testimony to the creativity and industry of a generation of activists, some of whom became officials and could count on the loyalty of many members. Local circumstances inevitably meant that the district unions varied in their ability to recruit and in their relationships with employers. Yet everywhere miners had developed some sense of a shared identity at the level of their coalfield. The diversity meant that an effective national unity was more problematic. The creation of the Miners' Federation of Great Britain (MFGB) in 1889 was itself an acknowledgement that a national agenda had to be shaped by an awareness of the variety of district experiences. Moreover the hard-won solidarity was inevitably provisional. Threats to markets or adverse geology could threaten profitability, and employers could react by attempting to reduce labour costs through attacks on wages or by seeking to reorganise working practices.[12]

Industrial tenacity usually cohabited with an attachment to Liberalism. Following the 1884 county enfranchisement, geographical concentration allowed some miners to elect their own nominees, and from 1885 they did so through the Liberal Party: a link that became more extensive with the subsequent democratisation of local government.[13] In several coalfields, including the North East, South Wales and the East Midlands, the Liberal networks for miners' leaders also embraced Protestant Nonconformity.[14] Only in Lancashire and much of Scotland, where miners were divided by ethnicity and religion, was the Liberal attachment not an effective option once that party had become from 1886 the supporter of Irish Home Rule. These coalfields shifted early to political independence, not so much

because of sympathy for socialism, but because independence allowed
for a political expression of solidarity free from ethnic and religious
rivalries. Elsewhere the shift from Liberalism was slow and sometimes
reluctant and ambiguous. The MFGB affiliated to the Labour Party
at the beginning of 1909 following two members' ballots on the issue.
Although the second vote gave a majority for affiliation, the East
Midlands coalfields remained firmly opposed.[15] A few of the Miners'
members refused to move from Liberal to Labour and many more
made only a token shift. Some of the latter remained openly linked to
Liberal organisations and became targets for local socialist criticism.
Others kept a diplomatic distance from official Liberalism but otherwise their politics were unchanged. Appropriately, Saville noted 'how
tough and tenacious the labourist tradition was amongst the mining
communities'.[16]

He acknowledged the achievements of this politics, citing the
comment of EP Thompson in his 1965 polemic with Perry Anderson.
The latter had proclaimed the three decades following the defeat of
Chartism as 'a deep caesura' in British working-class history.
Thompson's response pointed, arguably, to some of the factors facili-
tating what Saville presented as labourism.

> For the workers, having failed to overthrow capitalist society,
> proceeded to warren it from end to end. This 'caesura' is exactly the
> period in which the classic class institutions of the Labour
> Movement were built up – trade unions, trade councils, TUC, co-
> ops … which have endured to this day. It was of the logic of this new
> direction that each advance within the framework of capitalism
> simultaneously involved the working class more deeply in the status
> quo.[17]

Such involvement meant that working-class organisations became, in
Thompson's phrase 'antagonistic partners' within capitalism, effectively demonstrating the fractured consciousness that Saville found
characteristic of labourism. For Saville the defensive character of this
countervailing network was critical. It offered some protection against
the insecurity endemic to capitalism, and through its achievements
engendered self-respect. Saville presented these points of resistance as
specific to and therefore limited by occupational and geographical
contexts. This disparate configuration meant that in the wider society

the working class accepted a subordinate role. He employed Anderson's terminology. They had 'become a corporate class'.[18]

Saville's argument should be placed in its political context. The concept of labourism had a long history. Theodore Rothstein's *From Chartism to Labourism*, published in 1929, had its origin in writings that went back more than two decades, and which connected with the controversies surrounding the formation and politics of the Labour Representation Committee (LRC) and its lack of socialist commitment.[19] Although the range of Marxist writing on the British labour movement in the 1930s was limited Saville was influenced by the publication of the one volume *Marx-Engels Selected Correspondence* in 1934, and by their attempts to explain the weakness of an independent working-class political movement after the franchise extension in 1867.[20] After 1945 John Saville became an active member of the Communist Party Historians' Group, and in particular of the section concerned with nineteenth-century Britain. Like his comrades Saville felt that the radical hopes that had accompanied the defeat of fascism had rapidly withered. He found the Attlee government's domestic record 'weak and ineffective', but his most thorough contempt was reserved for the administration's foreign policy.[21] As the Cold War deepened, members of the Historians' Group felt increasingly beleaguered; yet despite or perhaps because of this, their discussions and increasingly their publications began to develop a credible challenge in some areas to historiographical orthodoxy. [22]

Within its agenda the nineteenth century section addressed the task of explaining the post Chartist character of British labour. One approach was through the concept of a labour aristocracy; another was through the analysis of labour ideology in the half century prior to 1918.[23] This agenda was evident in two contributions to a series of documentary collections, *Labour's Formative Years 1849-1879* and *Labour's Turning Point 1880-1914*, edited by James Jeffreys and Eric Hobsbawm respectively. John Saville helped Jeffreys with the compilation of documents for the earlier volume prior to his move to Hull in 1947.[24]

These intellectual and political experiences were central to Saville's developing ideas about British Labour, a response not just to its historical establishment but also to a Labour Party engaged in self-congratulatory celebration of a forward march of Labour expressed in rising electoral support and the record of the Attlee government. The official Labour version was typically teleological in its confidence that history was on its side. Yet the communist historians' response offered a variant on the same teleological optimism. They sought inspiration in an insistence on the radical pedigree of the English people whilst acknowledging that this radicalism had been largely contained within the labour movement that had developed since the demise of Chartism. The CPGB's claim to be the heir to this radicalism and its present and future instrument was captured not least in the figure of Tom Mann and his pilgrimage from socialism through syndicalism to communism.[25] For many within the Historians' Group the crises of 1956 shattered faith in the instrument, but the diagnosis of the labour movement's limitations often remained intact. Saville and others' understanding of labourism became a significant theme in the politics of the New Left, the more so because of the aspirations of the revisionists within a Labour Party which by 1959 had experienced defeat in three successive elections.

The concept was subsequently central to Ralph Miliband's *Parliamentary Socialism* (1961) to which John Saville had made a substantial intellectual contribution.[26] The pyrotechnical indictments of British exceptionalism by Perry Anderson and Tom Nairn also employed the term. Labourism highlighted the crippling limitations of British Labour, its empiricism and parochialism, its distaste for theory, its enervating attachment to the rituals of hallowed institutions and practices, and the dominance of sectional trade unions who were inextricably entangled within the confines of capitalism.[27] For many on the left the record of the 1964-70 Wilson governments, above all on economic and industrial issues and on Vietnam, simply confirmed this diagnosis. By 1967 Saville was insisting on 'the incompatibility of Labourism and socialist politics … the Labour Party has never been, nor is it capable of becoming, a vehicle for socialist advance … the destruction of the illusions of Labourism is a necessary step before the emergence of a socialist movement of any kind and influence becomes practicable'.[28]

Three years later, just before the Wilson government lost office, he made the historical comparison that perhaps would energise his writings on labourism. He suggested parallels between the challenge for socialists in 1970 and the one that faced their Victorian predecessors. For the latter 'the problem was to break the hold of the Liberal Party over the working class, or those sections that were politically articulate'. However an organisational breach had been accompanied by 'the same types of political activity but with different labels and with a different set of ideas on the part of the rank and file'.[29] The immediate political context doubtless made the concept of labourism seem more apposite. It stressed the limitations of a party whose politics were shaped by trade-union practices and whose culture, with its residual liberalism and socialist utopianism, offered minimal resources for understanding how power was distributed and exercised. Yet Saville's analysis rested on assumptions and claims that require careful examination.

The emphasis on the weakness of independent working-class politics should be set against an acknowledgment of the slow growth of the male electorate. In 1914 only about sixty per cent of males over twenty-one had the parliamentary franchise, a percentage little changed since 1885. How far this limitation was discriminatory against the working class remains contentious.[30] How far any such exclusion thereby handicapped the prospects for an independent working-class political party is debatable. Similarly, durable trade union membership was typically restricted to a narrow occupational range and, given industrial concentration, predominantly to particular geographical regions.[31] These limitations suggest that the scope for political innovation was relatively constrained. Moreover the construction of an independent politics was never just a matter of persuading activists and the politically aware to break with Liberalism. Many working-class electors, including many trade unionists, were or had been Conservative voters. One of the arguments used by supporters of political independence within the Miners' Federation against Derbyshire and Nottinghamshire miners who wished to keep their Liberal links used precisely this identification. Many former Tory miners in Lancashire and Scotland had been persuaded to vote Labour, an achievement that could be jeopardised if miners elsewhere insisted on maintaining their Liberal connections.

The miners demonstrated that pre-existing trade unions could be as much a constraint as a resource for the building of an independent working-class politics. By the 1890s, alongside coal, the skilled trades, cotton textiles and the railways had developed their own forms of trade unionism, as, with varying degrees of fragility, had some new unions of the so-called unskilled. For many craft unions effective workplace organisation shaped their political interests along specific

and typically radical Liberal lines.[32] The cotton unions had established robust systems of bargaining and used their organisational
strength to lobby established political parties.[33] Yet these patterns
could be subverted. Technical change could threaten the status of
craftsmen, adverse legal decisions could lead unions to seek redress
through parliament in a context in which Liberals showed little
capacity for winning elections. Municipal workers organised in
general unions had an interest in political representation. Railway
workers, like miners, wanted parliamentary action on health-and-
safety issues and because most employers refused recognition. Their
geographical dispersal made unlikely any effective mobilisation in
alliance with the Liberals. Such complexities facilitated the pragmatic
shifts towards independence that characterised the formation and
growth of the LRC. Affiliation of individual unions to the committee
was often the work of a few and rarely the consequence of consent by
a majority; this was an ambiguous and sometimes conspiratorial shift
that necessarily involved the continuation of older practices. Thus the
1903 Gladstone-MacDonald Pact, which guaranteed a limited
Labour presence in parliament, ensured that Edwardian Labour,
although independent, was very much a junior partner of a revived
and sometimes socially progressive Liberal Party.

MARQUAND AND COUNTERFACTUAL ALTERNATIVES

The concept of labourism has not been the monopoly of left critics of
the Labour Party. It has also been used by those sceptical of Labour
culture and organisation from a self-consciously social-democratic
perspective that was shaped heavily by the legacy of Edwardian Liberal
progressivism. The most thorough exponent from this position has
been David Marquand: biographer of Ramsay MacDonald, former
Labour MP and founder member in 1981 of the Social Democratic
Party.[34] Marquand presented the Labour Party as 'the instrument of
the labour interest rather than as the vehicle for any ideology'.
Although usually led by professionals and committed from 1918 to 'a
rather inchoate socialism', it was, he wrote:

> a trade union party, created, financed, and in the last analysis,
> controlled by a highly decentralised trade union movement, which
> was already in existence before it came into being. Above all, its ethos

– the symbols, rituals, shared memories and unwritten understandings which have shaped the life of the party and given it its unmistakeable style – have been saturated with the ethos of trade unionism'.[35]

The contrast with John Saville is obvious. Marquand endorsed Labour's commitment to parliament, its gradualism and its readiness to respect indigenous sentiments. But he viewed labourism as imposing a serious limitation on progressive politics. From the 1920s Labour had a durable electoral base amongst the unionised working class in older industrial sectors. Marquand saw this Labour core as defensive and parochial. This strength offered protection at difficult moments but was one cause of an inability to connect with other social experiences.[36] These characterisations resonate with Saville's politically very different indictment. Unlike Saville, Marquand offered a credible counterfactual to set against his indictment of labourism.

His alternative was the developing politics of the Edwardian 'progressive alliance' composed of an ideologically ecumenical Liberal Party, its creative and influential social wing epitomised by Lloyd George, and a much smaller Labour Party backed by the trade unions. The latter was predominantly working-class in its parliamentary presence and organisationally independent, but at one with the pre-war Liberal government on most immediate controversies. The alliance was underpinned by an electoral arrangement that was unpublicised but largely effective. Industrial disputes, especially after 1910, could breed some trade union antipathy towards Liberal ministers; but this, and Labour concern at the constraints of the alliance, were balanced by assessments that heightened electoral ambitions would precipitate three-cornered contests that would benefit the Conservatives.[37]

The alliance's disintegration was due in Marquand's view to the conjuncture of three developments, all resulting from or accelerated and intensified by the 1914-18 war: the 1916 split in the Liberal Party; Labour's break from the wartime coalition and its decision to fight the 1918 election as an independent force; and the massive growth in trade unionism that had begun pre-war, and had continued under wartime conditions, engendering a new self-confidence in Labour ranks. The 1918 election found a more ambitious Labour Party and a divided and confused Liberal Party facing a much expanded electorate. The outcome of the election, and subsequent Labour gains in the 1919 municipal elections, suggested a new political order, although there remained an uncertainty about the substance and permanence of any new alignment. This lasted until October 1924 and arguably until October 1931.

LIBERALS, LABOUR AND THE DMA

The extent to which the development of Liberal-Labour relationships was shaped by the growing significance of socio-economic issues and class identities for electoral choice remains controversial. What is clear is that regional and occupational varieties were important and that political changes cannot simply be read off from industrial experiences.[38] Saville's emphasis on miners' politics offers a valuable route into this territory. The Derbyshire Miners' Association (DMA) was formed in the winter of 1879-80. After 1900 it expanded rapidly and had a membership of over 42,000 at the time of the 1912 national coal strike. The coalfield's prosperity meant relatively consensual industrial relations, comparatively high wages and the development of a financially strong union. The Liberalism of the association's officials and of many members was hardly surprising.[39] James Haslam, the DMA's general secretary, had fought Chesterfield as a Liberal-Radical in the 1885 election but had lost to a Liberal coal-owner. When the victor broke with Gladstone over Irish Home Rule, Haslam failed to gain local Liberal support as an official candidate. He dutifully accepted this decision and eventually became the Chesterfield member in 1906 as a Liberal funded by his union. DMA parliamentary representation doubled the following year when its assistant general secretary WE Harvey was elected on the same basis in North-East Derbyshire.[40] Understandably their transfer to the Labour Party following MFGB affiliation was reluctant and superficial. They were returned as Labour candidates in the two 1910 elections but campaigned effectively as Liberals through their speeches and in their friendly relationships with local Liberal activists and officials. Personal preferences aside they had little choice. They depended on union and Liberal organisation. A distinctively Labour presence was minimal. The same situation had been evident in July 1909 when the death of the sitting Liberal coal-owner meant a by-election in the adjacent Mid-Derbyshire seat. No official Liberal stood. The forces of Progress were represented by JG Hancock, an official of the Nottinghamshire Miners' Association (NMA). Although a thorough Liberal, MFGB rules required that he run as a Labour candidate. Hancock's Labour attachment was however rudimentary.

Inevitably this situation provoked criticism from local socialists who began to pressurise the Labour Party head office with evidence of the Miners' members' attachment to Liberalism.[41] In response the accused could highlight the blend of opposition and indifference shown by local miners in the two MFGB ballots on Labour Party affiliation. Moreover, by 1909 four of the nine Derbyshire constituencies were represented by trade unionists. The three Miners' members were complemented by Richard Bell of the Amalgamated Society Railway Servants (ASRS), who had won Derby as a LRC candidate with local Liberal support in 1900 and had retained the seat as a Liberal backed by the trades council and sponsored by his union in 1906. He would be succeeded in January 1910 by Jimmy Thomas, funded by the ASRS standing on the Labour Party platform, but again with local Liberal benevolence. Clearly in Derbyshire a harmonious Liberal-Labour relationship had produced a relatively strong trade union representation.[42]

From mid-1913 these arrangements began to unravel. The Derbyshire Miners had been thoroughly involved in the national strike the previous year but the subsequent political events cannot be easily linked to whatever wider solidarity that conflict might have engendered. Rather, the DMA was compelled to rethink its political strategy in a context where the familiar Liberal sympathies were becoming untenable for any miners' union candidate. Haslam's death in July 1913 led to farcical confusion over the political attachment of his successor, the DMA agent Barnet Kenyon.[43] Kenyon fluctuated between Labour and Liberal allegiances before finally settling in the Liberal Party in February 1914. For himself the choice was predictable. He was of the same trade union generation as Haslam and Harvey, a Primitive Methodist preacher who was involved in local government and the co-operative movement. Such a record and the values that it represented could still evoke sympathy within the DMA but other considerations proved decisive for the association's future development.

The evasiveness of Hancock and some other Miners' members was already leading to exchanges between the Labour Party and the

MFGB. Party officials had to exercise tact. MFGB affiliation had been a major prize and the link should not be damaged by appearing to interfere in MFGB affairs. However the MFGB leadership was becoming less amenable towards Liberal sensitivities. The pioneering generation of Lib-Lab leaders had been largely replaced by men committed to political independence. Symbolically in 1912 the Lib-Lab president Enoch Edwards had been succeeded by the Scottish socialist Robert Smillie.[44] The annual MFGB conference in October 1913 spent considerable time debating the Chesterfield shambles. The insistence that all district unions had to endorse political independence was clear. Despite indications that the DMA wished to defend Kenyon, by early 1914 its officials, and a majority of its activists, had accepted with varying degrees of enthusiasm and resignation that membership of the MFGB carried with it political as well as industrial obligations. Any future candidates must stand as Labour Party nominees.[45]

Implementation of the decision came rapidly. Harvey died in late April 1914. As his successor in North-East Derbyshire the DMA nominated its president James Martin.[46] Martin was to all appearances another Barnet Kenyon in age, religious enthusiasm, community activities and committed Liberalism. There was one crucial difference. 'In all essential things I am a Liberal, but as the Derbyshire Miners' Association is connected with the Miners' Federation of Great Britain, I, as President of the County Association, can take no other stand than to support the Labour principles of the Miners' Federation.'[47] Martin's endorsement in a poorly attended lodge vote facilitated Liberal accusations that the DMA had become the target of extremist manipulation. The Liberals refused to accept the replacement of Harvey by a Labour nominee who, whatever his personal views, would not deal formally with the Liberal organisation. Instead they selected JP Houfton, the managing director of the Bolsover Collieries, backed by the coal-owner and Liberal member for Mansfield Sir Arthur Markham, the uncrowned king of Chesterfield. 'Beware of Socialist Wreckers' proclaimed the local Liberal press.[48] Perhaps the Derbyshire version of the progressive alliance had involved an element of condescension. Markham's sister Violet, who engaged forcefully in the campaign, later reflected that 'we thought it unfair and ungenerous that Labour should proceed to bite the Liberal hands that fed it'.[49] The increasingly bitter campaign led one cautious

DMA official, Frank Hall, to claim that industrial differences made political alliance impossible. 'It is evident that you don't quite realise what a Trade Union is, nor yet the reasons why they have been compelled to enter into politics. It is an anomaly for the Derbyshire Miners' Association as a trade union to form an alliance with the coal-owners politically.'[50] Yet despite some appearances it was not a simple contest between capital and labour. Amongst the mining electorate Houfton might well have polled better than Martin but the latter attracted enough votes to produce a Conservative victory.[51]

Yet for all its ambiguities the clash was decisive; the DMA in response to Martin's defeat began the task of developing independent political organisation in coalfield communities. The crumbling of the old order was underlined when Labour Party tolerance of Hancock's calculated ambiguities and evasions became exhausted and he was expelled from the party, as was the Warwickshire Miners' Member William Johnson. The imposition of political solidarity through trade union machinery meant that the DMA and NMA could provide the basis for Labour organisation in districts where it had been at best minimal. The organisational shift did not of itself entail a rapid transfer of loyalties amongst the mining electorate. Such a transfer subsequently occurred in the context of wartime and post-war changes within the mining industry. Such a thorough shift was rarely found amongst other occupational groups. More fundamentally the MFGB's firmly pro-Labour stance made at most a limited contribution to the broader disintegration of the progressive alliance. From 1918 the Nottinghamshire and Derbyshire mining seats became increasingly firm Labour strongholds but this development came in the broader context of national political developments and the wartime and post-war economic changes.[52] Through all these vicissitudes Barnet Kenyon survived until 1929 as Liberal Member for Chesterfield, facing little serious competition and appealing to the electorate on a blend of personal service and pathos.[53] Whether this indicated the residual strength of post-war Liberalism or a specific appeal based on community identification with an individual is unclear[54].

The tracing of this complex trajectory in one industry and one region highlights diversity, the interplay between the local and the national within trade unions and political parties, and continuities and changes. Despite the change in political label the post-1918 leaderships in Nottinghamshire and Derbyshire showed continuities of style and industrial policy with their predecessors. This appeared strongly in the Nottinghamshire leader George Spencer, Labour member for Broxtowe from 1918, one-time Wesleyan preacher and leader from 1926 of the breakaway Nottinghamshire and District Miners' Industrial Union (the 'Spencer Union'). Spencer in his dark formal suits personified self-consciously decent and respectable trade unionism; his industrial politics also expressed the particularism of the Nottinghamshire coalfield with its frequent prioritisation of local benefits over the imperatives of national policy.[55] The coming man in the DMA during the 1920s had a typical background in Liberalism and Methodism, but Harry Hicken came from a younger generation and his politics were shaped, not in the culture of Victorian Liberalism, but in the radicalisation of sections of the coal industry that began around 1910 and continued through the war and into the 1920s. Sermons gave way to socialism, Methodism to Marx. After the North-East Derbyshire by-election in 1914 he expressed his own shift as one motivated by policy not organisational loyalty. 'No one was a more earnest Liberal than I in 1906. And if the Liberals had adhered to their programme I venture to say I should be a Liberal today.'[56] As leader of the DMA from 1928 Hicken combined radical discourse and a visceral militancy with the sagacity needed to defend his union against both employers and the 'Spencer Union'.[57] Beyond these variations organisational independence was itself an ideological statement about working-class self-reliance and self-respect.

Labour's post-1918 attempt to reconstruct the politics of progress under its leadership was unpalatable for many Liberals who resented the rise to government of a party closely connected to the trade unions. Liberal choices during the crisis of 1931 owed something to the frustrations of the self-consciously talented. Yet despite the social tensions between Liberal and Labour the latter was shaped significantly by a liberalism that was about much more than a partisan pedigree. The Victorian and Edwardian state had significant pre-democratic features – the monarchy, the House of Lords, the persistence of a governing class that in complex respects predated the advent of capitalism. Yet at least so far as its activities in Britain were concerned, the state was relatively liberal. Strikers and other demonstrators were rarely killed by the state or by anyone else. Workers' organisations were not declared illegal. Activists were rarely subjected to arbitrary interference in their ability to organise or to propagandise. Alongside the ceremonials of monarchy and parliament such liberalism mattered. The Taff Vale judgement provoked consternation amongst trade unionists precisely because it violated this accepted pattern. The 1906 Trade Union Act restored the balance. With the state once again peripheral to workplace relationships the labour movement could endorse a political system that for all its pre-democratic features permitted scope for collective action in the industrial sphere.[58]

ASSESSING THE 'IDEOLOGY OF LABOURISM'

The legacy is important but insufficient for explaining the specific pattern of British working-class politics. The contrasts with imperial Germany were many: the form of the state, contrasting social structures, the divergent strengths and characters of liberalism, the view shared by Marx and Weber that Germany had not undergone an authentic bourgeois revolution. These could help to explain the contrasting discourses of British Labour and the German social democrats, Labourism and rejectionist Marxism. Yet the similarities are also striking. In both cases working-class politics involved fighting elections to parliament and other levels of government. Associated trade unions sought to build organisations, secure recognition and gain benefits. In each case party and unions became involved in practices that required bargaining and compromise. The rhetoric – labourist or Marxist – was seemingly not decisive. Edward Thompson made a similar point in his polemic with Perry Anderson. 'Beneath all differences in ideological expression, much the same kind of imbrications of working-class organisations in the status quo will be found in all advanced capitalist nations.'[59] Discourse had its limits.

This conclusion raises the question of the standard against which the 'Ideology of Labourism' should be assessed. Saville's investigation of credible counterfactuals within the British case was restricted to a brief assessment of the failure of British intellectuals to respond to capitalism with an effective critical analysis.[60] In his analysis of the Wilson governments he had acknowledged the problems facing socialists in the 1970s to be as formidable as those posed in the 1890s. 'What we need are new styles of work as socialists: new methods of organisation: new forms of socialist agitation; but how and in what

ways the old techniques and old organisational forms can be
supplanted are not easy questions to answer.'⁶¹ The value of analysing
actually existing working-class politics through a concept of labourism
that contrasts the actual against a never realised and imprecise alternative is questionable. This problematic basis has often been
complemented by inadequate appreciation of context. 'Labourism'
often withers into an ahistorical characterisation that conflates significant nuances. To characterise an instance as 'labourist' is not to
explain it.

'Labourism' as a rigorously defined category could indicate one
possibility in a project of comparative historical sociology that could
address within its agenda the problems posed by John Saville.⁶² Saville
noted the valuable contribution that the initial *Dictionary of Labour
Biography* made to an understanding of the labourist tradition. His
monumental achievement over the next nine volumes was to offer an
unparalleled resource for an understanding of the British labour
movement in its complexity that could challenge the claims of 'The
Ideology of Labourism' and much more beside.

Notes

1. Joyce M. Bellamy and John Saville, eds, *Dictionary of Labour Biography*
   (henceforth *DLB*), vol. 1, Macmillan, 1972, pxii.
2. John Saville, 'Notes on ideology and the miners before World War I',
   Bulletin of the Society for the Study of Labour History, 22, 1971.
3. Saville 'Notes on Ideology'.
4. John Saville, 'The ideology of labourism' in Robert Benewick, RN Berki
   and Bhikhu Parekh, eds, *Knowledge and Belief in Politics The Problem of
   Ideology*, Allen & Unwin, 1973, pp213-26.
5. See Malcolm Chase's chapter in this volume.
6. John Saville, *The Politics of Continuity British Foreign Policy and the
   Labour Government 1945-46*, Verso, 1993.
7. Saville, 'Ideology', p213.
8. Saville, 'Ideology', pp213-14.
9. Saville, 'Ideology', pp214-15.
10. Saville, 'Ideology', pp215-16. On Taff Vale see John Saville, 'Trade
    Unions and Free Labour: The Background to the Taff Vale Decision', in
    Asa Briggs and John Saville, eds, *Essays in Labour History*, Macmillan,
    1960, pp317-50.
11. For one example see Alan Fox, *A History of the National Union of Boot and
    Shoe Operatives 1874-1957*, Blackwell, 1958, chs 14-22.

12. For the diversity of miners' experiences see Roy Gregory, *The Miners in British Politics 1906-14*, Oxford University Press, 1968.

13. See for example Chris Williams, *Democratic Rhondda Politics and Society 1885-1951*, University of Wales Press, 1996, chs 1-2. A harbinger was provided by Morpeth, represented by the Northumberland Miners' leader Thomas Burt from 1874. A borough constituency with a wider franchise from 1867, its electorate also included a number of mining villages.

14. See for example Robert Moore, *Pitmen Preachers and Politics: The Effects of Methodism in a Durham Mining Community*, Cambridge University Press, 1974; Huw Beynon and Terry Austrin, *Class and Patronage in the Making of a Labour Organisation: the Durham Miners and the English Political Tradition*, Rivers Oram, 1994; Hester Barron, *1926 Miners' Lockout: Meanings of Community in the Durham Coalfield*, Oxford University Press, 2010.

15. In the second ballot held in 1908 the overall vote favoured affiliation by 213,137 to 168,446. However in the East Midlands coalfields (Derbyshire, Leicestershire, Nottinghamshire) the vote went against by 24,088 to 9,120.

16. Saville, 'Ideology', p219.

17. Anderson, 'Origins of the Present Crisis' (1964), reprinted in idem, *English Questions*, Verso, 1992, p23; Thompson, 'The Peculiarities of the English' (1965), reprinted in idem, *The Poverty of Theory and Other Essays*, Merlin, 1978, p71.

18. Anderson, 'Origins', pp32-3. For 'antagonistic partners' see Thompson, 'Peculiarities', p71.

19. Theodore Rothstein, *From Chartism to Labourism Historical Studies of the English Working Class Movement*, Lawrence & Wishart, 1983 edn with an Introduction by John Saville.

20. *Selected Correspondence of Marx and Engels*, edited by Dona Torr (1934).

21. John Saville, *Memoirs From the Left*, Merlin, 2003, p87. The focus of his *The Politics of Continuity* suggests the centrality of foreign policy to his hostility to the post war Labour Government.

22. For the CPGB Historians' Group see Eric Hobsbawm, 'The Historians' Group of the Communist Party', in Maurice Cornforth, ed., *Rebels and their Causes: Essays in honour of AL Morton*, Lawrence & Wishart, 1978, pp1-47; Bill Schwarz, '"The people" in history: the Communist Party Historians' Group, 1946-56', in Richard Johnson et al, eds, *Making Histories: Studies in history-writing and politics*, London 1982) pp44-95; Saville, *Memoirs from the Left*, pp86-89.

23. Hobsbawm, 'Historians' Group', pp36-7.

24. Saville, *Memoirs from the Left*, p86. Both collections of documents were published by Lawrence & Wishart in 1948.

25. See Schwarz, '"The People" in History', pp66-74. Dona Torr was a key figure in the construction of this alternative teleology. See her *Tom Mann*

and His Times, Lawrence & Wishart, 1956, and the entry by Antony Howe in Keith Gildart and David Howell, eds, *Dictionary of Labour Biography* vol. 12, Palgrave, 2005, pp275-82.

26. Ralph Miliband, *Parliamentary Socialism A Study in the Politics of Labour*, Allen & Unwin, 1961.

27. In addition to Anderson's 'Origins' see Nairn's several contributions to *New Left Review* (nos 23, 24, 27 and 28) in 1964-5.

28. Saville, 'Labourism and the Labour government', in Ralph Miliband and John Saville, eds, *Socialist Register 1967*, Merlin, 1967, p68.

29. Saville, 'Britain: prospects for the seventies', Ralph Miliband and John Saville, eds, *Socialist Register 1970*, Merlin, 1970, p210.

30. Ross McKibbin, 'The franchise factor in the rise of the Labour Party', *English Historical Review*, 91, 1976; Duncan Tanner, 'The parliamentary electoral system, the "Fourth" Reform Act and the rise of Labour in England', *Bulletin of the Institute of Historical Research*, 1983, pp205-19; Tanner, *Political Change and the Labour Party 1900-18*, Cambridge University Press, 1990, ch 5.

31. For distribution of trade unionists see HA Clegg, Alan Fox and AF Thompson, *A History of British Trade Unions since 1889. Volume1: 1889-1910*, Oxford University Press, 1964, chs 1, 12.

32. Alastair Reid, *The Tide of Democracy: Shipyard Workers and Social Relations in Britain 1870-1950*, Manchester University Press, 2010.

33. Peter Clarke, *Lancashire and the New Liberalism*, Cambridge University Press, 1971, ch4.

34. Marquand, *The Progressive Dilemma*, Heinemann, 1991, p17.

35. See for example Marquand, *Progressive Dilemma*, ch 6.

36. Marquand, *Progressive Dilemma*, ch 1.

37. For material on progressivism see Clarke, *Lancashire and the New Liberalism;* Tanner, *Political Change*; Ross McKibbin, *Parties and People: England 1914-1951*, Oxford University Press, 2010, chs 1-2

38. Tanner, *Political Change*, for detailed presentation of this point.

39. JE Williams, *The Derbyshire Miners*, Allen & Unwin, 1962.

40. See *DLB* vol. 1 for entries on Harvey and Haslam by JE Williams.

41. For correspondence on complaints see Labour Party archives LP/MF/11, a file also containing much on the Nuneaton MP William Johnson.

42. For Bell see David Howell, *Respectable Radicals: Studies in the Politics of Railway Trade Unionism*, Ashgate, 1999, ch 5

43. See *DLB* vol. 1 for entry on Kenyon by JE Williams.

44. See the *DLB* entries for Edwards (vol. 1, by Joyce Bellamy and John Saville) and for Smillie (vol. 3, by Saville). The Hanley by-election following Edwards's death saw division between Liberal and Labour and a heavy Labour defeat.

45. See DMA Council and Executive minutes August 1913-May 1914. There is also material in the *Derbyshire Times* and the *Derbyshire Courier*.

46. See *DLB* vol. 1 for entry on Martin by JE Williams.
47. *Derbyshire Courier*, 9 May, 1914.
48. *Derbyshire Courier*, 16 May, 1914.
49. Violet Markham, *Friendship's Harvest*, Max Reinhardt, 1956 edn, p19.
50. *Derbyshire Courier*, 16 May 1914; for Frank Hall, see the entry by Williams in *DLB*, vol. 1.
51. G Harland Bowden: 6,469; JP Houfton: 6,155; J Martin: 3,669.
52. In Derbyshire, Clay Cross, Ilkeston and North-East Derbyshire were won by Labour in 1922, and subsequently retained with the exceptions of Ilkeston and North-East Derbyshire in 1931. In Nottinghamshire Broxtowe and Mansfield were won in 1918 and retained except for Mansfield in 1922.
53. Kenyon was unopposed in 1918 and 1922, and had no Conservative opponent in 1924.
54. Kenyon was not unique. John Ward, founder of the Navvies' Union, held Stoke-on-Trent as a Liberal until his defeat by Cynthia Mosley in 1929.
55. *DLB* vol. 1 has an entry on Spencer by John Saville; see also Robert J Waller, *The Dukeries Transformed: The Social and Political Development of a Twentieth Century Coalfield*, Oxford University Press, 1983.
56. *Derbyshire Times*, 13 June 1914.
57. For Hicken see entry in *DLB* Volume 1 by JE Williams
58. See Ross McKibbin 'Why was there no Marxism in Britain?', *English Historical Review*, 99, 1984, pp299-331; for the legislative response to Taff Vale see Saville, 'The Trade Disputes Act of 1906', *Historical Studies in Industrial Relations*, 1, 1996, pp11-46.
59. Thompson, 'Peculiarities', p71.
60. Saville, 'Ideology of Labourism', pp222-5.
61. Saville, 'Britain: prospects for the Seventies'.
62. Such comparative work can be either within one society or cross-national; for the former see for example David Gilbert, *Class Community and Collective Action Social Change in Two British Coalfields 1850-1926*, Oxford University Press, 1992; for the latter Leighton James, *The politics of identity and civil society in Britain and Germany. Miners in the Ruhr and south Wales 1890-1926*, Manchester University Press, 2008.

The politics of continuity

John Callaghan

T*he Politics of Continuity* is Saville's analysis of Britain's role in the origins of the Cold War, an account of the real and the perceived in British foreign policy during 1945-6, the months when the hardening of Cold War positions took place. From the outset he rejects the idea that the Cold War was triggered by an event or episode or short-term crisis. Britain and the USA were involved in every continent of the world in 1945, a broken Soviet Union was not. But much of the world had moved to the left as the war ended. In America anticommunism was already well in place by 1945, and it became 'a populist movement of national significance in the later 1940s', but in Britain Bevin's foreign policy met with opposition from within the Parliamentary Labour Party (PLP) and 'from quite significant sections of the public', and 'notably from within sections of the trade union movement', even though 'the propertied classes had always been anti-communist and anti-Soviet'.[1] It was this tension in the British case which gave grounds in 1945 for socialists like Saville to think that a different foreign policy was possible from the one actually pursued. Bevin acknowledged the force of these hopes by projecting the image of a man trying to reach agreement with the Russians. But it was a false image, Saville insisted, because the course of confrontation was already set.

Conventional explanations for this course of confrontation argue that 'there was a real danger of the Soviet Union and other Communists taking advantage of the weakness of Western Europe to extend their power'.[2] Britain and the USA merely stood up to this challenge. Britain's world role, in this account, is a function of its determination to prevent the spread of Soviet power. Thus, according to Bullock: 'If the British were persuaded that Bevin was right to join the United States in organising Western Europe's recovery and security, it was not because they wanted to see their country playing a major role in the world but because they were convinced that there was no alternative'.[3] Though the Labour government 'had already begun on the process of withdrawal in Asia and the Commonwealth', Bullock thinks that it found 'substantial reasons … for not pushing it further until the dangerous instability of the situation after the war had been replaced by a new balance of power'.[4] Bevin did not saddle Britain with an unsustainable world role on this reasoning; he merely provided his successors 'with the indispensable basis of security in the Western Alliance'.[5]

By contrast Saville's account reminds us that the British imperial world role was constructed and maintained before anyone had even heard of the Bolsheviks. Throughout the Second World War it was tenaciously defended, often in response to American criticism as well as the criticism of nationalists and others. In seeking contact with the mind of the main British decision-makers Saville takes us immediately to the centrality of Empire in the calculations of senior Foreign Office (FO) officials. Empire was the basis of Britain's great power status and its world role. On the maintenance of this status there was 'complete and thoroughgoing agreement' within the wartime FO. Among this stratum there was also marked 'continuity in place and position'. The social origins of recruitment were stable, and perception was 'conditioned by social class' developed in schools like Eton and confirmed by departmental traditions, affluent lifestyles and conservative social circles. This was a process that produced and sustained a uniformity of view, whatever the differences that any one political question might occasion. But 'tradition and continuity' were also characteristics of British political life in general during the twentieth century, and the country was unique among European participants in the world wars in retaining its administrative structures intact. Recruited young, men like Sir Alexander Cadogan, Gladwyn Jebb and Sir Orme Sargent stayed long in the central bureaucracy and rose to its highest levels, unimpeded by personal faults of economic illiteracy (Cadogan), or neurotic fear of foreign travel (Sargent), and unchallenged in relation to the prejudices of their class.[6]

These men shared certain illusions. One of the several conceits of the Foreign Office and the diplomatic elite concerned the superiority of British diplomacy, especially when compared to the USA, in the wealth of its experience, and the subtlety and persuasion of its advocacy. The FO also held the 'curious belief that the Americans did not have any serious ideas about their own future in the world once war came to an end'.[7] The USA's fitful encouragement of colonial nationalism was merely baffling to British officials, while the strength of that nationalism was always seriously underestimated by them. American GNP rose from $91 billion in 1939 to $210 billion in 1944 and its industrial capacity almost doubled in the course of the war. Throughout the conflict Washington understood its strength and Britain's weakness. It could hardly be otherwise, given Britain's material dependence on the Americans for everything from food to machine tools. Yet the idea of American naivety, even stupidity, in foreign affairs was a recurring theme of FO analysis. The illusion that it was Bevin's far-sighted intervention that turned Marshall's Harvard speech into a real policy initiative is a minor application of this theme beloved by British, though not American, historians.[8] In fact US military planners had begun to identify the USSR as the next major threat by 1944. But in 1945 there was nothing within the American decision-making elite comparable to the anti-Soviet unanimity to be found in the British Foreign Office.[9] A more focused anti-communism had to await another year in Washington.

Indeed the Atlantic partnership was often subjected to strains and stresses by American criticisms of Empire, to which a 'superior' diplomacy in London mobilised the rhetoric of trusteeship and economic development, with luminaries such as Lords Lugard and Hailey, Sir Edward Grigg, Field Marshal Smuts and Keith Hancock to the fore as propagandists. Saville showed that the ruling assumptions in military and political planning for the post-war era were imperial assumptions. Whatever the constitutional position of India, for example, it was assumed that in matters of defence it would fall under British dominion. There was no sense of the permanence of British decline as a great power in the FO, and even when the events of 1945-7 underlined British 'financial nakedness', as a circular letter to all British embassies and missions abroad put it on 12 February 1947, it was argued that: 'Only if we were to find ourselves alone with our political objectives widely divergent from those of the United States would our financial nakedness be fully apparent to the world'.[10]

These defenders of Britain's world role perceived 'potential aggression and consistent hostility' in the behaviour of the Soviet Union from the moment the war ended. Saville has no difficulty in showing that they had always taken a hostile view of the Bolsheviks. Russia was locked out of the peace congress in 1919, sections of the British press were loud in their denunciations of the new regime, and even Ramsay MacDonald remarked on the fervour of anti-communism in the FO among its leading figures such as Eyre Crowe. The anti-communist ideology of the British elite informed attitudes to Spain during the civil war, and the 'red rat of Bolshevism' affected policy towards Hitler. Saville allowed that the Russians themselves conducted policies 'at best clumsy and inept, often brutal' and were obsessed with their own security. Hitler's invasion of the USSR on 22 June 1941 changed everything for a while, but in the last year of war British official perceptions of Moscow 'began to move back into their traditional forms'.[11] The chiefs of staff saw only one potential enemy after the war – the Soviet Union. A secretive and isolated country, but one of 'enormous power and resources', they thought in 1944, and potentially expansionist and aggressive in the future. The top brass was initially told to desist from such talk except in polite and circumlocutory terms; with clandestine friends in high places, the Russians were sure to have been kept informed of British discussions and there was no desire to alarm them. But after the Yalta conference in February 1945 'a much harder line' emerged from the FO, as anxieties about the eastern Mediterranean began to dominate the thoughts of its leading personnel. Orme Sargent in April 1945 wanted a 'showdown', rejecting spheres of influence such as those which Churchill had negotiated in Moscow as recently as October 1944. These thoughts, approved by Cadogan, were elaborated in a lengthy memorandum, 'Stocktaking after VE Day', in July 1945. Sargent argued that Britain as a great power had to confront the USSR across the whole of Europe and in doing so enlist the support of the USA 'upon some principle or other' that would pay deference to American moralising propensities while serving British interests. Failure to do so, according to Sargent, would enable the USSR, having consolidated its dominance of eastern Europe, to encroach upon southern Germany, Italy, Greece and Turkey. His thinking was an early example of the domino theory, a logic that was to be repeated many times in the years to come. The Second World War had not yet ended but the imperial planners expected Britain to resume its world role and saw the Soviet Union as the main future threat to it. Furious expressions of dissent were expressed on the left wing of the Labour Party at the first signs of this policy when Ernest Bevin, an old and continuing opponent of intervention in Spain, where Franco was still killing his left-wing opponents, publicly defended British military intervention in Greece in December 1944.[12]

CONTAINMENT AND COLD WAR

Saville argued that the 'pervasive' anti-communism of the FO was given a more sophisticated ideological thrust by virtue of developments in the USA, where a populist anti-communist temper was developing, as we have seen, fuelled by domestic spy scandals and party competition as well as overseas disputes with Moscow. George Kennan made an enormous impact in Washington with his despatch from the US embassy in Moscow – the so-called Long Telegram of 22 February 1946 – ascribing an ideologically driven foreign policy to Stalin and perceiving a world conspiracy orchestrated from the Kremlin, inevitably detrimental to the interests of the USA. The fact that this was widely hailed as a lucid and cogent analysis speaks volumes about the pitch of anti-communism that had already been reached among Truman's leading colleagues by the beginning of 1946, let alone their Republican opponents. Saville rightly observes that Kennan made no mention of the devastation of the Soviet Union in his 1946 despatches, or of the fear of Germany that obsessed the Soviet leaders, and fixed their minds on eastern Europe as a question of security, rather than of ideological ambition. Kennan knew about the crippled state of the Soviet economy and also of the Kremlin's anxieties about national security. He made much of them in other contexts.[13] But he compounded the impression created by the Long Telegram by feeding the Secretary of the Navy, James V. Forrestal – himself a visceral anti-Communist – with more analyses of the same sort, and by anonymously placing a new document with *Foreign Affairs* under the title 'The Sources of Soviet Conduct', where it was predictably interpreted as official policy. A month after the Long Telegram, Frank Roberts of the British embassy in Moscow, and a friend of Kennan's, supplied three long despatches to Bevin pointing to the same conclusions, but with the novel spin that the Soviets had special reasons to detest 'a social democratic Britain'. Roberts, like Kennan, also expressed more nuanced thoughts about future relations with the Soviet Union and accepted that it faced terrible problems of reconstruction. But he also emulated Kennan by keeping such complications out of the advice tendered to policy-makers in the spring of 1946. Instead these despatches emphasised the Soviet threat. Both analysts were quick to deduce that any Soviet successes – in say Persian Azerbaijan – would have profound knock-on effects and lead to falling dominoes across entire regions.

In practice neither the FO nor the State Department attached any importance to either the physical destruction suffered by the Soviet Union or the anxieties of its leaders about a resurgent Germany. Instead they focused on Stalin's alleged ideological fixations and his ambitions for world domination. Christopher Warner, Superintending Under-Secretary of both the Northern and Southern Departments of the FO, talked about 'The Soviet campaign against this country and our response to it' – described by Saville as 'probably the most important single document in 1946'. Like Kennan, Warner's focus was on ideology, and the inherently aggressive policies towards the West that the Kremlin chiefs allegedly derived from it. Britain, the weaker of the two Atlantic powers, was depicted by Warner as the target of an implacable Soviet war all over the globe. Bevin used these arguments in correspondence with Attlee, when the Labour leader questioned aspects of British policy.[14] By the time that a 'Committee on Policy Towards Russia' was convened on 2 April 1946, key figures on both sides of the Atlantic believed that a failure to stop communism even in remote locations would lead to the loss of whole continents. Such notions continued to be expressed in Anglo-American elite circles well into the 1960s.

Yet the chiefs of staff assumed that no war with the USSR was likely within the next five years. Kennan and Roberts also doubted that there were any Soviet intentions or capacity to invade Western Europe. Clark Kerr reported on a friendly interview with Stalin in January 1946; so did General Walter Bedell Smith, the new US ambassador to Moscow, that April. Maurice Peterson, Britain's new ambassador to Moscow, reported on constructive talks soon afterwards, as did a Labour Party delegation in August 1946, which had been treated to one of Stalin's observations about the opportunity for peaceful socialist construction in Britain.[15] Stalin's comments would not have surprised the Bulgarian communist leader and former head of the Comintern, Georgi Dimitrov, whose diaries were full of Stalin's scepticism about both the prospects of communists abroad and even of the doubtful utility overseas of Bolshevik ideology, as well as the evidence of his readiness to peacefully coexist with capitalism.[16] The inflexible ideological drive to world domination' of Kennan's and Warner's 1946 despatches is not supported by this evidence, nor that of Alexander Werth's interview with Stalin published in the *Sunday Times* on 24 September. But nor was it supported by Stalin's attitude to the post-war settlement in Italy and France in 1945 and 1946, or by Moscow's detachment from the civil war in Greece, or its support for a deal in China between the communists and the Kuomintang.

THE MIND OF ERNEST BEVIN

The Labour foreign secretary was unimpressed by any of this. 'It was his trade union experience that shaped him irreversibly, and even here he developed slowly', commented Saville.[17] Bevin subscribed to labourism, which Saville famously analysed as a late nineteenth-century ideology subordinate to the dominant ideas of the bourgeoisie. It combined an economistic, corporate and defensive class conscious that could be militant in matters of wage bargaining, with belief in the neutrality of the state and acceptance of the domi-nant ideological and institutional order.[18] Bevin always assumed that the British state was at the command of parliamentary majorities. After 1926 his position in the Trades Union Congress (TUC) had grown more powerful, as did his influence in the Labour Party after 1931. He boasted of the TUC's having become 'an integral part of the state' in 1937, and during the war years he spearheaded the corporate relationship between labour, business and the government. At no point was Bevin influenced by the tradition of 'trouble-making' on Labour's foreign policy left wing. On the contrary, both Bevin and Attlee arrived in government with their anti-communism already well established, and could be counted as 'front-runners in world anti-Communism' until the US political leadership caught up with them in 1947.[19]

Bevin regarded the British empire, as he told the Commons in February 1946, as 'the greatest collection of free nations' in the world. Its dismantling, he thought, 'would be a disaster'.[20] After his first speech on foreign affairs in the House of Commons, on 20 August 1945, Lord Halifax wrote to him from the British embassy in

Washington conveying American appreciation of the continuity in British policy as displayed in that speech. Bevin made no changes to FO personnel on grounds of incompetence or reactionary political views, and his senior advisers soon came to appreciate him for his loyalty and his capacity to represent the departmental view in cabinet and make it government policy. Among Bevin's weaknesses were his capacity for hatred, his vanity and his intolerance of criticism. According to his officials and almost all historians Bevin was independent-minded and knowledgeable of foreign affairs, possessing a vision in broad terms of the policy he wanted to pursue. But Saville challenged both of these assertions.[21] Bevin had little practical experience of foreign affairs and had no idea of what a Labour foreign policy would look like, much less a socialist one. He emerged from the war committed to continuity of policy and enjoyed the public support of his Tory opposite number, Anthony Eden, on this basis.[22] It is true that he picked up ideas on the empire – notably during a Pacific cruise from Canada to Australia in 1938, in the company of Lionel Curtis, Keith Hancock, Sir Alfred Zimmern and Lord Lothian – and that he became an advocate of pooling the resources of the colonial empires as a way of overcoming tensions between the great powers. He saw no conflict of interest in helping the Colonial Office to wean emergent trade unions in the colonies away from politics and nationalism. He also became a loud advocate of colonial development, and seriously entertained the idea that Britain could recover its economic independence from the USA and defeat colonial nationalism by sponsoring economic development in the Middle East and Africa. Bevin assumed throughout these activities and speculations the permanence of Britain's world role based upon empire.

Saville suggested that Bevin's work in the FO was inevitably affected by the fact that he relied on officials for the composition of almost all written communications. As Duff Cooper remarked 'the mere setting of words on paper was for him a long and arduous process'.[23] When he was forced to do so, the result, as Christopher Mayhew admitted, was often incoherent and obscure. Saville inferred that most of Bevin's memoranda and instructions were never drafted or altered by him and concludes:

> Certainly he was not a man to be over-ruled if his own assessment was at issue, but given the range and complexity of the problems to

be considered each day, and given above all the general agreement about fundamentals between Bevin and his officials, it follows that it was the Foreign Office in its individual and collective judgement which pronounced on most questions; and it further underlines the accepted view that the most important characteristic of Bevin's conduct of foreign affairs was the continuity of approach with his predecessors.[24]

This analysis is reinforced when account is taken of Bevin's poor health – including 'angina pectoris, cardiac failure, arterio-sclerosis, sinusitis, enlarged liver, damaged kidneys and high blood pressure', to quote Bullock's list of the foreign secretary's complaints. Certainly Bevin suffered repeated bouts of illness and long absences from the office, especially during the last two years of his life, when his value to the FO was largely as a figurehead who enjoyed enormous authority in the cabinet and governing party.

We may doubt Saville's contention that Bevin's foreign policies 'were probably more anti-Soviet than a Conservative government would have pursued', and his judgement that Churchill and Eden were 'never as fervently ideological as Ernest Bevin'.[25] By his own account, Saville argued that whoever had entered office in July 1945 would have found 'anti-Sovietism pervasive throughout the Foreign Office', together with the resolve to defend Britain's imperial and world role. Eden and Churchill would have been at home in this atmosphere and, like Bevin, would have found the dominant views wholly compatible with their own personal and private opinions.[26] In relation to the Greek crisis Bevin had accepted 'wholly the anti-communist thesis' from the beginning, though there was never any evidence of Soviet interference in what was essentially a civil war.[27] And though he never publicly equated Stalin and Hitler, as the outgoing TUC secretary Citrine did, Saville says 'there can be little doubt that on this crucial question he was at one with him'.[28] Certainly, within six months of taking office Bevin compared Hitler's and post-war Soviet foreign policy on three occasions, and Saville concluded that: 'There can be little doubt that Bevin saw little difference between the Nazi and Soviet regimes …'.[29] This was his conviction from the start of his tenure as foreign secretary. When the historian AJP Taylor made a BBC broadcast on 24 September 1945, after the London Conference of Foreign Ministers, arguing that the

Soviets were entitled to a Mediterranean base, and that, had the Bolshevik revolution not occurred, they would have got much more from the Versailles peace conference in 1919, Bevin's response, and that of his officials, was one of outrage – indicative, Saville argued, of their early anti-Sovietism.

But Bevin knew in July 1945 that the expectation of Labour activists was that the government would seek friendship with the USSR. Until the summer and autumn of 1947 opposition to Bevin's policy within the labour movement was 'vigorous and widespread'. He had to tread warily; but '[t]here is no basis for any argument that Bevin was "estranged" from his senior officials in 1946 or that he ever seriously sought accommodation with Soviet Russia'.[30] He did, however, have to get the USA on board. 'In the early years of Bevin's tenure of office his diplomacy was directed towards committing America to a general and particular support of the various positions the United Kingdom was adopting in respect of its policies towards the Soviet Union'.[31] Within less than six months of taking office Bevin explained to John Foster Dulles and senator Vandenberg that Stalin was like Hitler, and Soviet pressure on Persia, if not checked, would lead Moscow to the oilfields of Mosul.[32]

THE ATTLEE REBELLION

Attlee was the only senior figure in the Labour government to question aspects of Bevin's foreign policy. Saville depicted him as a man who gained experience of foreign issues working on the opposition front bench from 1931. During the war he sat on three major committees – the War Cabinet, the Defence Committee and the Lord President's Committee; he also chaired the Suez Canal Committee and the Armistice and Post-War Committee. He was thus exposed to intelligence reports, surveys and specialist reading on foreign issues throughout the war. He told Churchill in the summer of 1945 that he accepted continuity of policy in foreign affairs. Attlee's mounting hostility to the USSR did not surprise Saville, but the Labour leader also recognised Britain's diminished status in world politics and questioned assumptions about Britain's grand strategy and world role, and it is for those reasons that he is considered at length in *The Politics of Continuity*.[33] Attlee first registered his dissent from the conventional assumptions of Britain's world role as chairman of the Suez Canal

Committee in March 1945, when he expressed the view that air warfare had rendered redundant the old arguments in favour of British involvement in the Middle East.

His questionings during the first two years of his premiership were kept from most of his colleagues, and even escaped the later attention of biographers such as Harris and Bullock.[34] Yet they began in the early spring of 1945, when Attlee suggested international control of the Suez Canal and a sharing of the Middle East defence burden, and they continued until the spring of 1947. During the Potsdam conference he told Eden that his ideas about Middle Eastern and imperial defence were derived from the naval era, now finished, and assumed a world of warring great powers, as well as Britain's ability to pay the full cost of the world role – assumptions Attlee could not share. He told Churchill that from a Soviet point of view Egypt was merely a British satellite, and British determination to have a voice in Middle Eastern affairs invited the Soviets to claim similar privileges. He also questioned the FO determination to acquire Cyrenaica in September 1945, on both cost grounds and strategic irrelevance. Against these arguments the FO consensus argued that any concessions to the Soviets would inevitably whet their appetites for more. Thus Soviet bases anywhere in the Mediterranean would mean Soviet-controlled governments in adjacent states. Bevin shared the FO's 'vacuum theory' and had no sympathy for Attlee's critique of Britain's role in the Middle East – he even entertained fantasies that the British position in the Middle East could be consolidated by financing the social and economic development of the local populations. Ignorance of, or gross underestimation of, Arab nationalism was a feature of Bevin's reasoning, but, as Saville observed, it was also near universal among the FO and military experts. Bevin even imagined in 1948 creating 'one great Middle Eastern army' under British control.[35]

Attlee suggested in March 1946 that Britain should be regarded as 'an easterly extension of a strategic area the centre of which is the American Continent rather than as a Power looking eastwards through the Med to India and the East'.[36] This provoked an exposition of the 'vacuum theory' from worried FO officials. The USSR, according to the orthodox, would step into the Mediterranean as Britain withdrew from it, and would then proceed into Africa, while Italy, France and Spain fell under her control. Bevin implored Attlee to see that social democracy in the Mediterranean area would disappear and would come under siege in its British redoubt. The chiefs of staff added that the Middle East was needed for bases that could launch aerial attacks upon the USSR. So 'Attlee was confronted with almost the whole weight of the Whitehall administrative machine. Indeed, as far as is known, he did not have support of any significance for his critical appraisal except from Dalton and the Treasury'.[37] His rebellion was defeated, possibly after an ultimatum from the chiefs of staff, but also because his authority within cabinet was always dependent on Bevin's support.[38]

THE REAL AND UNREAL

Among the hard facts of 1945 is to be counted the physical destruction of the USSR. 'Above all other considerations, it was the terrible and hideous experience of the years of war that barred the possibility of another conflict coming from the Russian side. Large parts of their country were in ruins, and the pall of twenty million dead – or was it twenty-five million? – spread over those who survived.'[39] Saville cited Jürgen Förster's judgement, one that few would question now, that Operation Barbarossa was 'the most monstrous war of conquest, enslavement and extermination' in modern times.[40] The resulting destruction was so enormous that it was bigger than Stalin was prepared to acknowledge. Saville believed that the senior FO staff were 'innocent of any serious appreciation of economic affairs', and that neither they nor the chiefs of staff 'understood the consequences of six years of war'. But it should be added that they also chose to ignore reporters who did understand something of the weakness of the USSR in 1945, such as Kennan and Roberts, on those occasions when they deigned to mention it.[41] The USSR had also demobilised around ten million of its armed forces by the end of 1947, and Saville allowed that its rate of demobilisation was faster and more far-reaching 'than was recognised at the time', while the movement of the Red Army into Western Europe or the Middle East – an event the public was invited to regard as likely – 'was not practicable on a large scale'.[42] Again, some people recognised that there was no Soviet intention or ability to invade western Europe at the time of the Great Fear, including George Kennan, but such views were not allowed to influence the rhetoric of anti-communism. In terms of cold war myths, the idea of an expansionist Soviet Union intent on world domination is one of the grosser fabrications of the propagandists. But it was also one of the most effective.

On Saville's own evidence there was only one 'substantial critic' of foreign policy within the political-administrative elite and that was Attlee, and his criticisms were largely confined to the extent of Britain's world role. He chose to keep these questionings out of cabinet and did not seek allies. There was criticism of policy towards the Soviet Union in the party, including within the PLP, but a motion critical of Bevin at Labour's June 1946 conference, we are told, had no possibility of success, 'since the trade union block vote was always in these years at the service of the Labour leaders'.[43] Furthermore, the elite were not alone in their suspicions of the USSR. As Saville acknowledged, 'gross violations of justice, and the harshness of the Stalinist regime, began to be appreciated in parts of the organised labour movements …'.[44] While 'there is no simple formula … to explain the ways in which the idea of an aggressive communism hardened into an undeviating dogma', one factor, Saville admitted, 'was indisputably the conduct of Russian foreign policy'.[45] He also sees that there was some justification in Bevin's equating of British communist manoeuvres with those of Soviet foreign policy.[46] The media could be expected to present Russia in a negative light, 'but in large and small ways the Russians presented themselves as impossibly obdurate and intransigent', and came out badly in relation to 'innumerable matters of human rights and civil liberties'.[47] Russian ineptitude was appreciated as an aid to policy-makers in London and Washington, as the testimonies of Eden, Acheson and the former American ambassador Joseph E Davies all observe.[48] But there is another hard fact lurking behind these observations; the Stalin regime was actually a ruthless, blood-stained dictatorship, though the extent of its remove from socialist ideals was appreciated by hardly anyone on the British left in 1945. The depiction of the Soviet leaders as a bunch of untrustworthy, unscrupulous thugs was rooted in facts, and if the comparisons drawn with the Hitler regime were not credible in matters of foreign policy, they were close enough in other respects to carry the day.

Saville acknowledged that 'popular opinion in general, among both the working class and the middle class, was never in any doubt concerning the importance of Empire to the British way of life'.[49] Nor was the leadership of the Labour Party. This was one of the illusions of the age, perhaps. The loss of India no more crippled the British economy than the loss of Indonesia ruined the Netherlands. Ten years after independence both metropolitan countries were more prosperous than they had been before the war began. But the picture in 1945 was grim. The British economic predicament included the greatest current account deficit in its history. Keynes, one of the first to warn of this 'economic Dunkirk', also realised that much of the American loan he negotiated in December 1945 was 'primarily required to meet the political and military expenditure overseas'. There had been no serious discussion about how Britain's reduced financial circumstances might revise its grand strategy.[50] Marshall Aid from 1948 contributed to Britain's ability to maintain its overseas commitments, while slowly relaxing domestic austerity and building exports. The sterling balances of Britain's colonial possessions, their dollar earnings and Britain's physical control of their trade also contributed to UK recovery, by virtue of a more ruthless exploitation than they were accustomed to. Yet the appearance sedulously cultivated by the coalition government – and maintained by succeeding Labour governments and even recent historians of those governments – was the exact reverse; namely that Attlee's 'ragged-trousered philanthropists' were guilty only of generosity (and of the bungling 'groundnuts scheme' in East Africa). Saville had to quote Arthur Lewis's *Financial Times* article of 15 January 1952 to find a contemporary who understood the real situation.[51] If knowledge of what was happening in respect of the sterling balances held by Britain's colonies was slight – as it was – the political activists were not much better informed about the political situation in the colonial world.[52]

While there was a striking absence of any serious attempt to understand the post-war world in the FO, especially of the forces of nationalism, there was also widespread ignorance in Britain as a whole. The European colonial powers were determined throughout the war to restore their lost possessions, but faced two problems in doing so – the USA and the strength of colonial nationalism. Though Roosevelt championed anti-colonialism and invoked Indo-China to illustrate the worst aspects of imperialism, he did so without forcing through firm policy changes, and with diminishing rhetorical force as the war ended. The British, by contrast, steadfastly defended the return of the French colonies in a spirit of defending and forging common imperial interests – but also to ensure that France could be counted as a future ally on European matters. US policy-makers, by contrast, had to contend with different voices, including the opposition of the Joint Chiefs of Staff to trusteeship, because of their desire for unrestricted control over the islands taken from the Japanese, and the indifference of the State Department's European Office on matters of colonial nationalism. The Foreign Office, meanwhile, stressed the role of France as a stabilising force in south-east Asia in preparations for the San Francisco conference of May 1945. This completely ignored the fact that the Vietnamese were opposed to the return of the French, and that 'there was no viable French administration which had not collaborated with the Japanese'.[53] Furthermore, the French were in no position to reinstate colonial control – lacking the men and materiel – and so it was done by SEAC from 8 September 1945. But since there were not enough troops of the Allied powers on the spot, the defeated Japanese were brought back into service for police work, and, later, even for active combat against the nationalists. 'All the reports that came out of Indo-China in these early days emphasised the hatred of the French by the peoples of Vietnam', and Saville made clear that the attitudes and behaviour of the local French population was chiefly responsible for this.[54] As a British report pointed out, they combined 'almost hysterical fear of the Annamites ... with an intense hatred and desire for revenge' which would block any liberal policy and its acceptance by the Vietnamese. French repossession of Saigon was completed by 19 December 1945. But the whole episode was eclipsed in the world press by the conflict accompanying the Anglo-Dutch effort to restore Dutch rule in Indonesia

Saville provided a persuasive account of the British establishment's imperial world-view in the 1940s, and of its determination to restore the country's global role based upon its Empire-Commonwealth. He reminded us that Soviet communism had always been a problem for Britain's foreign policy-makers until Hitler forced the two countries into the alliance of 1941-5. Saville was equally persuasive in arguing that the Soviet Union was in no position, and in no mind, to embark upon a policy of expansion beyond the eastern European buffer zone in 1945-6. It had already bitten off as much, if not more, than it could chew. But there was a world communist problem in 1945-6 that Saville was well aware of but did not discuss. That consisted in the fact that powerful communist movements had developed in Asia and

Europe during and immediately after the war. Nationalism threatened imperial interests too, and, as the examples of China and French Indo-China demonstrated, it could fall under communist leadership. Did the precise relationship between Stalin and these communist and radical nationalist movements matter to British and American policy-makers? Their dominant assumption was that the communist parties were wholly subordinate to Moscow, and that communists would seek to dominate anti-colonial national movements. The British in particular had enough experience of dealing with Soviet diplomacy and Comintern policy in the colonies to have no reason to place any faith in deals struck with Stalin. The post-war arguments over the Middle East and the Mediterranean were a reminder of this, if any were needed, at a time when the balance of power in Europe seemed out of kilter, to Stalin's advantage. From an imperial perspective, tensions and diplomatic conflict with the Soviet Union were inevitable in these circumstances.

Saville talked about how the radical tradition, which Labour inherited, supplied a line of criticism of British foreign policy from 1900, but of how the consensus established within the coalition government after 1940 broke that pattern:

> The agreement on foreign politics was a new departure – or largely a new departure – for the Parliamentary Labour Party as well as for the broader labour movement … it was only during the Second World War, and the years that followed, that basic agreement with the Tories was accepted by the leadership, supported by the majority votes of the right-wing trade unions at Party conferences. Whatever the equivocations of the pre-1939 decade – and there were many – there was nothing comparable with the accord on fundamentals that emerged after 1940.[55]

Hitler and the war emergency helped to forge that foreign policy consensus, and 'Munich' – signifying appeasement and betrayal – had already come to symbolise how not to deal with a ruthless dictator by the time the war ended. There were no leading figures in British public life who openly doubted Britain's world role on the basis of its Empire-Commonwealth in 1945. On this matter there had always been consensus.[56] No pre-war Labour front bench had ever stood for anything else. It is hard not to conclude that the possibility of an alternative foreign policy was one of the illusions of 1945 and 1946, while the one that actually came to pass was over-determined. What turned this into the Cold War was the attitude of the USA and the Soviet Union.

Notes

1. John Saville, *The Politics of Continuity: British Foreign Policy and the Labour Government 1945-46* London: Verso, 1993, p2.
2. Alan Bullock, *Ernest Bevin: Foreign Secretary*, Oxford: Oxford University Press, 1985, p845.
3. Ibid, p845.
4. Ibid, p847.
5. Ibid, p847.
6. Sir Orme Sargent became Permanent Under-Secretary (PUS) at the Foreign Office in 1946; Sir Alexander Cadogan preceded Sargent as PUS in the years 1938-46 and became Britain's ambassador to the UN in 1946; Gladwyn Jebb attended the Teheran, Yalta and Potsdam conferences as a Counsellor in the Foreign Office. After the Second World War, he served as Executive Secretary of the Preparatory Commission of the United Nations in August 1945, being appointed Acting United Nations Secretary-General from October 1945 to February 1946 until the appointment of the first Secretary-General Trygve Lie.
7. Saville, *Politics of Continuity*, p65.
8. Saville, *Politics of Continuity*, pp64-70, 154.
9. Saville, *Politics of Continuity*, p72.
10. Saville, *Politics of Continuity*, p80.
11. Saville, *Politics of Continuity*, p42.
12. Recent histories of the Greek civil war suggest that it emerged from political polarisation within Greece rather than anything to do with plans for the expansion of communism; see M. Mazower, 'Historians at war: Greece, 1940-1950', *Historical Journal*, 8, 2, 1995, pp499-506. For a more detailed analysis of the situation in Greece see John Sakkas's chapter in this volume.
13. See George Kennan, *Memoirs, 1925-1950*, New York: Pantheon, 1967, pp393, 402; D. Mayers, *George Kennan and the Dilemmas of US Foreign Policy*, Oxford: Oxford University Press, 1988, pp105-6, 109-110, 120.
14. Saville, *Politics of Continuity*, p52.
15. Saville, *Politics of Continuity*, pp55-57.
16. I. Banac, ed., *The Diary of Georgi Dimitrov, 1933-49*, New Haven: Yale University Press, 2008, pp13, 271, 291, 303, 305, 352-3.
17. Saville, *Politics of Continuity*, p81.
18. John Saville, 'The ideology of labourism' in Robert Benewick, RN Berki

and Bhikhu Parekh, eds, *Knowledge and Belief in Politics The Problem of Ideology*, Allen & Unwin, 1973, pp213-27; see also Saville, 'Ernest Bevin and the Cold War' in John Saville and Ralph Miliband, eds, *Socialist Register 1984*, Merlin, 1984, pp68-100; also the chapter by David Howell in this volume.

19. Saville, 'Ernest Bevin', p96; also Oliver Harvey, ed. J. Harvey, *The War Diaries of Oliver Harvey*, Collins, 1978, pp62-3, for Bevin's and Attlee's anti-communism.
20. Saville, *Politics of Continuity*, p4.
21. As does Peter Weiler, *Ernest Bevin*, Manchester University Press, 1993.
22. See Anthony Eden, *Full Circle: The Memoirs of the Rt. Hon. Sir Anthony Eden*, Cassell, 1960, p5; Frank Roberts, 'Ernest Bevin as Foreign Secretary', in Richard Ovendale, ed., *The Foreign Policy of the British Labour Governments, 1945-51*, Leicester University Press, 1984, p23; David Dutton, *Anthony Eden: A Life and Reputation*, Arnold, 1997, p317; Robert Rhodes James, *Anthony Eden*, Weidenfeld and Nicolson, 1986, pp319-20; D.R. Thorpe, *Eden: The Life and Times of Anthony Eden First Earl of Avon*, Pimlico, 2004, p349.
23. Saville, *Politics of Continuity* p103.
24. Saville, *Politics of Continuity*, p105.
25. Saville, *Politics of Continuity*, pp4, 6.
26. Saville, *Politics of Continuity*, p43.
27. Saville, *Politics of Continuity*, p100; see G. Alexander, *The Prelude to the Truman Doctrine: British Policy in Greece, 1944-1947*, Oxford University Press, 1982.
28. Saville, *Politics of Continuity*, p107.
29. Saville, *Politics of Continuity* 107.
30. Saville, *Politics of Continuity*, p62.
31. Saville, *Politics of Continuity*, p62.
32. Saville, *Politics of Continuity*, p63.
33. Saville, *Politics of Continuity*, p119.
34. Bullock, *Ernest Bevin: Foreign Secretary*; Kenneth Harris, *Attlee*, Weidenfeld & Nicolson, 1982.
35. Saville, *Politics of Continuity*, p134.
36. Saville, *Politics of Continuity*, p136.
37. Saville, *Politics of Continuity*, p147.
38. Viscount Montgomery, *Memoirs*, Collins, 1958, p436.
39. Saville, *Politics of Continuity*, p57.
40. Saville, *Politics of Continuity*, p209.
41. See J. Zametica, 'Three Letters to Bevin: Frank Roberts at the Moscow Embassy, 1945-46' in J. Zametica, ed., *British Officials and British Foreign Policy*, Leicester University Press, 1990, p87; Kennan, *Memoirs*, pp393, 402; D. Mayers, *George Kennan and the Dilemmas of US Foreign Policy*, Oxford University Press, 1988, pp105-6, 109-110, 120.

42. Saville, *Politics of Continuity*, p7.

43. Saville, *Politics of Continuity*, p19.

44. Saville, *Politics of Continuity*, p41

45. Saville, *Politics of Continuity*, p58.

46. Saville, *Politics of Continuity*, p99.

47. Saville, *Politics of Continuity*, p58.

48. Acheson observed in a letter to Truman that 'in a tight pinch we could generally rely on some fool play of the Russians to pull us through'. D. S. McLellan and D. C. Acheson, eds, *Among Friends: Personal Letters of Dean Acheson*, Dodd, Mead and Company, 1980, p84.

49. Saville, *Politics of Continuity*, p21.

50. Saville, *Politics of Continuity*, pp152-3.

51. Saville, *Politics of Continuity*, p159

52. Saville, *Politics of Continuity*, p255, n33 discusses this in relation to the sterling balances, demonstrating that the exploitative nature of these 'forced loans' was only discussed in relation to India by 1946, in a single Fabian pamphlet by A. C. Gilpin. But India was soon to become independent and able to look after its own interests; the Crown Colonies were not.

53. Saville, *Politics of Continuity*, p190.

54. Saville, *Politics of Continuity*, p193.

55. Saville, *Politics of Continuity*, p117.

56. J. Callaghan, *The Labour Party and Foreign Policy: A History*, Routledge, 2007.

Abbreviations

AEU	Amalgamated Engineering Union
ASRS	Amalgamated Society Railway Servants
CIA	Central Intelligence Agency (US)
CND	Campaign for Nuclear Disarmament
CPGB	Communist Party of Great Britain
CPI	Communist Party of India
CSCA	Civil Service Clerical Association
CSP	Congress Socialist Party
DMA	Derbyshire Miners' Association
EAM	National Liberation Front (Greece)
ECCI	Executive Committee of the Communist International
ELAS	(Greek) National Popular Liberation Army (Greece)
FAK	Front Anti-Komunis (Indonesia)
FO	Foreign Office (UK)
FORD	Foreign Office Research Department (UK)
FRUS	Foreign Relations of the United States
IES	Department of State Exchange of Persons Program (US)
IIA	International Information Administration (US)
INC	Indian National Congress
IRA	Indian Revolutionary Association
ITJ	Islamic Student Society (Pakistan)
KKE	Greek Communist Party
LAI	League Against Imperialism
LHASC	Labour History Archives and Study Centre,
LRC	Labour Representation Committee
LSE	London School of Economics
MFGB	Miners' Federation of Great Britain
NA	National Archives (London)
NEC	(Labour Party) National Executive Committee
NLR	*New Left Review*
NMA	Nottinghamshire Miners' Association

NR	*New Reasoner*
NSC	National Security Council
NUM	National Union of Mineworkers
OCB	Operations Co-ordinating Board (US)
OSS	Office of Strategic Services (US)
PLP	Parliamentary Labour Party
SEAC	South East Asia Command
SOE	Special Operations Executive
SSRC	Social Science Research Council
TUC	Trades Union Congress
ULR	*Universities and Left Review*
USDAW	Shop, Distributive and Allied Workers
USIA	US Information Agency
USIS	US Information Service
VFS	Victory for Socialism
WEA	Workers' Educational Association

The Socialist History Society

The Socialist History Society was founded in 1992 and includes many leading Socialist and labour historians, both academic and amateur, in Britain and overseas. The SHS holds regular events, public meetings and one-off conferences, and contributes to current historical debates and controversies. The society produces a range of publications, including the journal *Socialist History*.

The SHS is the successor to the Communist Party History Group, established in 1946. The society is now independent of all political parties and groups. We are engaged in and seek to encourage historical studies from a Marxist and broadly-defined left perspective. We are concerned with every aspect of human history from early social formations to the present day and aim for a global reach. We are particularly interested in the struggles of labour, women, progressive and peace movements throughout the world, as well as the movements and achievements of colonial peoples, black people, and other oppressed communities seeking justice, human dignity and liberation.

Each year we produce two issues of our journal *Socialist History*, one or two historical pamphlets in our *Occasional Papers* series, and members' newsletters. We organise several lectures and meetings in London each year, as well as occasional conferences, book-launch meetings, and joint events with other sympathetic groups in London and elsewhere.

Join the Socialist History Society!

Members receive all our serial publications for the year at no extra cost and regular mailings about our activities. Members can vote at our AGM and seek election to positions on the committee, and are encouraged to participate in other society activities.

Annual membership fees (renewable every January):

Full UK £20.00

Concessionary UK £14.00

Europe full £25.00

Europe concessionary £19.00

Rest of world full £30.00

Rest of world concessionary £24.00

For details of institutional subscriptions, please e-mail the treasurer on francis@socialisthistorysociety.co.uk.

To join the society for 2011, please send your name and address plus a cheque/PO payable to Socialist History Society to: SHS, 50 Elmfield Road, Balham, London SW17 8AL. Subscriptions can also be paid online. Visit our websites on www.socialisthistorysociety.co.uk and www.socialist-history-journal.org.uk.

Notes on contributors

Tony Adams is Principal Lecturer in History at Manchester Metropolitan University. He has published on the history of urban politics, industrial relations, and co-operation, and is a former editor of the *Manchester Region History Review* and the *Labour History Review*.

John Callaghan is Professor of Politics and Contemporary History at the University of Salford. His publications include *Labour and Foreign Policy* (Routledge, 2007) and *Cold War, Crisis and Conflict: the history of the CPGB 1951-68* (Lawrence & Wishart, 2003).

Malcolm Chase has written widely on Chartism, including articles in *English Historical Review, Labour History Review* and *Northern History*. His book *Chartism: A New History* was published by Manchester University Press in 2007. He is Professor of Social History at the University of Leeds.

Madeleine Davis lectures in the School of Politics and International Relations at Queen Mary University of London. Relevant publications include 'The Marxism of the British New Left', *Journal of Political Ideologies* (2006), and 'The Origins of the British New Left' in Klimke and Scharloth (eds) *1968 in Europe* (2008). She is currently working on a book on The British New Left.

Sobhanlal Datta Gupta was until his retirement Surendra Nath Banerjee Professor of Political Science, University of Calcutta. His primary research interest is in international communism and the intellectual history of Marxism. His books include *Comintern and the Destiny of Communism in India: 1919-1943* (2006) and (as editor) *The Ryutin Platform: Stalin and the Crisis of Proletarian Dictatorship* (2010).

David Howell is a co-editor of the *Dictionary of Labour Biography* and Professor of Politics at the University of York. He has published widely on British labour history including studies of the Lancashire miners and the railway unions. His most recent books are *MacDonald's Party* (2002) and *Attlee* (2006).

Dianne Kirby is a Senior Lecturer in the School of English, History and Politics at the University of Ulster. John Saville supervised her doctorate on 'The Church of England and the Cold War, 1945-55' at the University of Hull and she has since published extensively on the religious dimension of the Cold War.

Colin Leys is emeritus professor of politics at Queen's University, Canada, and an honorary professor at Goldsmiths College, London. His books include *The Rise and Fall of Development Theory* (1996), and *Market Driven Politics; Neoliberal Democracy and the Public Interest* (2001). He was co-editor of *The Socialist Register* from 1997 to 2009.

Kevin Morgan is a former editor of *Socialist History* and a founding editor of *Twentieth Century Communism: a journal of international history*. His writings on communism and the labour movement include *Communists in British Society 1920-91* (2007) and studies of Harry Pollitt, Ramsay MacDonald and the Webbs. He is Professor of Politics and Contemporary History at Manchester University.

John Sakkas is Associate Professor of Mediterranean and Modern Greek History in the Department of Mediterranean Studies, University of the Aegean, Greece. His most recent publication is 'Greece and the mass exodus of the Egyptian Greeks, 1956-66', *Journal of the Hellenic Diaspora* (2009).

Index

219